A STRANGER AND YOU WELCOMED ME

A STRANGER *and* YOU WELCOMED ME

HOMILIES AND REFLECTIONS FOR CYCLE B

EDITED BY
Deacon Jim Knipper

PUBLISHED BY :

Clear Faith Publishing
781 Caxambas Drive
Marco Island, FL 34145

ISBN: 978-1-940414-30-0

Cover & interior design by Doug Cordes
Cover art & interior illustrations by Br. Mickey O'Neill McGrath, OSFS

The mission of Clear Faith Publishing is to spread joy, peace and comfort through great writing about spirituality, religion and faith that touches the reader and serves those who live on the margins. Portions of the proceeds from this book are donated to organizations that feed, shelter, and provide counsel for those in need. For more information, please visit us at: www.clearfaithpublishing.com.

CONTRIBUTING AUTHORS

Kevin Ahern
Bill Bausch
Margaret Blackie, PhD
Rev. Nadia Bolz-Weber
Greg Boyle, SJ
Rev. Mark Bozzuti-Jones, PhD
Rev. Margaret Bullitt-Jonas, PhD
Donna Ciangio, OP
Rory Cooney
Katherine Cordova, SCHC
Dave Davis
Becky Eldredge
Robert Ellsberg
Massimo Faggioli
Michelle Francl-Donnay
Deacon Ron Hansen
Marty Haugen
Dan Horan, OFM, PhD
Mike Joncas
Deacon Greg Kandra
Deacon Jim Knipper
Mike Leach
Rick Malloy, SJ
Ricky Manalo, CSP, PhD
James Martin, SJ
Shirin McArthur
Megan McKenna
Brian McLaren
Penny Nash
Dennis Plummer
Jan Richardson
V. Gene Robinson
Richard Rohr, OFM
Tim Shriver
Mary Sperry
Fran Rossi Szpylczyn
Pat Wenrick
Phyllis Zagano, PhD

DEDICATION

In loving memory of
my beloved grandson,
Julian Tao Knipper
29 April 2017 – 31 August 2020

I WILL ALWAYS LOVE YOU...
"SO MUCH, FOREVER TIME"

"I had crossed the line. I was free; but there was no one to welcome me to the land of freedom. I was a stranger in a strange land."

—**HARRIET TUBMAN**

"If you preach the gospel in all aspects with the exception of the issues which deal specifically with your time, you are not preaching the gospel at all."

—**MARTIN LUTHER**

"We do not think ourselves into new ways of living, we live ourselves into new ways of thinking."

—**RICHARD ROHR, OFM**

"It is no use walking anywhere to preach unless our walking is our preaching."

—**ST. FRANCIS OF ASSISI**

"Jesus teaches us another way: Go out. Go out and share your testimony, go out and interact with [others], go out and share, go out and ask. Become the Word in body as well as spirit."

- **POPE FRANCIS**

CONTENTS

PREFACE

IT WAS NINE YEARS AGO THAT I LAUNCHED Clear Faith Publishing—with the goal of publishing just one book of homilies that featured many of the excellent homilists who had come into my life at various points. During my early adult life, I was blessed to have been witness to great preaching during my college years by the Jesuits at the University of Scranton and later on by my home pastor, Fr. Bill Bausch (who is still one of our Contributors today). Serving as a deacon in Princeton, New Jersey for the past twelve years connected me to a number of talented lay leaders and clergy who have incredible skills in breaking open the Word and encouraging listeners on how to better understand what the Gospel calls us to do.

We listen to the Gospel stories time and time again in worship over the years, often without hearing or recognizing the impact that they could have on our lives. Thus, the goal of a good homily is to unwrap these stories, written so long ago, so we can relate them to our lives today and gain some wisdom on how to live: in the love of Christ and for the love of others.

So it was that I launched *Hungry, and You Fed Me: Homilies & Reflections for Cycle C* in November 2012, committing to donate the net proceeds of all sales to four identified charities that feed the hungry. The book was met with such great success that we followed with *Naked, and You Clothed Me* and *Sick, and You Cared for Me,* for Cycles A and B, respectively, with an expanded number of authors and using the moniker, "Homilists for the Homeless." Over the years, this set of books won numerous awards and raised a total of over $100,000 for twelve charities.

With that, our small publishing company was in full swing, with a mission to spread joy, peace, and comfort through great writing about spirituality, religion, and faith. Our publications touch readers and serve those who live on the margins by continuing our financial support of organizations that feed, shelter, and provide counsel for those in need.

Soon we began publishing works for authors such as Br. Mickey McGrath; Megan McKenna; Rev. Dr. Dave Davis; William Byron, SJ; Fr. Bill Bausch; and many others. But the question we would get most often was, "When will you do another series of books for the three liturgical cycles?" Thus, we took advantage of the COVID-19 quarantine period to begin just that. With an expanded and diversified group of Homilists for the Homeless, we are pleased to launch the new series with this edition for Cycle B.

We hope you will enjoy these homilies and reflections, including a section of funeral homilies—another request we have frequently received over the years. May each homily open your heart, mind, and soul to the very presence of Christ in our lives. May every reflection encourage you to feed the hungry, clothe the naked, and welcome the strangers who come into your life.

Finally, may the love of Christ, which dwells within each of us, thereby be encouraged, called forth, and shared with a world that cries for healing, forgiveness, and care for one another, especially for the least of our sisters and brothers.

DEACON JIM KNIPPER
02 NOVEMBER 2020
ALL SOUL'S DAY

Advent

1ST SUNDAY *of* ADVENT

BRIAN McLAREN

"May he not come suddenly and find you sleeping."

1ST READING:
ISA. 63: 16-17, 19B; 64:2-7

2ND READING:
1 COR. 1:3-9

PSALM:
80:2-3, 15-16, 18-19

GOSPEL:
MARK 13:33-37

I'LL BET YOU'VE HAD THE EXPERIENCE OF nearly falling asleep at the wheel. For me, it's most likely to happen late at night on an interstate. The dotted lines between lanes seem to hypnotize me and soon . . . I'm . . . yawning . . . and . . . WHOA! WOW! YIKES! I find myself drifting off and am suddenly jolted back into awareness. I pull over, maybe get a cup of coffee. It's scary and dangerous!

The same thing happens to us on many levels. We go on autopilot in our marriages and our marriages gradually drift off the road. We fall asleep on our jobs and make a serious mistake. We fall asleep as parents and don't realize how much trouble our kids have gotten into until a police officer knocks on the door or we get a call from the school.

We can also fall asleep at the wheel spiritually. We think, "I go to church, I give my offering, I sing the songs, I say the creeds." But our rituals and habits hypnotize us, like those broken lines between lanes, and we don't realize that our spirits have nodded off to sleep. Soon, we're driving off the shoulder into apathy, complacency, or greed, or we're driving into oncoming traffic with bitterness, resentment, arrogance, or even racism and hatred.

That's why Jesus uses such strong language and such disturbing stories so often. Many people think he was predicting the literal end of the world, but, more likely, he's warning people of "the end of the world as we know it" that will come inevitably if we fall asleep and take our blessings for granted.

In today's gospel, Jesus tells one such disturbing story. He asks us to imagine a typical estate of his day, where slavery was the norm. But then something very abnormal happens: The master goes away and leaves his slaves in charge.

It's a startling statement when you consider it: He put his slaves in charge.

In another parable, Jesus explains what can happen. "The master's gone," the employees say. So, they start exploiting one another. They forget they're accountable. They forget that they're not ultimately in charge. They forget that the master will one day return—at an unexpected moment—and they'll be called to account.

So, listen: It doesn't matter who you are—a humble worker, low on the social pyramid; or a corporate titan; or even president of a nation. You are not ultimately in charge. One day, you will be held accountable.

This message is especially important for us today, because we live in a dangerous time when we are running off the road and heading into oncoming traffic in many ways. Think about it:

We've fallen asleep in regard to the planet. We take more resources than the earth can replenish. We pump in more toxins than it can decontaminate. We heat it up. We pollute it with trash. We drive more and more species to extinction because we destroy their habitats—and call it development! So, we're just driving along, half asleep, thinking we're in charge. And some of us, if someone tries to rouse us and remind us of our accountability, we get cranky and tell them to shut up and go away.

It's similar in relation to poverty. If we're rich, we have no idea how difficult it is for people in poverty. We're used to it. We're sound asleep when it comes to injustice. We think this level of inequity is normal and OK. We fall asleep and refuse to be awakened.

It's the same in relation to peace. We spend so much on weapons and war. Think of how much good a portion of that money could do, if it were invested in preemptive peacemaking instead of preparing for war. We're in our dream world and God wants to rouse us to reality.

It's the same in relation to the dignity and equality of all peoples. If we're white, we fall asleep about our own privilege and participation in structural racism. If we're Christian, we buy into all sorts of nightmarish fantasies and conspiracy theories about Muslims, Jews, or atheists. If we're so-called able-bodied or neuro-typical, we fall asleep toward our brothers and sisters who suffer from physical or mental challenges.

How have we cared for this planet? We think we're in charge, but we'll be held to account.

How have we cared for the poor, the vulnerable, the homeless, the sick or diversely abled, and the racial, ethnic, and religious minorities? The majority might think that they rule, but they will be held to account.

How have we worked for peace—politically and also personally? Closer to home, how have we treated those closest to us—our family members, our coworkers, our neighbors, the person we see at the store or coffee shop each day? We may think we're in charge, but we will be held to account.

I say that not to make you feel guilty. I say that not to make you afraid. I say that because all of us can go on autopilot and soon . . . we . . . drift . . . off . . . the . . . road.

The crash that's coming will be so horrible that Jesus is willing to disturb us to save us from it. So, once more, I hope you're listening. I hope you're alert and awake. I hope you're willing to be disturbed.

In God's name, wake up! *Wake up!* WAKE UP!

2ND SUNDAY *of* ADVENT

THE REV. PENNY A. NASH

"Immediately..."

1ST READING:
ISA. 40:1-5, 9-11

PSALM:
85:9-14

2ND READING:
2 PET. 3:8-14

GOSPEL:
MARK 1:1-8

THE GOSPEL OF MARK, THE FIRST OF THE four gospels to be written down, hasn't always gotten a lot of respect.

It's short, it has an ambiguous ending, it doesn't feature people's favorite parables like the Prodigal Son or the Good Samaritan. Its vocabulary is fairly limited and it uses the word "immediately" over and over—immediately Jesus went here and did this and then immediately, quickly, breathlessly—most of the sentences start with "and"—Jesus went there and said that. And this, and that, and another. The pace is relentless.

And Mark doesn't have a sweet birth narrative to ease us into the story of the savior. No shepherds, no magi, no angels. No genealogies.

For centuries, Biblical scholars pretty much ignored Mark, calling it rough, primitive, obscure; not understanding its power and purpose. But, oh, Mark is my favorite of the gospels, because it doesn't want us to get distracted from the message. It doesn't want us to loll around in a scene too long, lest we lose the point, lest we think the story is about anything other than the shocking, urgent, mysterious revelation of God Almighty in the human person of Jesus Christ—and how hard that is for any of us to grasp.

Mark gets right to the point. The beginning of the good news of Jesus Christ the Son of God reaches back to the prophets. This may be a shocking story, but it's not without a familiar context. The Christian arrangement of the Old Testament ends with the prophet Malachi, who says that before the awesome day of the Lord's return, God will send the great prophet Elijah (that wild, hairy man who wore a leather belt and called down fire from heaven) to reconcile the people to one another in preparation for God's mighty return.

Add to that the potent and poignant story of the people of God as told by the prophet Isaiah, who assures a people languishing long in exile—after the destruction of the Temple and the whole nation of Israel—that God will break through all barriers, will make a safe and straight way through the wilderness, and bring God's people home.

And so, in the beginning, but out of the history of God's people, now comes John the Baptizer, hairy and leather-belted, a new Elijah, to continue the prophetic witness, to prepare the way for us.

God is still speaking through the prophets, and this prophet proclaims that something is about to happen, that someone greater than all the prophets, someone powerful and mighty, comes this way. Someone who will break through all barriers to get to us, we who are bent under heavy loads, and someone who will comfort us and lead us safely home.

No need to linger over any pretty scenes or literary buildup. That's our Mark.

Do you see how urgent this is? Do you see how awe-some this is, that God Almighty comes to us in our brokenness, busting through the chaos of this world and heralded by a wild man who talks about holy fire? No wonder we surround the story with lowing cattle and angels and fir trees and candle lights. It's almost too raw to bear on its own.

In Advent, we are given the time and space to stop and pay attention to something that for most of us is actually kind of unbelievable, and yet we remember, somewhere, somehow, that it is true. That God bends toward us, that God's move is always toward us, even when we are looking the other way or have lost sight of the strength of God's mighty arm and the goodness of God's gentle embrace.

But we are most likely to remember that it is true if we have had some kind of experience of it ourselves.

Ah, experience of God. Experience of this awesome one who is heralded by a wild man talking about holy fire. Some of us may not be so sure about that. We're respectable people. Sometimes people tell me they don't think they've had any kind of experience of God, really. But I wonder if maybe they haven't learned to recognize it yet.

Paradoxically, mysteriously, God is both wild and gentle, both present and absent, both intensely personal and warmly communal.

Not all of us have experienced the relentless fierceness of God's power—I think of stories of whole communities transformed by forgiveness in the wake of violence like the work of the Truth and Reconciliation Commission in South Africa or the behavior of the Amish people after the school shooting in Pennsylvania or people keeping vigil on death row.

I think that some of us, individually, worry we might not be able to withstand that fierceness, but most of us have experienced God in some way. For myself, I think about trudging along a beach, pouring out my frustrations and worries in half-formed sighs that pass for prayer, and then a single, perfectly formed shell washes up just in front of me, out of the blue, like a gift, a calling card saying, "I'm here and I hear you."

I remember the fingers of my newborn baby curling over mine and the rush of love going out of me that took my breath away. I think about that stirring impulse inside me that makes me want to give and love and connect to others, in both their pain and joy, and gives me the strength to do so. I remember feeling mysteriously accompanied on the road through a snowstorm by a little red truck marking and clearing the way ahead of my car.

I think about the rays of light coming out of the clouds after a storm and the stirring birdsong and the fragrance of roses and I marvel at the raw power of the love and delight that flows all around the universe and flows through me if I will but stop and know it.

These experiences of mine may seem small and sentimental, but I know that they are connected to that same power that transforms the world on a much larger scale. And that power is ultimately about breaking through the things that keep us from loving God and loving one another so that we can be healed. As we read through the Gospel of Mark this year, we will see for ourselves how much emphasis this Gospel puts on Jesus's power of healing and restoration.

And so, I invite you to marvel with me about this God who bulldozes through all obstacles and tenderly gathers together all of God's people and leads them safely home. And then, I invite you to take time in the coming weeks to slow down, to stop even, to be still and seek—look for—the experience of God and God's promise. To not let the parties and events and even the beauty and good cheer of the season take up all of our time and energy and so distract us from that real experience of God.

And I also invite you to share in the prophet's work yourself. God is still speaking through prophets of all sorts, not just the ones who call fire down from heaven, and God commands us to comfort God's people today. Therefore, I invite you to seek to experience God not just for your own wellbeing but for the wellbeing of the world—because you cannot offer love and hope to others until you know love and hope yourself.

You don't have to look far to see how many people have lost hope. Who don't know love. Who are exhausted and bent over in pain or hunger or fear or shame. Whose relentless grief is overwhelming them now.

And so, immediately, today, listen to the prophet's urgent command, charging you and me to break through whatever barriers we need to break through with our own holy fire to offer hope, to offer love, to offer God's comfort to God's people through our own hands.

For this is only the beginning of the good news of Jesus Christ the Son of God.

3RD SUNDAY *of* ADVENT

FRAN ROSSI SZPYLCZYN

Rejoice! Rejoice! O Israel rejoice! To you shall come Emmanuel!

1ST READING:
ISA. 61:1-2, 10-11

PSALM:
LUKE 1:46-50, 53-54

2ND READING:
1 THESS. 5:16-24

GOSPEL:
JOHN 1:6-8, 19-28

THE BELOVED HYMN "O COME, O COME Emmanuel" is sealed in our hearts and minds, isn't it? The lyrics embody encouragement in a season of darkening days at a time when we are asked to wait patiently and trust in the promise of the coming messiah.

The topic of patient persistence hit home for me of years ago when I read some books and articles about climbing Mount Everest. It was said that most people fail in their quest to summit at the very last stage of the climb. They make it so close and then things fall apart near the top because it has been so long, plus the dire conditions as they draw closer. It is often darker, colder, far more difficult, not to mention the ever-decreasing amount of oxygen in the air and the physical toll of such a journey.

Although it could sound a little Lenten in spirit, it ultimately reminds me of Advent as we wait for the light to be born and it can be easy to grow discouraged. Culturally it is a season of busy-ness full of shopping, writing cards, preparing lists, thinking about holiday parties and dinner menus. Many of us are doing those things and stressing out about spending money that we don't really have and time that is in equally short supply. Add to that the calendar year will conclude, and many of us may be weighed down with the reminders of resolutions unmet and goals left incomplete. Either way, we might feel nothing but discouragement at a time when we feel like we should be happy. All the while, we know that spiritually are invited to wait and watch in quietude. There is a lot of dissonance as all of these elements intersect.

In our own time, there is the likelihood of even greater disconnection and discontent as we muddle through this particular Advent season. Our awareness may be focused squarely on the shorter, darker days and challenging circumstances of the current environment, not the coming light. That may make sense on the surface, but the Gospel is never about the surface alone!

Today we celebrate Gaudete Sunday, the Third Sunday of Advent. We are at the halfway point, rounding the bend to Christmas. On this Sunday we are pink and not purple or deep blue. We have more light and hope, we are encouraged and urged to joy. The meaning of Gaudete is the cry for joy, the cry we hear in the first reading from Isaiah, which says: "...He has sent me to bring good news to the afflicted, to bind up the brokenhearted, To proclaim liberty to the captives, release to the prisoners, to announce a year of favor from the Lord and a day of vindication by our God."

This is the Good News of the coming of Christ! God wants us to be encouraged and lifted up, knowing we are in the homestretch. We must be reminded, and we must remind others, that Emmanuel, the god-with-us, is coming. It will not be too much longer, and we are asked to be joyful and have faith.

It is easy to lose our way whether through seasonal depression, general blues, or just the discouragement that comes from a long slog on a hard road. Not unlike the climbers of Everest, we are near the summit, but we don't have a clear sense of it. Things may be more rarified, the air thinner, our ability to be patient, or to make good decisions might be altered. God is urging us to stay focused, keep our eyes on the east, awaiting the coming light and joy of Jesus' birth!

In this season of patient, watchful expectation, particularly in a year when patience is worn thin, may we heed the words of both the hymn and the readings for today. Rejoice, rejoice always, rejoice in the name of God. Know that God-with-us is on his way, take heart, hold on, be joyful.

May we not allow too many of the distractions of sadness, sorrow, and seemingly darker days dispirit us. Let us lean into the wisdom of the ages and the hope of faith as the cry of Isaiah echoes through the centuries. The prophet reminding us to rejoice and know that glad tidings and good news are in those very echoes. Let our holy imaginations, illuminated by the pink Advent candle, give us a glimpse of the light that is coming our way.

May the remaining steps on our Advent journey be lit with the hint of joy that the dawn of Christ will bring! We will not lose our way so close to the end. May we have confidence that God will be with us as we make the final steps of our annual trek. Rejoice and be glad, salvation is near!

4TH SUNDAY *of* ADVENT

DEACON JIM KNIPPER

"The hungry he has filled with good things."

1ST READING:
2 SAM. 7:1-5, 8-12, 14, 16

2ND READING:
ROM. 16:25-27

PSALM:
89:2-5, 27, 29

GOSPEL:
LUKE 1:26-38

SO, WHILE WE ARE ONLY HOURS AWAY FROM celebrating the birth of the Christ Child—and all the celebration and lights and gifts which go with that—I want to take a few minutes for us to just ponder God's gift of the incarnation. Incarnation begins with today's Gospel, as we hear Mary's ultimate "yes" to the angel, who tells her that she carries a child who will be called the Son of God. God takes on flesh and makes the movement toward us, reminding us that there is no separation between each of us and God. It is God's ultimate affirmation of God's abundant love for us—love so great that God comes and walks among us.

But, for what reason? Some theologians will immediately point to the end of Jesus' life and the crucifixion, saying that Christ only came here to solve a problem and to die for our sins. Other theologians will say that any problem which existed was solved on day one, with the birth of Christ, and that by focusing so much on the end of his life, we miss the core message of the depth and breadth and meaning of the incarnation: that God so loves the world and loves you and me that God continually comes to us; that God came not to teach us about kingship, but, rather, kinship. And if we miss that point, we will miss the central thread that weaves through all of Christ's teaching.

And if we had just extended this morning's Gospel passage a few lines, the prominence of kinship would be evident. For right after Mary's "yes" to be the mother of the Christ Child, her first action is to immediately head out "in haste" to visit her cousin Elizabeth, who is also with child. Mary's focus was on kinship. And in that encounter, Mary describes how the child that she carries—the incarnate God—will cast down the mighty from their thrones and lift up the lowly. He will fill the hungry with good things and the rich will be sent away empty.

It seems, at times, that we live in a world where many would rather adapt and conform and restrict and limit everything so that the focus is comfortably centered on them—yet it is clear from the start that this incarnate God enters into our midst with the aim to upset the status quo. As we see, Jesus is always about widening the circle of compassion and dismantling the barriers that we put up to exclude others. He stood with the sinners, the prostitutes, the lepers, the outcasts, and the unclean—lifting up the lowly and filling them with good things.

This, my sisters and brothers, is what the kinship of God looks like. It means being part of God's embrace: getting off our thrones and entering into kinship with each other, not kingship over each other. With the incarnation of God, it would seem that God was not interested in being a God "up there" (wherever that may be), but rather a God who is among us, with us, and encouraging us to delight and to never lose hope. This is a message that needs to be echoed throughout our kinship networks.

Father Greg Boyle is a Jesuit priest who has spent decades ministering to those who have lost hope, living within the gangs of Los Angeles. Father Greg is the founder of Homeboy Industries, a nonprofit that provides job training, tattoo removal, and other services for those newly released from prison and former gang members (who are fondly called "homies"). The Los Angeles-based group helps more than 10,000 people per year. His first book, *Tattoos on the Heart*, spent years on bestseller lists, followed by his next book, *Barking to the Choir*.

In the Introduction of his new book, Father Greg writes:

> Kinship is the game-changer. It is the Pearl of Great Price. It is the treasure buried in the field. Let's sell everything to get it. Yet we think kinship is beyond our reach.... Yet Gospel Kinship always exposes the game, jostles the status quo in constant need of conversion, because the status quo is only interested in incessant judging, comparisons, measuring, scapegoating, and competition. And we, the Choir, are stuck in complacency.[1]

It is through the connectedness of kinship, in a time when our world lies "in sin and error pining," that we can recognize the incarnate God and allow our soul to feel its worth.

In his first book, Father Greg tells the story of when he and three of his homies were invited to the White House by Laura Bush to speak at a conference on helping America's youth. This part of the story picks up on the flight home after a successful visit. One of the homies, Alex, handles tours of the Homeboy facilities during guest visits. Covered with tattoos, he has undergone thirty-seven laser surgery treatments, with some ninety more to go in order to remove them all.

While inflight, Alex says he needs to use the bathroom, so Father Greg points him to the back of the plane. Some 45 minutes later, Alex returns to his seat and the conversation goes like this:

> "*Oye, qué pasó, cabrón*—I thought you fell in?"
>
> "Oh," Alex says, with his signature innocence, "I was just talkin' to that lady over there."
>
> I turn around and see a lone flight attendant standing in the back.
>
> Alex winces a bit.
>
> "I made her cry. I hope that's okay."
>
> "Well, Alex," I brace myself, "that might depend on what you actually said to her."

1 Gregory Boyle, *Barking to the Choir: The Power of Radical Kinship* (New York: Simon & Schuster, 2017), 10.

> "Weellll," Alex begins, "She saw my Homeboy Industries shirt and all my tattoos and, weellll, she started to ask me a gaaaanng a' questions, so....
>
> He pauses with a whiff of embarrassment.
>
> "So, I gave her a tour of the office."
>
> At 34,000 feet, Alex walks this woman through our office. He introduces her to our job developers, explains our release program, and hands her goggles to watch tattoos being removed.
>
> "And I told her that last night we made history...for the first time in the history of this country, three gang members walked into the White House. We had dinner there...I told her the food tasted nasty."
>
> He pauses and gets still.
>
> "And she cried."
>
> I get still myself.
>
> "Well, *mijo*, whaddaya 'spect? She just caught a glimpse of ya. She saw that you are somebody. She recognized you...as the shape of God's heart. Sometimes people cry when they see that."
>
> Suddenly, kinship—two souls feeling their worth, flight attendant, gang member, 34,000 feet—no daylight separating them. Exactly what God had in mind.[2]

Indeed—this is what Mary had in mind when she said "Yes!" This is what God had in mind when God came to this world in the flesh. I think it is what St. Paul had in mind when he wrote that we are to pray always—for all this is...kinship. It is about relationship and not requirements. It is about being connected and not about be corrected. It is living a life, not

2 Gregory Boyle, *Tattoos on the Heart: The Power of Boundless Compassion* (New York: Free Press, 2010), 204–205.

settling with a partial God, but to live in the incarnation, to bear fruit from Mary's "yes," to be open to an expansive, ever-loving God, and to allow our soul to feel its worth.

So, as we bring our Advent to a close, may you be open to the transformation which we all need, by realizing that our union with God is found in the depths of everything—especially in our wounds, our failings, our faults, and our losses. For God is right here, right now, always and forever—regardless of any achievement or performance on our part—always present, always loving, lifting us up and filling our hunger with good things.

Christmas

CHRISTMAS: MIDNIGHT

DAVE DAVIS

"Do This!"

1ST READING:
ISA. 9:1-6

PSALM:
96:1-3, 11-13

2ND READING:
TITUS 2:11-14

GOSPEL:
LUKE 2:1-14

ZEAL. IT'S SUCH A BIBLICAL WORD—ZEAL. Who uses that word? You come upon a refreshingly happy and enthusiastic salesperson this time of year. The one who is fighting off exhaustion by being happy, responding to cranky customers by being kind. The person looks you right in the eye, with a smile, and says, "Thanks for coming in and have a great holiday!" No one walks away from that and says to themselves, "Wow, what zeal!"

"The zeal of the Lord of hosts will do this." Zeal? Most English translations of the Bible stick with the word "zeal" here in Isaiah 9:7. There are not a lot of options that show up in the Hebrew dictionary—synonyms for zeal. Maybe most translations stick with "zeal" because no one could figure out another word to use. That old "Good News" paraphrase says, "The Lord Almighty is determined to do this." The dictionary defines zeal as "enthusiastic diligence"; not just enthusiasm, but "enthusiasm for a person, object, or cause." "The enthusiastic diligence of the Lord of hosts will do this." Well, that pretty much explains it all, doesn't it? Or drains the meaning right out of it. Zeal. There's got to be more to it. More meaning, more theology in it.

Zeal.

Years ago, I attended a performance of Bach's *Brandenburg Concertos.* The concertos were played by members of the Lincoln Center Chamber Music Society in New York City. Interestingly, all the musicians stood while they played, except those whose instruments require otherwise. Watching and listening to a chamber group play, I am always struck by how they communicate with each other, how they have to listen to one another, how they watch one another, how connected they are. This time, I was also struck by how they at times smiled at each other while they were playing. And how much some moved their entire bodies into the music, working it, playing it. Playing with such... zeal. It was sort of mesmerizing, sort of like watching a dance.

Then you realize that they weren't just bouncing around like bobble-head dolls; even the "enthusiastic diligence" was coordinated. It matched the music. You know how Bach takes a theme or melody and works it from instrument to instrument; from the first violin, to the second, to the violas, to the cellos, the flutes, to the oboes, and back again to the violins. The visible zeal coming from those musicians did the same thing. Their stronger, more exaggerated movements followed the pattern. You could watch it in their expressions, their whole bodies, their beings (there, there, there, there). The zeal, their zeal, it's in the notes. The zeal is in the music. The zeal comes from Bach! It's part of the DNA of it all.

Zeal. There's more to it.

The zeal of the Lord of hosts. Light shining on those who walk in darkness. Joy rising after the night's sorrow. Justice and righteousness kissing each other. Faithfulness rising from the ground. Righteousness looking down from the sky. Wordless comfort for those with broken hearts. Unconditional forgiveness for the lost son now home. A loving touch for the sinner the world would sooner stone. Strangers welcomed like angels. The unclean fully embraced. New life rising where there once was none. A child born for us. All of it—it's all part of God's zeal. The zeal is in the notes, the gospel notes. It's in salvation's music that tells of God's steadfast love. The zeal is who God is. Our salvation is part of God's DNA. All that God has done, God is doing, God will do... this. Zeal.

Zeal is more than the enthusiasm of the Lord of hosts. Zeal is God's very being. And there is this breathtaking coordination to the "enthusiastic diligence" when it comes to the God of our salvation. For the grace of God moves through God's people. Selfless love there, and there, and there. These waves of movement. The movement of God's healing love. A grieving heart cradled there, and there, and there. A waning spirit lifted there, and there, and there. The one in need cared for there, and there, and there. A voice for justice cries out there, and there, and there.

An enthusiastic diligence for the kingdom coordinated by the very Spirit of God. The zeal leaps right from the child's manger. God's zeal, the zeal of the Child born for us, the zeal of Immanuel, the zeal of the Messiah, the zeal of the One for whom the angels sing, that zeal at work for you, in you, through you. Zeal. Zeal. The word drips with meaning. The word is fraught with salvation. "The zeal of the Lord of hosts will do this." God has done, is doing, will do—this.

I know it must have happened somewhere, in some church, during some Christmas pageant one year. The pageant, as it unfolded, let's just say there were some significant kinks. Mrs. Wasley was only in her first year as the volunteer in charge, and if we're honest, it will probably be her last year. Nightmare would be too strong of a word to ever use for a Christmas pageant. After all, the term "perfect Christmas pageant" is an oxymoron, a contradiction that flies in the face of the incarnation whereby God took on and made holy all of the frailty of this broken vessel of our humanity. Christmas pageants were made to have rough edges. However, at this church, on that evening, as the pageant played on, Mrs. Wasley was just a bit taken back by the sharpness of those edges.

Maybe there were a few things she would have done differently. For instance, maybe it wasn't such a good idea to have all the second and third graders be animals, especially after Billy asked if they could make animal noises, and Mrs. Wasley said, "Yes, Billy, that might be very realistic." Or maybe somebody could have pointed out to Mrs. Wasley that it takes a bit of time to dress and move and fix the hair of the heavenly host, especially when it is made up of thirty-two angels who are all between two and four years old. And maybe in working with the fifth-grade narrators, Taisha and Jerod, who were actually very fine readers, Mrs. Wasley shouldn't have suggested at the dress rehearsal that they memorize the last scripture lesson so it could have more impact.

Let's just say it was a rough afternoon in Bethlehem. Mary had been sick all morning and the bucket next to the manger was not to feed the animals, it was for her to use. Joseph may have been a "righteous man" and "unwilling to expose Mary to shame," but he was also thirteen and decided about ten days ago he wasn't going to enjoy this pageant at all. So, Mrs. Wasley knew it was going to be a struggle, but when the animals arrived behind those shepherds, any hope of heavenly peace vanished. They took over the whole chancel and elevated "lowing" to a new high-volume art form that seemed to combine beatboxing, slam poetry, and body noises.

And the angels, well, the angel moms and dads working backstage in the fellowship hall were so intent on getting hair and halos right that they completely missed their cue, so the heavenly host arrived way after the congregation had sung "Angels We Have Heard on High," even after the narrator Taisha said, four times, "And suddenly there was a multitude of the heavenly host with the angel," even after the Magi! But when they arrived, they looked good—their halos were perfect and their hair was just right.

Right near the end, right before everyone was to sing "Joy to the World, the Lord is come," the narrators, Jerod and Taisha, fought their way to center chancel stage for the last scripture reading. It was from Isaiah, "For a child is born to us." They stepped on and over an abundance of sheep and cows, even some dogs and cats and one child who came as a mouse. Angel parents in the congregation were paying no attention to what the narrators were about to say; they were making up for lost googling time and rapidly wearing down their phone charges. Mary was reaching for the bucket and Joseph had rolled his eyes so many times they just about fell out of his head.

So, the narrators dutifully put down their script as Mrs. Wasley had instructed two hours ago. And they started to recite Isaiah 9:2–7. Aisha had the first part and she did it beautifully, though no one could hear over the barnyard noises still going on. Jerod, now determined to be heard, started with a shout. A shout loud enough that it caught some attention from the animals, the angels, and the paparazzi parents. "For a child is born to us, a son is given to us." Jerod had this nailed. He ran through those names perfectly. Mrs. Wasley told him that was the most important part: "Wonderful Counselor, Mighty God, Everlasting Father, Prince of Peace."

Unfortunately, that was as far as Jerod got with trying to memorize over the mac and cheese and ham they fed the cast between the dress rehearsal and the performance. He started to trip up just after Prince of Peace, and he sort of garbled out something about justice and righteousness. And then he stopped. He just plain stopped, right there in front of God and everybody. The sanctuary was now utterly, uncomfortably, awkwardly, painfully silent. Mrs. Wasley was reaching for her script so she could give the cue. Random parents were grabbing pew bibles to look up Isaiah 9 so they could help. The silence was deafening and seemed like it went on forever.

But Jerod, much to his credit, didn't give up. He didn't panic. He seemed to gather himself. And with a maturity beyond his years, knew that if he said something loud and with authority, most everyone would assume he was right.

And so Jerod, with enthusiastic determination and in the strongest of prophet's voice, looked up to heaven, and with a unique conflation of scripture and a Nike commercial, Jerod boldly proclaimed and begged and pleaded, "God? . . . Just do this!"

As the silence held, and before the organist could decide whether to start "Joy to the World" or not, a voice could be heard coming from a few pews back. Someone said, in a stage whisper, "That might be the best Christmas prayer I've ever heard!"

God, just do this!

Zeal. The Zeal of the Lord of hosts will do this.

NATIVITY *of the* LORD: MASS DURING *the* DAY

DAN HORAN, OFM

"The Word became flesh."

1ST READING:
ISA. 52:7-10

PSALM:
98:1-6

2ND READING:
HEB. 1:1-6

GOSPEL:
JOHN 1:1-18

CHRISTIANS OFTEN TEND TO TREAT THE solemnity of Christmas in one of two common ways. Either they consider it an annual birthday party for a newborn baby or they see it only as the first sign of God's saving power for the human race. Both of these perspectives make some sense and have at least some grounding in the tradition, but neither fully conveys the significance of the Incarnation in quite the way that today's readings invite us to consider. Not only is Christmas more than a baby's birthday party, it is also more than a celebration exclusively for human beings.

For starters, the closing line of today's first reading, which is echoed in the responsorial psalm—that "all the ends of the earth can see the salvation of our God"—speaks to the absolute novelty and wide-reaching significance of the birth of Christ. Yes, Jesus of Nazareth was a human person, the messiah whom Christians proclaim is the Eternal Word made flesh. Given that Christmas literally celebrates his birth, we can certainly recognize it as a birthday. However, what God accomplishes in and through Christ goes far beyond the species Homo sapiens. The general tenor of the passage from Isaiah and Psalm 98 is that the whole world ought to be so overwhelmed by God's saving power, which is motivated solely by divine love, that everyone and everything should break out into song.

But what exactly are we lauding? What is the whole created universe eager to celebrate?

This is where the second reading and gospel come into focus. The opening of the Letter to the Hebrews recounts the enduring presence of God from the beginning of creation. It is not that our ancestors in ages past had no understanding of God or had some exclusively false sense of who God is or is not. It's just that they never had the opportunity to see God in God's fullness, to reach out and touch God, to walk with God, to hear God and to speak to God with our human language and completely within our finite context. But, "in these last days, he spoke to us through a son, whom he made heir of all things and through whom he created the universe, who is the refulgence of his glory, the very imprint of his being, and who sustains all things by his mighty word," the Letter to the Hebrews exclaims. The Creator of heaven and earth, all things visible and invisible, has been fully revealed in the person of Jesus Christ. The one in and through and unto whom all things were created has become part of that very same creation.

This sense of the divine in creation is made clearer in the Gospel of John. In verse 14, we hear the climactic announcement that "the Word became flesh and made his dwelling among us, and we saw his glory, the glory of the Father's only Son, full of grace and truth." That phrase *and the Word became flesh* is frequently brushed past quickly since we human hearers tend to project ourselves and our experiences into the story of God's revelation. And yet, the author of John's Gospel chose the Greek word *sarx* ("flesh") deliberately. The passage could have just as easily said that the Word became "human" (*anthropos*) or "man" (*andra*), but instead the word *sarx* was chosen.

Sarx means earthly materiality, creatureliness, corporeality that includes but is not limited to human creatures. Elsewhere in scripture, the term is used more generally and its deliberate usage in John's prologue should give us pause if we are inclined to think it pertains to humanity alone. No one contests that the Word became *sarx* as the fully human person Jesus of Nazareth. Rather, the question remains, as the late Australian theologian Denis Edwards put it: "What relationship is there between the wider natural world, the world of galaxies and stars, mountains and seas, bacteria, plants and animals, and the life, death, and resurrection of Jesus Christ?"[1] The answer to this question is contained in the fuller theological, broadly ecological meaning of Christmas!

God entered the world as one like us, fully human in all things but sin, and precisely being fully human, Jesus Christ was part of a complex and interrelated cosmic web of creation. The Word's entrance into creation is good news not only for humans, but also for all creatures and all creation that, as St. Paul expresses in his Letter to the Romans, is longing for that day of salvation that involves nonhuman creation as much as it does humanity (Romans 8:19–23).

As the American theologian Sr. Elizabeth Johnson once wrote, "We evolved relationally; we exist symbiotically; our existence depends on interaction with the rest of the natural world.... The flesh that the Word of God became as a human being is part of the vast body of the cosmos."[2] God's entrance into creation as *Emmanuel*—"God with us"—is the greatest sign of divine love for all of God's creatures, humans included, which are interrelated and interdependent in this evolutionary world.

Contemporary theologians have been unpacking the significance of this fascinating truth. A Danish theologian named Niels Henrik Gregersen even coined the term "deep incarnation" to represent this profound dimension of our faith. In one of his articles, he wrote: "the incarnation of God in Christ can be understood as a radical or 'deep' incarnation, that is, an incarnation into the very tissue of biological existence and the system of nature."[3] In other words, everything in the created world, those things visible and invisible, known and yet-to-be-discovered, is implicated in God's decision to become *flesh*; all of God's creatures are touched by and benefit from God's gift of love and life in the Incarnation.

All of a sudden, Christmas as a human holiday seems far too small a feast for the magnificence of God's becoming *sarx*. This is something that St. John Paul II understood, too. In his 1986 encyclical *Dominum et*

---

1 Denis Edwards, *Deep Incarnation: God's Redemptive Suffering with Creatures* (Maryknoll, NY: Orbis, 2019), xv.

2 Elizabeth A. Johnson, *Ask the Beasts: Darwin and the God of Love* (London: Bloomsbury, 2014), 196.

3 Niels Henrik Gregersen, "The Cross of Christ in an Evolutionary World," *Dialog: A Journal of Theology* 40:3, Fall 2001, 192–207.

vivificantem, the former pope wrote: "The Incarnation of God the Son signifies the taking up into unity with God not only of human nature, but in this human nature, in a sense, of everything that is 'flesh': the whole of humanity, the entire visible and material world."[4] He then goes on to reflect on the "cosmic significance" of the Incarnation, recognizing that Christ elevates not merely human nature but *all nature.*

Indeed, God so loved the world that God chose to enter into it as part of it. In doing so, God became part of the very fabric of creation, of which we too are a part. But so is every other aspect of creation. On this Christmas day, especially as we gather in the midst of an ongoing global climate crisis, may we recognize the cosmic significance of the Word becoming flesh, humbly recalling our place as fellow members of God's family of creation and working to respect, preserve, and protect our creaturely sisters and brothers in Christ.

---

4 John Paul II, *Dominum et vivificantem*, May 18, 1986, 50.

FEAST *of the* HOLY FAMILY

MEGAN McKENNA

"They took him up to Jerusalem to present him to the Lord."

1ST READING:
GEN. 15:1-6, 21:1-3

2ND READING:
HEB. 11:8, 11-12, 17-19

PSALM:
105:1-9

GOSPEL:
LUKE 2:22-40

TODAY IS THE FEAST OF THE HOLY FAMILY and most of us will immediately think of Jesus, Mary, and Joseph as this family. But in reality, *the* Holy Family is our God, the Trinity: our Father, the Spirit, and the beloved child, Jesus. We are all made in this image of God and so our families reveal and express God's Holy Family and our own experience of the Trinity. That means that every family is HOLY. Your family is HOLY. My family is HOLY. And so, we celebrate all families today and look in awe and wonder at how each and every one of our families reveals something of our God, the Trinity, to us and to the world.

Our first reading is from Genesis, our beginnings, and it is God Yahweh assuring Abram that his family will be as numerous as the stars of the heavens. And in spite of the fact that he and Sarai originally had no child, they will have their own family. (Sarai has given her slave to Abram and Ishmael is born. According to law at that time, Ishmael is the son of Sarai and Abram.) The second segment skips past the story of the three strangers who are treated with such great hospitality, and we are told that "The

LORD took note of Sarah as he had said he would; the LORD did for her as he had promised." When the child is born, they name the child Isaac. Their families will be intermeshed for all time, up till now.

Psalm 105 recounts and sings of the marvelous wonders that God does for all their offspring. He remembers them and his promises to them as history advances, through a thousand generations.

The letter to the Hebrews speaks of Abraham, who "generates" not solely physically, but through faith and obedience to God's covenant. Even when he is tested by offering his son Isaac to God, he obeys, and all his descendants bear his legacy of faith. He is a faint symbol of Jesus, who was raised from the dead, God's beloved child, given now to all peoples in resurrection life. He is our brother in the power of the Spirit, given to us by our Father.

The gospel brings us to Jesus's human family: Joseph, his adopted father, and Mary, his mother, bound together in care of the child given to all the world. In every family that reflects the Holy Family of the Trinity, there is one who fathers: who protects, fosters, supports in the larger world, physically sustains, and teaches. At the time of Jesus, it was the father that would teach a boy how to be a man and a Jew, obey the law, pray, and know and imitate the God of the covenant in mercy, kindness, justice, compassion, forgiveness, and tenderness—how to be like God. The woman, the mother, would raise the girl to be a woman and a Jew, teach her how to pray, to be obedient to the covenant and wait on the promises of the One to come, and, in theological terms, receive "the Spirit" and take the seed of faith to maturation and fullness of practice in every aspect of her life. Together, the father and mother would pass on their tradition and belief as people of the covenant, as people belonging to God.

The gospel begins with an example of this obedience to the tradition and laws of their faith. Mary and Joseph go to the Temple to complete her purification after giving birth, and to offer their first-born child to God with an offering of turtle doves (the gift offering of the poorest in the community). This has long been called the Feast of the Presentation, the handing over and dedication of the child to God's service.

But, while there, they meet two people, both elderly, Simeon and Anna, faithful, long-suffering, and enduring prophets. They have been waiting for this child to come. Simeon sings of this child who belongs not just to his parents, or even to the Jewish people, but to all nations. He will be a sign of contradiction as he reveals who God is for everyone. And Anna rejoices with the child in her arms and preaches to everyone who will listen of the glory of God in his gift of the promise. Then, we are told of Jesus, that he "grew and became strong, filled with wisdom; and the favor of God was upon him." And we are told that Mary and Joseph were struck with amazement as they learned who this child would be.

The gospel states strongly that family (in Jesus's Good News to the poor) is not constituted by marriage or blood ties (even Joseph is father by adoption and choice). There must be others in the Holy Family, born of faithfulness, tradition, and wisdom, that enable the children to grow strong and be filled with wisdom and know God's favor upon them. In sacramental terms, we might think of them as godparents at baptism, but family must be more than blood kin or connection by marriage. Dorothy Day, founder of the Catholic Worker movement, would say that every household [family] should have a room set aside for strangers to rest and abide awhile. Outsiders, even total strangers like the visitors to Abram and Sarai's tent, are essential members of the Holy Family.

There must be aunts, uncles, cousins, friends of the parents, other couples, people who are not married, and other friends who make up the family. If it "takes a village to raise a child," it takes many add-ons to make a family, especially one that is to reveal the Holy Family, the Trinity that is our God. The father—whoever fulfills that role—is the shadow of God as fathering, and the mother—whoever fills that role—is the shadow of the Spirit instilling and indwelling; as the child or children mirror Jesus, the beloved child of our God.

There are many stories in Native communities about the creation of butterflies. They all tell of a gift of the Creator that is shared especially with young ones, who, when they see butterflies, *reach, stretch* out arms, hands, eyes, and spirits, seeking to grasp hold of them, attracted by their movement, gracefulness, colors, and elusiveness. They are seen as essential for the child to grow, to mature, and to reach past where they live, the ones with whom they dwell and who share their household and daily life. Without the butterflies, children would be stunted in their development; they would be deprived of otherness, difference, and strangeness—all necessary to learn about oneself (to grow in wisdom). And, as the three strangers come to announce good news to Sarai and Abram, and Simeon and Anna (and even the shepherds in Luke's gospel) announce good news to Joseph and Mary, these strangers, these butterflies, are needed to bring the family their connection to the larger world and whatever history may be waiting for them.

Jesus himself will tell his disciples: "Who is my family—my mother, brothers, sisters? . . . Anyone who hears the word of my Father and puts it into practice is mother, brother, and sister to me." [Mark 3:33–35, author's interpretation.]

So, who is in your family? Your family is holy. My family is holy. *All families are holy.* In fact, the presence of "strangers," those not usually included in family by blood or marriage, are the ones that help—more than others, perhaps—to make our families *holy*, as our God is holy. Take a look around at your family, those here today and those "at home," farther away. With Mary and Joseph, marvel at what you are hearing and how utterly amazing it is that God makes us family, and draws us into his holy family, the Trinity of Three in One.

Remember, your family is holy. All families are holy.

SOLEMNITY *of the* BLESSED VIRGIN MARY

MICHELLE FRANCL-DONNAY

And Mary kept all these things, reflecting on them in her heart.

1ST READING:
NUM. 6:22-27

PSALM:
67:2-3, 5, 6, 8

2ND READING:
GAL. 4:4-7

GOSPEL:
LUKE 2:16-21

THESE DAYS IN PARTICULAR—POISED BETWEEN seasons, teetering on the edge of a new year—lend themselves to pondering, to treasuring the year past in our hearts. What astonished us? What brought us to tears? What made us howl with laughter? What suffused us with joy? What brought us closer to God?

We contemplate, too, what the new year will bring. Will it astonish us? What new griefs will we have to bear? Where will we find God? When will we desperately need God?

Luke tells us that Mary pondered all the events that surrounded Christ's birth in her heart. I imagine her cradling a young Jesus in her arms, still astonished at the visit from Gabriel, still overwhelmed with joy, still worried what Simeon meant when he promised her heart would be pierced. What, I'm sure she wondered, would the next days and months bring? How would she cope?

How can we follow Mary's example and prayerfully ponder our past, present, and future with God? In his *Spiritual Exercises*, St. Ignatius of Loyola suggested a short daily practice called the Examen, a way to recognize God at work in every aspect of one's life. Take ten minutes at the end of the day, advised Ignatius, and seek out God's handiwork in your life.

Ignatius's prayer process begins by recognizing that we are always in the presence of God. Don't be timid. Ask God to help you pray, to bring his light to bear on your day. The line that opens today's psalm well captures what Ignatius hopes for those praying the Examen: *O God, be gracious and bless us and let your face shed its light upon us.* [Psalm 67:2]

Next, says Ignatius, tell God you are grateful. Ignatius thought ingratitude—not pride or greed—was the ultimate root of all sin. If we cannot see that all we have—our very lives and all that surrounds us—comes from God, then we are blind to God. God is our true treasure. So, be specific. Search your day for one or two luminous moments for which you are particularly grateful, and give God thanks for these gifts.

The meat of the Examen is a review of the day. Take it hour by hour, noticing with God where you felt his presence, where you felt particularly beloved. Where did you love in return? The point is not to scour for sins, small or large, but to become more and more familiar with how God is at work in your life. This is what God desires for us, as he asked Aaron to bless the Israelites, and, by extension, us. *May the Lord uncover his face to you* reads the last line of Aaron's blessing in one translation. May you see the Lord.

It is often the small things that turn out to be most important: the moment when someone unexpectedly waved you ahead in a long line at the grocery store, or the sense of awe you experienced walking out the door into a beautiful afternoon. As C. S. Lewis noted in his *Letters to Malcolm: Chiefly on Prayer*, "We must not be too high-minded. I fancy we may sometimes be deterred from small prayers by a sense of our own dignity rather than of God's."[1] Don't be too high-minded; share it all with God.

We are humans, and inevitably we fail in our love for each other and for God. So notice, too, the moments that make you wince as you review the day. Ask God to forgive you and prayerfully seek his advice on what

1 C. S. Lewis, *Letters to Malcolm: Chiefly on Prayer* (New York: HarperCollins, 1964), 29.

remedy you might make. Who should you apologize to? Is it once again time to seek out the sacrament of reconciliation? What might you do differently next time? Ask God for the grace to walk anew in his pathways.

Pay attention to your feelings during the review of your day. What part of this prayer stirred your heart the most? Talk it over with God. Ignatius recommended doing this as one friend might speak with another, heart to heart. Finally, look to tomorrow. What are you worried about? What are you looking forward to? Close your prayer by asking for God's grace and strength for what is to come.

As we begin this new year, resolve to take up the habit of sharing your day with God, treasuring its joys as Mary did, and pondering anew how you might, in this moment, grow closer to God. Like the shepherds and all who heard their stories, allow yourself to be astonished at what God has done for you, the small miracles as much as the large.

May the Lord bless you and keep you, may his face shine upon you, and may you have peace, today and all the year to come.

The EPIPHANY *of the* LORD

REV. JAN RICHARDSON

"And behold, the star that they had seen at its rising preceded them."

1ST READING:
ISA. 60:1-6

PSALM:
72:1-2, 7-8, 10-13

2ND READING:
EPH. 3:2-3, 5-6

GOSPEL:
MATT. 2:1-12

ONCE UPON A TIME, ON A SOJOURN TO ALASKA, I found myself in a room of maps. The room was in the Anchorage Museum, and the maps were part of an exhibition in which artists from across the United States had turned the idea of mapmaking inside out. In their hands, the traditional boundaries of cartography stretched, dissolved, shattered. There was little here that resembled a foldable piece of paper that would help a person get from Point A to Point B.

Wandering the room, I saw maps that took the form of sculpture, of pottery, of books. There was a map that opened like a scroll, a map that was a diptych, a map that had been made by weaving. Few of the maps depicted actual geographical locations. These were maps for charting worlds of imagination, fantastical realms, personal history, the strange and wondrous inner terrain of the soul and spirit. The maps told stories of things both seen and unseen. Their contours set me on the road to an enduring fascination with cartography.

I have a hunch that this fascination owes in large measure to the fact that I have so few maps for my life. In my vocation as an artist, writer, and ordained minister, I have traveled a path for which I have had no model, no blueprint, no chart. Even as the absence of a map has been part of the struggle of the path (*I have to make it up as I go along*), it has also been part of the joy (*I get to make it up as I go along!*).

Because I have had few maps for my life, I used to think of myself as someone who had a high tolerance for mystery—that I was adept at living with the unknown, carrying the questions, and taking the time to dream and discern my way toward the next place in my path. Then my husband died, just a few years after we were married, and darkness suddenly fell with a stunning intensity. In the wake of Gary's death, my capacity for mystery has been severely tested.

Sometime after Gary died, I found myself remembering the enchanted map room in Alaska. I began to wonder what it might look like to make a map in the dark, one that would help me navigate this strange and unfathomable terrain. I wanted a map *of* the dark, a map stitched together of mystery and shadows, questions and wonderings. I began to dream of a map with wounds, with holes; a map that bears witness to what has been torn away, even as it allows space for light and illumination to enter, and for new paths to emerge from the dark.

For those who feel like we spend much of our lives navigating in the dark, Epiphany Day is a day of festival. It is a time when we remember the Magi, those ancient travelers who undertook their journey with only the barest beginning of a map. They were wise to the heavens, and observers in the sharpest sense of the word, but they had no ready-made chart that laid out their course. As the Gospel of Matthew tells it, all that the Magi had to illuminate their terrain and guide their way was a star. This was where their map began: with a burning light, with a step taken, and with the company of those who were drawn in the same direction, that they might welcome the Christ who had come as light made flesh.

Whatever the texture of the darkness we journey through—the painful darkness of loss, grief, and suffering, or the hopeful darkness of anticipation, mystery, and dreaming—Christ waits to meet us there. In his presence, even the darkness can become a place of discernment, of creating, of imagining: a place where a way is made and a map begins.

FOR THOSE WHO HAVE FAR TO TRAVEL

A Blessing for Epiphany

If you could see
the journey whole,
you might never
undertake it,
might never dare
the first step
that propels you
from the place
you have known
toward the place
you know not.

Call it
one of the mercies
of the road:
that we see it
only by stages
as it opens
before us,
as it comes into
our keeping,
step by
single step.

There is nothing
for it
but to go,
and by our going
take the vows
the pilgrim takes:

to be faithful to
the next step;
to rely on more
than the map;
to heed the signposts
of intuition and dream;
to follow the star
that only you
will recognize;

to keep an open eye
for the wonders that
attend the path;
to press on
beyond distractions,
beyond fatigue,
beyond what would
tempt you
from the way.

There are vows
that only you
will know:
the secret promises
for your particular path
and the new ones
you will need to make
when the road
is revealed
by turns
you could not
have foreseen.

Keep them, break them,
make them again;
each promise becomes
part of the path,
each choice creates
the road
that will take you
to the place
where at last
you will kneel

to offer the gift
most needed—
the gift that only you
can give—
before turning to go
home by
another way.

BAPTISM *of* OUR LORD

BECKY ELDREDGE

"You are my beloved Son; with you I am well pleased."

1ST READING:
ISA. 55:1-11

PSALM:
ISA. 12:2-6

2ND READING:
1 JOHN 5:1-9

GOSPEL:
MARK 1:7-11

HOW OFTEN DO WE SEARCH FOR WHAT defines us? As humans, we have a relentless desire to answer the question, "Who am I?" We define our identity in a multitude of ways, but most often by what we have or by what we do. What happens, though, if what we have or what we do changes? This can happen to us in times of great transition, such as when relationships change, when our health or a loved one's health weakens, when we lose our jobs, or when our finances are not secure. Any one of these losses can cause us to spiral into a search for the answer to, "Who am I *now*?"

Our Baptism invites us to embrace the fact that the truest sense of who we are is inseparable from God.

When our identity is wrapped up in the false securities of the world, a change in one of them might cause our understanding of our identity to crumble. Chances are that at some point in our lives we will be stripped of the very things to which we cling to define us. When these things change, we can lose a sense of who we are. We might also hold onto positive or negative words spoken to us by others to define us. Others' affirmation can give us a sense of who we are. At the same time, we can also struggle with our own sense of self-worth because of voices in our lives telling us we are not good enough.

Jesus knows a thing or two about losing the false securities of the world. As he grew in wisdom and understanding of his call, he stepped into deep waters of faith in God that superseded any earthly securities of worldly leaders, of his religious community, and of his family. I often wonder what Jesus wrestled with in his life. Did he yearn to answer the same question we often seek to answer—"Who am I?" Did he, like so many of us do, seek to define himself by what others said he was? How did he make sense of what people around him said as he grew up and entered his public ministry? How did he sort through all the voices around him that told him who they thought he was or who they expected he should be? How did he make sense of what he had, the relationships in his life, and the steady changes he walked through?

In today's Gospel, I think we get a glimpse of what might have helped Jesus walk through his ministry and life assured of who he was. Let's take a look at this defining moment of Jesus's life:

> On coming up out of the water he saw the heavens being torn open and the Spirit, like a dove, descending upon him. And a voice came from the heavens, "You are my beloved Son; with you I am well pleased."

In this profound moment of Jesus's life, God makes Jesus's identity clear. It is rooted in God's love. God made it clear Jesus's identity was inseparable from God's love. This understanding of God's love for him seemed to carry Jesus through the rest of his life.

Monty Williams, SJ, in his book *The Gift of Spiritual Intimacy*, defines spiritual intimacy as our "truest sense of ourselves as inseparably rooted in God."[1] Spiritual intimacy with God is understanding that who we are is inseparable from God. It is about identity in relationship with God and not based in what we have or what we do. Once we know who we are in

1 Monty Williams, *The Gift of Spiritual Intimacy: Following the Spiritual Exercises of Saint Ignatius* (Toronto: Novalis, 2009), 11.

God, we can walk through anything. Jesus shows us we can even walk through death, because we know that even though everything around us changes, we know who we are.

Jesus experienced the truest sense of who he was at his Baptism. It was the foundational grounding in his identity. We experience the truest sense of who we are at our Baptism also. We are claimed by Christ at our Baptism. It is in the marking of the sign of the cross on us that we are visually marked as belonging to Christ—a belonging that never goes away. It is assuring us of our lifelong identity as beloved sons and daughters of Christ. This is an unshakable identity that carries us through any change or transition in our lives.

Being claimed by God, just as Jesus was, means we are given the abundant promises that our readings speak of today. Promises such as we hear from the prophet Isaiah in both our first reading and psalm:

- that when we seek the Lord, he can be found
- that we are given the promise of new life
- that mercy and forgiveness are freely shared
- that clarity of our thoughts, our path, and our way forward are available to us
- that we can walk forward unafraid, due to the confidence that God is with us and we know who we are

Next to my desk hangs a canvas with nine words that capture the essence of my identity. *Who I am in God is who I am.* For the last ten years, these nine words have grounded and calmed me when life throws its expected and unexpected changes my way. I repeat this phrase often when I am feeling unsure of who I am. They bring me home, time and time again, to the identity given to me at my Baptism. They remind me that the truest sense of who I am is a woman inseparable from God.

This is the gift of spiritual intimacy with God. Our identity doesn't come from what we do, what role we play, where we live, or what we own, but in simply the person we are in God. This is true for each one of us. Our Baptisms mark our truest identity of who we are—inseparable from God.

Lent

ASH WEDNESDAY

RICK MALLOY, SJ

"Your Father who sees in secret will repay you."

1ST READING:
JOEL 2:12-18

2ND READING:
2 COR. 5:20-6:2

PSALM:
51:3-6, 12-13, 14, 17

GOSPEL:
MATT. 6:1-6, 16-18

THERE'S THIS PRIEST DISTRIBUTING ASHES in the subway, early on Ash Wednesday. A guy, reeking of booze and weed, who has obviously been Mardi Gras partying all night, sits on a bench nearby. The guy looks at a newspaper and calls out, "Yo, Padre, what causes arthritis?" The priest looks at him with great disdain and disgust and says, "Too much drinking, too much drugging, too much womanizing, and not enough praying." The guy looks back at the newspaper. Realizing his response hasn't been very merciful or compassionate, the priest says to the guy, "Look. I'm sorry. That was a little harsh. How long have you suffered from arthritis?" The guy looks up and says, "Oh, I don't have arthritis. It says here the pope does."

We all ought to have tee shirts with Matthew 7:1 emblazoned on them: "Stop judging, that you may not be judged." Today, of all days, we should realize the church is a hospital for sinners, not a showcase of saints. And the fact that we are all here shows that we know that.

So today, let's think about why we are here, what it all means for our transformation in Christ, and how forgiveness is central to Lent and to our faith.

Today is the day everyone shows up. Maybe it's because, for once, the Church is giving away something for free! "Ashes . . . how much?" "No charge!" All you need is the humility to present yourself, be signed with ashes from last Palm Sunday's burnt palms, and hear the words, "Remember you are dust, and to dust you shall return" (Genesis 3:19).

For many years, I have seen multitudes show up on Ash Wednesday, everywhere from college campuses, where we'd see four times as many students at Mass as on a regular Sunday, to parishes where overflow crowds fill the pews, and even in prison. Years ago, I served at Holy Name Church in Camden, New Jersey. In the 1990s, Camden was often the poorest and/or most violent city in the USA. Riverfront State Prison was in our inner-city parish, on the edge of the Delaware river across from Philadelphia.

One Ash Wednesday, I walk out of the prison "library," where I've just celebrated Mass and distributed ashes for about five times the normal number of Mass attendees. As I walk across the prison yard, a huge guy, six foot five inches, tattoos, very menacing looking—the whole hard-prison-look deal—approaches me.

"Yo, Padre. Hit me."

I look up at him, way up, and say, "What?"

"Hit me."

I look at him incredulously. Hit him? I'd rather play with snakes.

"Hit you?"

"Yo, those ashes . . . hit me."

"Oh." I finally get it.

So, I get out the container of ashes. "Remember that you are dust . . . ."

Immediately a crowd of prisoners draws near and encircles me. They all want ashes.

All of a sudden, every siren in the place goes off. Guards come running over with rifles raised. A booming voice comes over the loudspeaker. "Move away from the priest. Now! Do it now! Move! Father, are you OK?"

I put up my hands and yell, "Yeah, I'm fine. It's OK. They just want ashes."

Why does everyone want ashes? What is it in us that desires this sign and reminder of the truth of our death and dependence on God? Why do we so realize a felt need to pray, fast, and give alms? I think it has to do with our longing for transformation, for our innate desire for God, who we know, deep down, loves us and wants the best for us.

We need to pray, to enter into the silence of our hearts to find forgiveness, compassion, and grace. St. Thomas Aquinas says grace is the ability to do what we could not do before. We need to fast, get some things out of our lives and heads, so other realities can enter into our awareness. We need to give alms to help us realize that all is gift. Much of what we have is somewhat unmerited, and what others lack is often not because of their faults.

We want ashes because we want transformation and transformation is all about change. Once upon a time, there was an elderly Amish woman. She and her whole family went to a mall. They'd never been to one before. They were mesmerized by the stores, the lights, the food court. The old woman watches as an elderly man approaches two shiny metal doors. Doors open; he goes in; doors close. A minute later, the doors open and a guy looking like George Clooney exits. Now, we'd know this is an elevator, but she's never seen one. She sees another old guy go in the doors, and, poof, out comes a Matt Damon look-alike. A third old man goes in and out comes a Ryan Gosling type dude. She cries out to her daughter, "Hurry up. Get your father over here."

Transformation in Christ is not becoming a movie star lookalike or getting to be rich and famous. The transformation we long for is freedom from all that destroys and dies, freedom for everything that is graceful and good, freedom to be who we truly and deeply desire to be. God becomes what we are so that we might become what God is. That's not some Jesuit spin on theology. That's St. Athanasius in the fourth century: Catechism of the Catholic Church #460. You can look it up!

Forgiveness is a main method of transformation. God forgives us. We forgive one another. "Forgive us our trespasses as we forgive those who trespass against us." In the sacrament of reconciliation, we encounter the power and presence of the Holy Spirit and God's forgiveness.

In a world too often filled with trials and tribulations, we can hold on to celebration, consolation, and communion by practicing forgiveness. There's a story of two survivors of the Nazi death camps. One asks the other, "Have you forgiven the Nazis yet?" The other replies, "No. I'll never forgive those bastards." The first gently points out, "Then they will always have you in prison."[1] To refuse to forgive is like drinking poison and thinking it will harm the person who hurt you.

Forgiveness frees us. Forgiveness is what we contemplate and celebrate during Lent. Let's become a forgiving people. I often wonder how different our lives and world would be if on September 12, 2001, the President of the USA had said, "We have been attacked. Several thousand of our citizens have been brutally murdered. But many in our land are Christians, and all legitimate faith traditions call us to forgive and love. Justice necessitates peace and reconciliation. We will not retaliate in kind. We will struggle to forgive. We will work for peace, rather than an escalation and expansion of violence." What would the world we live in today be like if we had forgiven the terrorists, rather than gone to war?

We all want forgiveness. We all want to be freed from war and worry, fear and fighting, doubt and despair. We all want to live in the joy and justice of the daughters and sons of God. We want mercy and grace, faith and freedom, hope and healing. Ashes signal that we want the grace of transformation.

And oh, by the way, the pope doesn't have arthritis!

Let us pray.

---

1 Ernest Kurtz and Katherine Ketcham, *The Spirituality of Imperfection: Storytelling and the Search for Meaning* (New York: Bantam, 1992), 213.

1ST SUNDAY *of* LENT

REV. JAN RICHARDSON

"He remained in the desert for forty days."

1ST READING:
GEN. 9:8-15

PSALM:
25:4-9

2ND READING:
PET. 3:18-22

GOSPEL:
MARK 1:12-15

AT ONCE THE SPIRIT DROVE JESUS OUT INTO the desert, Mark tells us in the gospel reading for this day. He has just told us, only a few verses ago, of Jesus' baptism by his cousin John, and of how, as Jesus comes up from the water, he sees the Spirit descending from the torn-open heavens and hears a voice tell him, *You are my beloved Son.*

He has been initiated. He has been declared Beloved. And where we might expect that Jesus is now all set to take up his public ministry, he turns instead toward the desert, promptly confounding our expectations, as he will do again and again. With the baptismal waters of the Jordan still clinging to him, Jesus enters into the wilderness, the name *Beloved* ringing in his ears.

How else to enter into the forty-day place that lies ahead of him? How else to cross into the wilderness, where he will have no food, no community, nothing that is familiar to him?

How else, but to go into that landscape with the knowledge of his own name: *Beloved.*

Forty days.
Beloved.
Forty nights.
Beloved.
In the blazing day.
Beloved.
In the deep darkness.
Beloved.
In the solitude.
Beloved.
In the hunger.
Beloved.
In the temptation.
Beloved.
With the wild beasts.
Beloved.

And then Mark's Gospel tells us this: *and the angels ministered to him.* After the starkness and the solitude, after the long season of waiting and wrestling, the angels appear.

We do not know in just what way the angels minister to Jesus after those forty days of hungering and discerning and coming to know himself with such clarity. I imagine bread and wine; I imagine a small space of rest and ease at the end of his desert vigil. I imagine the angels finally turning Jesus—gently, firmly—back toward the landscape that now waits for him. I imagine him carrying something of the wilderness within himself as he emerges from its borders. And I imagine him holding fast to the knowledge that comes to those who travel in such spaces: In the desert, there is wild grace. In the wilderness, angels wait.

When Jesus comes striding back out of that terrain, his belovedness blazes within him; the desert has seared this belovedness into him. Whatever else has passed in these forty days, he leaves that landscape with this gift. He knows who he is and what he is here to do: to be belovedness embodied, and to bear this love into the world.

As we cross with Christ into the landscape of Lent and into the mystery that lies ahead of us, how might it be to enter this season with the same knowledge that Jesus carried: that our name, too, is *Beloved*? It might take time for *Beloved* to settle into our heart, our bones—forty days, at least—but that is what this season is for.

BELOVED IS WHERE WE BEGIN

If you would enter
into the wilderness,
do not begin
without a blessing.

Do not leave
without hearing
who you are:
Beloved,
named by the one
who has traveled this path
before you.

Do not go
without letting it echo
in your ears,
and if you find
it is hard
to let it into your heart,
do not despair.
That is what
this journey is for.

I cannot promise
this blessing will free you
from danger, from fear,
from hunger or thirst,
from the scorching of sun
or the fall of the night.

But I can tell you
that on this path
there will be help.

I can tell you
that on this way
there will be rest.

I can tell you
that you will know
the strange graces
that come to our aid
only on a road
such as this,
that fly to meet us
bearing comfort
and strength,
that come alongside us
for no other cause
than to lean themselves
toward our ear
and with their
curious insistence
whisper our name:

Beloved.
Beloved.
Beloved.

2ND SUNDAY *of* LENT

REV. DR. MARK BOZZUTI-JONES

"This is my Son, the Beloved; listen to him!"

1ST READING:
GEN. 22:1-2, 9-13, 15-18

2ND READING:
ROM. 8:31-34

PSALM:
116:10, 15, 16-19

GOSPEL:
MARK 9:2-10

IN THE GOSPEL OF MARK, WE HEAR THE GOOD news of God manifested in Jesus Christ. Mark tells the story of God's salvation in a deliberate way and presents a story in which every incident is connected to the whole. From the proclamation of John the Baptist to the final command of the Resurrected Christ, the reader and the church have one task and that is to listen to Jesus, who is the Beloved Son of God. The Baptism of Jesus, the Transfiguration, and the Resurrection are central events in this invitation to listen.

In the gospel accounts of the Transfiguration, Jesus commanded his disciples not to tell people about what they had seen, but there was no command not to tell people what they had heard. Truth be told, listening has a more foundational role in the Christian life. Discipleship is built on the solid rock of listening to Jesus Christ. When we listen deeply, only then can we proclaim the good news of God in Christ. And so, the message of the Transfiguration is to listen. *Jesus is the Beloved Son of God and we become beloved children of God when we listen to him.*

Listen to him. Give your attention to Jesus Christ, the Beloved. Give your heart, mind, soul, and strength to my Son. Listen to him. Give your life to him. *Listen to him.*

When we listen to God, we live like Jesus—live in such a way that we respect the dignity of every human being and work to be agents of God's compassion and justice. *Listen to him.*

How we listen as Christians—how we listen as a spiritual practice—is of utmost importance because how we listen shapes our prayer, our beliefs, and, most of all, our actions in the world. Listening requires discipline, attention, prayer, and spiritual accompaniment. In truth, the commandments could also be summed up this way: *Listen to God and listen to each other as you listen to yourself.*

Jesus listened deeply to God. In Mark's gospel, Jesus's ministry—his words and actions in the world—began only after he had listened to these words at his Baptism (Mark 1:11): "You are my beloved Son; with you I am well pleased." These words hold tremendous importance for the gospel of Mark and all the gospels. The Christian journey and commitment begin when we listen to God saying this to each of us: *You are my daughter, the beloved, with you I am well pleased. You are my son, the beloved, with you I am well pleased.*

In Mark's gospel, God's affirmation, "You are my Son, the Beloved, with you I am well pleased" becomes the principle and foundation of the gospel and Jesus's ministry. This is so important for Mark that Jesus is the first to speak after these words are spoken to him (whereas Matthew and Luke allow the devil and others to speak before we hear from Jesus). In Mark's gospel, after Jesus listened to these words at his Baptism, he proclaims, "This is the time of fulfillment. The kingdom of God is at hand. Repent, and believe in the gospel." (Mark 1:15).

We are called to believe and reaffirm our faith in the first words spoken in Mark's gospel by Jesus whenever we read the story of the Transfiguration and hear the words: *This is my Son, the Beloved; listen to him.*

Let us spend some time looking at and listening to the story of the Transfiguration. The story of the Transfiguration in Mark's gospel comes directly after Jesus tells his disciples and his friends that the Son of Man must undergo great suffering, be killed, and after three days rise again. This becomes Mark's way of reminding us that, before we enter into the mysteries of the glorious Transfiguration and Resurrection, we must pay attention to the suffering and pain in our world.

As followers of Jesus Christ, we are called to ask ourselves about the suffering, rejection, betrayal, and death in our world. To follow Christ all the way is for us to listen to the suffering, rejection, betrayal, and death of others. Without a doubt, the sin of racism is one way in which Blacks in America continue to suffer, face rejection, experience betrayal, and face death repeatedly. We cannot care about Jesus Christ without caring about the suffering in our world. Remember the first words spoken by Jesus after he was declared to be God's Beloved Son: *The time is fulfilled, and the kingdom of God has come near; repent and believe in the good news.*

The time is fulfilled, and so life takes on a whole different meaning and focus. *How are we being called to repent? How are we being called to allow God to change our hearts? How are we being called to see the face of God in each other?*

Before Jesus took them up to the mountain, he asked his disciples if it would profit them to gain the whole world and lose their life. To understand the pain and suffering of others is the way to follow Jesus. To pay attention to our own cross is the only way we can fully understand the power of the Resurrection. Life in Christ invites us to experience life on a new level, to experience a new way of being in the world—a new creation, a new world order, a new world. Mark hammers home this point by saying that Jesus took Peter, James, and John up the mountain six days later. We are called to remember that repentance and living the good news draw us into a whole new world in Jesus Christ.

And so, upon this high mountain, apart by themselves, Jesus is transfigured before them "and his clothes became dazzling white, such as no fuller on earth could bleach them. Then Elijah appeared to them along with Moses, and they were conversing with Jesus." This piece of information is important because it precedes the words of Peter. So, there is a lot of talking going on. "Then a cloud cam, casting a shadow over them and then from the cloud came a voice, 'This is my beloved Son. Listen to him"

They hear this voice and one wonders if the voice is not the most important event of the whole high mountain experience. The voice is clearly from God and the voice affirms everything that Jesus has been teaching. Listening to him brings life and is the most important thing.

Listen to him. Remember all he told you and all he will tell you. Mark makes it clear that they do listen to Jesus: "So they kept the matter to themselves, questioning what this rising from the dead meant" (Mark 9:10).

The Transfiguration links the Baptism of Jesus with his first words spoken in the gospel of Mark and connects them to the final words spoken by Jesus in the gospel of Mark. To remember the Transfiguration and to listen to the Resurrected Christ is to take the final words of Jesus very seriously: "Go into the whole world and proclaim the gospel to every creature" (Mark 16:15).

3RD SUNDAY *of* LENT

FR. BILL BAUSCH

"Stop making my Father's house a marketplace."

1ST READING:	**2ND READING:**
EXOD. 20:1-17	1 COR. 1:22-25
PSALM:	**GOSPEL:**
19:8-11	JOHN 2:13-25

JOHN, THE STORYTELLER OF THIS GOSPEL, set Jesus's words and action "in the temple." Yet, notice that when Jesus speaks of the same place, he calls it "my Father's house." Here is the central conflict and central theme of the gospel story. What's going on in the temple area is not appropriate for his Father's house. It has no place there. It must be overturned.

So, we see Jesus, who in another gospel described himself as "meek and humble of heart," making a whip from thick cords and cracking hard across the tables, overturning them, spilling everything and shouting, "Stop making my Father's house a marketplace." The moneychangers were there because people had to pay the temple tax for the sacrifices carried out each day. Because these Jews were from all over and brought with them Roman coins with Caesar's image on them—Caesar being considered a divinity—their coins had to be converted to the imageless temple money of the Jewish exchange. That was understandable. It was the gouging, the exorbitant rates, the fleecing of the pilgrims that got to Jesus—in the holiest of places yet! The temple precincts had become a veritable mall of ATMs, a circus of noise and transactions. Holiness had been replaced by hokum. Jesus was merely acting in the ways of the prophets of old.

Seven centuries before, the prophet Isaiah (1:11) declared God's scorn for such temple shenanigans: "'What do I care for the multitude of your sacrifices?' say the Lord. 'I have had enough of whole-burnt rams and fat of fatlings. In the blood of calves, lambs, and goats I find no pleasure.'" Prophetic anger is what Jesus was showing: outrage at what should not be, but was. God's honor and God's people should not be treated like that.

This incident tells us something about Jesus—and something about ourselves. You see, people can be measured by what angers them. True, anger can be dangerous. So can too much food, sun, and water. Anger that leads to reform and betterment is a respectable and desirable emotion.

So, it comes down to this: We are basically judged by what angers us and what does not. Anger becomes the primary Lenten emotion and forms the basis of a litany of reflective questions for this season. Ponder this: We get angry if we get stalled in traffic and miss the first episode of *The Sopranos*. But are we angry over injustice, over the millions of children starving in our own country, the land of plenty? Do we get angry over the massacre in Darfur, or the massive greed of so many politicians: Jack Abramoff seeding corruption, former US Representative Randy Cunningham pleading guilty to accepting million-dollar bribes? What about Michael Milken, Ivan Boesky, Ken Lay, and Bernie Ebbers fleecing their companies and our pocketbooks?

Are we angry that there are homeless in our land of mega-mansions? What about the graphic violence and mindless sex in the media, the corruption of sports, the vast and growing chasm between the very rich and very poor? Are we not just merely disgusted, a feeling that stays within us, while anger would move us to action outside of ourselves? Are we angry over how we buy into the culture's norms of success: high consumption, low reflection, fierce competition, tepid cooperation, rampant materialism? Are we angry over our selfishness and petty jealousies, our picayune lying and cheating, our lack of a generous spirit, our failure to develop a truly spiritual life?

It's time to turn the temple of our lives into "My Father's House."

Okay, let me tell a story that says what I just said, only more memorably.

On a late August night, a cabbie picked up a woman. He was responding to a call from a small brick complex in a quiet part of town and he assumed that, as usual, he was being sent to pick up some hungover partiers, or someone who just had a fight with a lover, or a worker heading to an early shift in the industrial part of town.

When he arrived at 2:30 a.m., the building was dark except for a single light in a ground-floor window. He saw no one. Now, under the circumstances, most drivers would just honk once or twice, wait a minute, and then drive away. But this cabbie was different. He had seen too many impoverished people who depended on taxis as their only means of transportation or people who needed assistance.

So, he got out, walked to the door, and knocked. "Just a minute," answered a frail, elderly voice. He could hear something being dragged across the floor and, after a long pause, the door opened. There was a small woman in her eighties, wearing a blue print dress and a pillbox hat with a veil pinned on it, looking for all the world like somebody out of a 1940s movie. By her side was a small nylon suitcase. He got a glimpse of her apartment, which looked as if no one had lived in it for years; the furniture was covered with sheets. There were no clocks, knickknacks, or utensils on the counters. In the corner was a cardboard box filled with photos and glassware. "Would you carry my bag to the car?" the woman asked. So, he took the suitcase to the cab, then returned to assist the woman, who took his arm as they walked slowly toward the curb.

When they got into the cab, she gave him an address, then asked, "Could you drive through downtown?"

"It's not the shortest way," he answered.

"Oh, I don't mind," she said. "I'm in no hurry. I'm on my way to a hospice."

When he looked in the rearview mirror, he noticed her eyes were glistening. "I don't have any family left," she continued. "The doctor says I don't have very long."

The cabbie then quietly reached over and shut off the meter. "What route would you like to take?" he asked.

For the next two hours, they drove through the city. She showed him the building where she had once worked as an elevator operator. They drove through the neighborhood where she and her husband had lived when they were newlyweds. They pulled up in front of a furniture warehouse that had once been a ballroom where she had gone dancing as a girl. Sometimes she'd ask the cabbie to slow down in front of a particular building or corner and would sit, staring into the darkness, saying nothing.

As the first hint of sun was lighting up the horizon, she suddenly said, "I'm tired. Let's go now."

They drove in silence to a small convalescent home, with a driveway that passed under a porch. Two orderlies came out to the cab. They were solicitous and intent, watching her every move. They were obviously expecting her.

The cabbie opened the trunk and took the small suitcase to the door. The woman was already seated in a wheelchair. "How much do I owe you?" she asked, reaching into her purse.

"Nothing," he said.

"You have to make a living," she protested.

"There are other passengers," he responded.

Almost without thinking, he bent over and gave her a hug. She held him tightly. "You gave an old woman a little moment of joy," she said. "Thank you." He squeezed her hand then walked into the dim morning light. Behind him, a door shut. It was the sound of the closing of a life.

Now, let the cabbie finish this story in his own words:

"I didn't pick up any more passengers that shift. I drove aimlessly, lost in thought. For the rest of that day, I could hardly talk. What if that woman had gotten an angry driver or one who was impatient to end his shift? What if I had refused to take the run, or had honked once, then driven away? On a quick review, I don't think that I have done anything more important in my life."

Then he added a summary of this homily. He said, "We're conditioned to think that our lives revolve around the great moments, but truly great moments often catch us unaware—beautifully wrapped in what others may consider a small one."

Transformation, friends, is the goal of Lent and it's Lent's small acts of kindness that gets us there.

4TH SUNDAY *of* LENT

MIKE JONCAS

"Whoever lives the truth comes to the light, so that his works may be clearly seen as done in God."

1ST READING:
2 CHR. 36:14-16, 19-23

PSALM:
137:1-6

2ND READING:
EPH. 2:4-10

GOSPEL:
JOHN 3:14-21

ONE OF THE HIGHLIGHTS OF MY CHILDHOOD that I looked forward to every year was the annual Christmas broadcast of Gian Carlo Menotti's *Amahl and the Night Visitors.* This short opera, written for broadcast on TV, narrated a lovely imaginative tale in which the biblical magi (identified as Three Kings), on their way to visit a child of prophecy, stop off at the home of an impoverished mother and her crippled son, Amahl. Though strangers, the magi are welcomed and entertained with the best the widow and her villagers can provide. After the entertainment, as all are sleeping, the mother steals some of the gold intended for the Christ Child and is attacked by the magis' page. Melchior, speaking for the rest of the magi, forgives the theft and, in one of the most beautiful passages in the opera, sings of the child they are all seeking:

On love, on love alone he will build his kingdom.
His pierced hand will hold no scepter.
His haloed head will wear no crown.
His might will not be built on your toil.
Swifter than lightning,
he will soon walk among us.
He will bring us new life,
and receive our death,
and the keys to his city belong to the poor.[1]

The mother, declaring that she has been waiting for such a king all her life, states that she would send a gift herself if she weren't so poor. Taking his cue from his mother's change of heart, Amahl offers his crutch as a present and is miraculously cured. The opera ends with Amahl joining the magi in their journey to Bethlehem. Even at a distance, contact with Christ brings about healing.

Today's gospel recounts another night visitor, this time in conversation with the adult Jesus. Nicodemus the Pharisee, identified as a religious authority among Judeans, visits Jesus under cover of darkness, fearing that his honor would be compromised if he visited this itinerant preacher in broad daylight. Like many who encountered Jesus, Nicodemus is baffled by Jesus's sayings, but he doesn't give up pondering them. Later in John's Gospel, Nicodemus will dare to stand against his own religious party, the Pharisees, defending Jesus's right to a hearing when the crowds are divided by his teaching in the Temple. Nicodemus has moved from being a night visitor to a daytime defender of Jesus the preacher. Nicodemus's final appearance in John's Gospel signals the outcome of his spiritual journey. After Joseph of Arimathea takes possession of Jesus's corpse by command of Pontius Pilate, Nicodemus brings myrrh and aloes to anoint the body and joins Joseph of Arimathea in wrapping the body in strips of linen for burial. From night visitor to daytime defender to servant of God's Son, Nicodemus now "lives the truth [and] comes to the light, so that his works may be clearly seen as done in God."

During these forty days of Lent, the Church, in a special way, accom-

1 Gian Carlo Menotti, *Amahl and the Night Visitors* (piano-vocal score), G. Schirmer, 1997.

panies the elect as they prepare for their full initiation into Christ with the Easter sacraments of baptism, confirmation, and first eucharist. They frequently begin their journey of faith as strangers to the Gospel, night visitors to the Word of God, confused and unsure of the longings of their hearts as they approach Jesus and his Church. They have come into the light, declaring their intent when they became catechumens to learn all they can about life according to Christ's Spirit. Now, as the elect, they rejoice with us that "God so loved the world that he gave his only Son, so that everyone who believes in him might not perish but might have eternal life." Like the magi in *Amahl and the Night Visitors,* they have come to believe that "on love, on love alone he will build his kingdom." Like Nicodemus, they seek to "live the truth and come to the light." With them and with Jesus in today's Gospel, we declare "that everyone who believes in him might . . . have eternal life" in him.

5TH SUNDAY *of* LENT

DEACON JIM KNIPPER

"Unless a grain of wheat falls to the ground and dies, it remains just a grain of wheat; but if it dies, it produces much fruit."

1ST READING:
JER. 31:31-34

PSALM
51:3-4

2ND READING:
HEB. 5:7-9

GOSPEL:
JOHN 12:20-33

FOR SIX YEARS PRIOR TO THE CORONAVIRUS pandemic, I attended the Los Angeles Religious Education Congress, where over 35,000 Catholics and other Christians gather each year to pray, to sing, to listen, and to see the Church come alive with a new set of eyes. Actually, that was the theme of a recent Congress: See/Ver—for scripture is filled with many references about our need to see differently:

- Jesus laid his hands on the blind man's eyes, his sight was restored, and he saw everything clearly. (Mark's account of the healing of the blind man in chapter 8)

- "Immediately things like scales fell from his eyes and he regained his sight." (Conversion of Paul, found in Acts 9:18)
- "While he was with them at table, he took bread, said the blessing, broke it, and gave it to them. And their eyes were opened and they recognized him." (Story of the Road to Emmaus in Luke 24:30)

As we come into the final weeks of our Lenten journey, my question to you is: How well do you see Christ in your life?

Unfortunately, I think many people miss the opening line in this week's Gospel, which starts out saying some Greeks came to worship at the Passover Feast and they asked to *see* Jesus. Greeks were gentiles, not Jews, and thus their reason to celebrate this feast had to be their attraction to this rabbi, Jesus. Their query seems to be more than just the act of star-crazed gentiles looking to get a glimpse of Jesus—but rather a desire to really know who this Jesus is . . . to know how to follow Jesus . . . to know what it means to see like Jesus.

And while some commentaries on this passage say that Jesus ignored the Greeks, I think it is just the opposite—rather, Jesus's answer is quick and to the point: You want to see what it means to be like me? The seed must die in order to produce fruit. In other words, by following Christ, we must experience daily dying, knowing that we will get it wrong and we will take two steps forward and then move backward . . . and false assumptions will be exposed, and the false self will die, and then the lens through which we see humanity and see God will change, allowing us to see in a new way.

Recently, I had the opportunity to hear Tim Shriver give a talk about his spiritual journey and his work as CEO of Special Olympics. His mother, Eunice Kennedy Shriver, and her concern about children who were intellectually disabled, created a deep desire in him to learn what these children could do in sports and other activities versus just dwelling on what they could not do. So, what began in 1962 as Camp Shriver with fifty kids in her backyard has now grown to be the world's largest sports organization for children and adults with intellectual disabilities, providing year-round training and competitions to more than four million athletes in 170 countries.

In his talk, Tim told us the following story. It was July 1995, and the old, dilapidated Yale Bowl was the venue for the Special Olympics World Games. For the first time in its history, the president of the United States was to attend the opening ceremony. The Secret Service had already determined that the old stadium was too porous to ensure protection of the president on the field. So, it was decided that President Clinton would arrive and be taken to the very top of the Yale Bowl, where a secure perimeter could be established, and that he would preside from there.

Tim recounts the scene in his book, *Fully Alive: Discovering What Matters Most*:

> For most of them, the experience of parading into that stadium must have seemed surreal. Coming as they did from institutions and isolated classrooms and lonely corners of despair in villages and towns around the world, most of them would never have been applauded for anything before. They were society's outcasts....Over and over, in the countless languages they spoke, they each would have heard "retard," "defective," "sick," "delayed," and, maybe worst of all, "in-valid." Success experiences were nonexistent.[1]

But this crowd roared as they entered the stadium, the president was in attendance, and the Yale Bowl came to life. Prior to the event, the athletes were each given one of those disposal cameras to carry with them into the Opening Ceremonies so they could capture the moment. And, as the ceremony was in full swing, a professional photographer saw a group of athletes, dressed in African garb, all with their disposable cameras raised up to take pictures of the president. But he quickly realized that they were holding their cameras backward. The lenses were flush against their noses as they looked through the viewfinders. He concluded that they must have never used these cameras before.

So, as Clinton was giving his welcoming address, the photographer cut through the crowds and made his way to the athletes in order to help them before they wasted all their pictures. Assuming that they did not know English, he motioned to them that, in order to get a picture of Clinton, they needed to flip the camera around. In response to his advice, one athlete, in perfect English, thanked the photographer and said, "But may I show

---

1 Timothy Shriver, *Fully Alive: Discovering What Matters Most* (New York: Farrar, Straus and Giroux, 2014), 4.

you something? If you turn the camera around and hold your eye up to the viewfinder and look backward, it still works. It works like a telescope and you can see the president very clearly. So we're using these little cameras so we can get a good view of the president. But thank you for helping us."[2]

"Look backward, it still works." Can you imagine the face of the photographer as he looked into the eyes of this young athlete, who had just opened his eyes in a new way by telling him that the camera works in reverse? The eyesight of this man was changed forever. The lens with which he sees the world was modified to where he no longer saw a dis-abled person, but rather one who is very cap*able*, in a way he did not see. Labels—which we all commonly attach to those different from us—were removed and this photographer saw with new and un-assuming eyes. *Look backward, and it still works.*

In other words, to use the Gospel language we just heard—a grain of wheat needed to die; a part of the photographer had to perish: the part that judges others, the part that feeds the ego, the part that blocks us from seeing.

Part of our Lenten journey is about learning to see God in our daily lives and discovering how to better understand and appreciate God's indwelling. But it requires a new way of seeing. For we are all different, all disabled in some fashion, and all have labels given to us by others and ourselves—labels which hold us back, labels which limit who we are, labels we must shed by seeing in a new way. *Look backward, and it still works.*

But it requires us to let go of our past mistakes—allowing the grain of wheat to die and living a daily pattern of death and resurrection. The first reading tells us of God's promise to always be our God, no matter how much we screw up, for God forgets our sins and promises a new beginning, time and time again.

So, as we head to the end of the Lenten season, may you remember that part of life is a daily dying to oneself.

And may your eyes be opened to see—in a new way—*all* the blessings that we each have.

And may you never forget that, in the eyes of God, as different and broken as each of us may be: *Look backward, and it still works.*

---

2 Ibid., 5.

PALM SUNDAY

RORY COONEY

Those preceding him as well as those following kept crying out: "Hosanna!"

1ST READING:
ISA. 50:4-7

PSALM:
22:8-9, 17-20, 23-24

2ND READING:
PHIL. 2:6-11

GOSPEL:
MARK 14:1-15:47

THE PEOPLE OF JERUSALEM WERE ACCUSTOMED to military parades, especially around the holy days. It was Passover week, and the religious festival was a vivid annual reminder that once there had been a Pharaoh instead of a Caesar, and God had taken the side of his ragtag people over the powerful Egyptian army and led them into freedom.

The last sixty years had seen one uprising after another in Judea. So the governor, Pontius Pilate, would lead the Roman garrison in full battle regalia from Caesarea Maritima on the western coast of Samaria into the fortress Antonia in the city of Jerusalem for the week surrounding the festival. Scarlet and gold, horses, lances, swords, and shields would enter Jerusalem from the west in a show of Roman imperial theology. To the Romans, there were many gods, but the one that mattered was the emperor, who was the "divine son" and guardian of the Pax Romana. Anyone in the provinces who challenged the power of the emperor knew the price for that treason and blasphemy was execution on the cross. Both the values of the empire—power and victory—and the tools of the empire—armies and violence—were on full display. There was no misreading them.

But, on this day, another procession enters Jerusalem for the week of the Passover festival. This one arrives from the eastern side, from Bethany. It is a procession of peasants, led by a healer and teacher riding on a donkey. For the man on the donkey, and probably for some of his followers, the meaning is clear. The prophet Zechariah (9:9–17) had spoken of the king of Jerusalem coming unarmed into the city, proclaiming a different message:

> Exult greatly, O daughter Zion!
>   Shout for joy, O daughter Jerusalem!
> Behold: your king is coming to you,
>   a just savior is he,
> Humble, and riding on a donkey,
>   on a colt, the foal of a donkey.
> He shall banish the chariot from Ephraim,
>   and the horse from Jerusalem;
> The warrior's bow will be banished,
>   and he will proclaim peace to the nations.

From the moment we met Jesus in Mark's gospel, he proclaimed an urgent message in his words and in his actions. "The time is *now.* God's rule is *right here.* Everyone needs to *turn around,* go in a new direction, and live in the good news of God's victory." Three times we have heard those words since Advent. All of the healings, exorcisms, confrontations with religious authority, miracles, and parables have led to this day, when Jesus parodies the imperial parade and announces the arrival of the peaceful reign of God in the city of peace itself.

Of course, it all goes off the rails. The Jerusalem priesthood wants no part of a revolution of any kind, and have had enough of this backwater miracle-worker's continual and righteous harping about the system of stipends and taxes that keeps revenue flowing into the temple—revenue that, so far, has kept the Romans and Herod content and out of the temple.

The people's cries of "Hosanna" (Psalm 118:25), not unlike "*eleison*" in Roman civil religion, were both a cry for rescue and a shout of praise. Their singing Psalm 118 to the donkey-riding king, with its allusions to the Davidic king coming to the temple, set off alarms among the leadership. Jesus and his movement had to be stopped before a riot began.

In nearly every encounter with Jesus—a call, a healing, or an exorcism—Mark records some kind of response. Jesus calls the fishermen and they "abandoned their nets and followed him." Same with the sons of Zebedee. He cures Simon's mother-in-law of a fever, and "the fever left her and she waited on them." Mark even records the responses of those who are unable to do what Jesus asks them, like the leper who was told not to say anything, but couldn't help publicizing the whole event. He calls Levi the tax collector away from his tables, then Levi follows and throws a dinner for him. The Pharisees and elders respond too, as when he heals the man with a withered hand in the synagogue on the sabbath. The man was almost a bystander, hadn't even asked to be healed. But after the healing, the Pharisees began looking for a way to put Jesus to death.

How do people respond to the cross? The twelve disappeared. The women disciples stand at a distance with Mary Magdalene. Joseph of Arimathea, perhaps more concerned with order than with solidarity with Jesus, requests the body from Pilate, who asks to be sure Jesus is dead. Then there's the centurion, who watches the one labeled "King of the Judeans" breathe his last. Are his words meant to be a testimony to Jesus's divinity, which would have been blasphemy for him and cause for his own execution? Or are we meant to hear them as ironic, as someone might say today, "Right. This guy sure looks like the son of a god." I tend to think the latter. His words are the last laugh of the empire. "Now," they think, "the sheep will scatter. The shepherd is dead. So much for that impostor."

On this Palm Sunday of the Lord's passion, we too are called to enter one of the processions into the City of Peace, Jerusalem. Will it be on a warhorse, surrounded by soldiers carrying assault rifles, threatening those who disagree with us, who don't look like us, who have different values than we do, with pain, torture, even death? Or will we follow Jesus, who enters the City of Peace to bring peace and not a sword, who in fact comes to banish the sword and every other weapon from the whole landscape of humanity?

Two emperors: Caesar and Christ. Two strategies for "keeping the peace": one through victory, one through justice. Two processions into the Holy City. How will we respond to Jesus on this day? Can we put away the sword and be people of peace? Can we turn our backs on the world that everyone says has to be violent because "that is the way it has always been," and go in a new direction, knowing full well that the path of peace leads through the cross?

Which procession do we join today? Jesus says it again: The time is *now*. God's rule is *right here*. Everyone needs to turn around, go in a new direction, and live in the good news of God's victory. What we decide will mark the beginning of the gospel for the next two millennia.

HOLY THURSDAY

DEACON RON HANSEN

"I received from the Lord what I also handed on to you."

1ST READING:
EXOD. 12:1-9, 11-14

PSALM:
116:12-18

2ND READING:
1 COR. 11:23-26

GOSPEL:
JOHN 13:1-15

ST. PAUL'S LETTER TO THE CHRISTIANS IN Corinth was written in 54 AD, so slightly more than twenty years after Christ's resurrection. Twenty to thirty years after the Apostle to the Gentiles reported what constitutes our second reading for this Holy Thursday, the evangelists Mark, Matthew, and Luke developed their own, non-eyewitness accounts of Christ's last Passover meal, interpreting an inherited Aramaic tradition that the first generation of Christians thought was faithful to what Jesus actually said and did.

"I received from the Lord what I also handed on to you," St. Paul wrote, so it would seem his learning of Jesus's time on earth was somehow infused into Paul at some point. He actually spent just a few days in the company of the Eleven who accompanied Jesus in his public ministry. But the commemoration of the Last Supper was already well-established by others then. As early as chapter 2 in the Acts of the Apostles, we find: "They devoted themselves to the teaching of the apostles and to the communal life, to the breaking of the bread and to the prayers."

Those prayers were probably adaptations of the *Haggadah*, a memorial rite on the feast of Passover, narrating the events of the Exodus that are announced in Holy Thursday's first reading. In biblical times, to "remember" meant not only to recall to mind whatever had been done by God, but also to effectively experience it again, to have the past authentically present. Remembering, the Jews would be conscious of God's intervention in their history and, in gratitude for that, be called to holy action now.

"Do this in remembrance of me," Jesus said. The Real Presence of Christ in the Eucharist has its origins in such Jewish thinking.

We know from his criticism of Simon the Pharisee (in Luke 7:44–46) that Jesus valued the Jewish customs associated with the gracious hosting of a meal, so we can presume that in his role as host of the Hebrew feast of *Pesach* (*Pascha* in Greek), Jesus would have kissed his guests in greeting them, anointed their heads with perfumed oil, and, as we see in the gospel of John, washed their feet just as slaves did then.

Thenceforward, apostleship and service would be forever linked.

Commencing the feast, Jesus would have first offered a prayer of thanksgiving to bless the fruit of the vine and then passed the cup, or chalice, of wine to his friends to share. Then the flat cakes of unleavened *matzah*—the so-called bread of affliction—would have been served along with a kind of leek that was dipped in a dish of salted water and vinegar. After that, the lamb would have been brought to the table.

With the pouring of a second cup of wine, Jesus would have continued the remembrance, concluding it with praise of the Eternal God in what Jews call the Great Hallel. All who were there would have then shared the wine and finished eating the *matzah* and lamb and, perhaps, stewed fruit. Jesus would have blessed a third cup of wine with the second half of the Hallel, singing a hymn that included our psalm for this evening. The feast would have ended just around midnight. And then, we're told, Jesus and his disciples went to a garden across the Kidron Valley from Jerusalem, on the hill of the Mount of Olives, in order to continue their prayer.

So much of our sacramental life depends on our liturgical reenactments of that Last Supper. Our sacrament of the Eucharist is first proclaimed in St. Paul's epistle to the Corinthians, a scene further developed by the evangelists. Also instituted is the sacrament of Holy Orders, for in addressing as "you" the Twelve disciples at the meal, Jesus was establishing a priesthood that was intended to "eat this bread and drink the cup," and feed us as well, *in saecula saeculorum,* into the ages of the ages.

Catholic theology teaches that sacraments effect what they signify, and so it is here. Our gifts of bread and wine are changed by Christ from being symbols of ourselves and our self-giving, to being Christ himself and his self-giving. They are no longer things; they are God. And in the extravagant gift if the Eucharist we are, as St. Augustine wrote, receiving ourselves, for our Baptism formed us into the body of Christ. Our "Amen," our "So be it," is a sign that we are both receiving and giving, that Christ has not just become present to us, but that we have become present to Christ, and are sent out as Christ's disciples to love and serve God and one another, with a blessing in the name of the Father, and of the Son, and of the Holy Spirit.

GOOD FRIDAY

THE REV. PENNY A. NASH

"Behold, the man!"

1ST READING:
ISA. 52:13-53:12

PSALM:
31:2,6,12-13,15-16,17,25

2ND READING:
HEB. 4:14-16; 5:7-9

GOSPEL:
JOHN 18:1-19:42

FOR MUCH OF MY LIFE, I KIND OF GLOSSED over the events of Good Friday. "Crucified, died, and buried"—that all goes together quickly, as a memorized and oft-repeated phrase, and then we get to the real good part: the Resurrection, God's action in history to raise Jesus from the dead, to overcome death and the grave, to open the way for us to eternal life, to show that nothing can separate us from the love of God. Yes, yes, all of that, yes. Resurrection will come.

But today, I cannot gloss over the "crucified and died" part. Jesus's death was not poetic or lovely; it was not like Beth in *Little Women,* who just faded away, gently and sweetly. It was not like Sampson, who brought down the Philistines and himself as a last act of power and vengeance, an angry self-immolation. It was not beautiful, and it was not about brute strength.

The events of today, Good Friday, were the result of blindness, fear, scorn, and hate, a willingness—maybe even an eagerness—of the powerful to draw a line and challenge anyone who crosses it, to say both to certain individuals and to whole groups, "You don't belong on my side of this line."

In the late nineteenth and early twentieth centuries, there were thousands of deaths of this sort. Mobs clamored for the death of men (and a few women) who dared to ignore the color line. Mobs captured these men and advertised the upcoming public hanging (and accompanying degradations) so that people could come and watch other people being lynched. People—black people—hung on trees, maybe after being tortured, while other people—white people—stood around, watching as if this is just what happens some days.

Sometimes folks posed for pictures at these spectacles, and photographers made and sold postcards of men and women and even children standing, smiling, next to the black dangling feet or maybe the mostly or partly whole but dead bodies of people killed in a show of power and control and its attendant sentiments: fear and hatred. "This is what we can do," the powerful said, "and we're not at all unwilling to do it to you, too, if you get out of line, if you cross our boundaries. You will pay. Look. See?"

Crown of thorns. Purple robe. Bruised and bloody face. *Ecce homo*: Behold the man.

What is power, what is life, what is death? How is it that this unspeakably cruel scene is supposed to draw us all together? How are these arms, stretched out upon the cross, able to gather us into a saving embrace when there are nails and blood and jeers and spitting and mocking in the way?

As far as I can tell, when the Scriptures say that Jesus, through the cross, would draw us all unto himself, it is in the same manner as a train wreck. We gather in fear, dread, and bewilderment. We look, and cannot look away. We watch, mesmerized and yet repelled, with focused attention, the smashup. Seeing something like that is supposed to make us say, "No. No more of this."

And still, clearly, Good Friday was not the end of the wrongful conviction of innocents, the end of mocking, the end of spitting, the end of hateful violence, the end of deadly power plays, violent seizures, the end of the powerful saying to the powerless, "We can kill you if we want to."

So, what is truth? as Pilate asked Jesus. What is the truth of this day, of this life? "I am the way," Jesus said, "and the truth and the life." In the beginning was the Word, and the Word was with God, and the Word was God. And the Word became flesh and made his dwelling among us, and we saw his glory, full of grace and truth.

Jesus is God made flesh. And Jesus, God made flesh, would not come out to battle evil with swords and clubs, would not use humiliation and violence as means to an end. That is the truth that stood in front of Pilate.

Jesus showed us another way of being, of living, that is about divine, abundant life for everyone in the midst of a world that is more at home with stories about scarcity and the fight for power and control by a few. Jesus came to show us God, and the world did not like the way he broke down the walls that the world puts up, the way he crossed the lines—and not only crossed them, but erased them.

And there are consequences for this kind of life, of crossing and erasing boundaries.

Ecce homo, behold the man.

Easter

EASTER SUNDAY

REV. RICKY MANALO, CSP, PHD

Mary of Magdala... saw the stone removed from the tomb.

1ST READING:
EXOD. 14:15–15:1

PSALM:
19:8, 9, 10, 11

2ND READING:
ROM. 6:3-11

GOSPEL:
MARK 16:1-7

TOMBS ARE EVERYWHERE.

Just look around; they are all around us. No, not those large marble burial chambers that we glimpse whenever we drive past a cemetery. I'm referring to tombs of injustice such as those that imprison people whose only crime is seeking asylum from persecution. A tomb where captives once wrote a letter detailing their filthy conditions at the height of the deadly COVID-19 pandemic, to no avail. One month later, 81 of the 120 detainees tested positive for COVID-19 and faced death in their shared tomb, with no way out.

I think of the countless people who are assaulted and confined in tombs of gender inequality, sexual-orientation discrimination, poverty, and racial and ethnic bias. Many women, and even men, are harassed and demeaned on a daily basis. African Americans endure systemic racism. Asian Americans are labeled as "Chinese viruses," LGBTQ people do not feel welcome by church doctrine in communities that demonize and entomb their existence. Powerless and alone, the entombed begin to believe lies about their worth, doubts about their abuse, and huddle further into their tombs of shame and fear. Such stories need to be heard and believed.

Yes, tombs are everywhere.

But the types of tombs mentioned above are not meant to be enclosed forever. Not today, of all days . . . not ever.

- Today, we celebrate Christ's freedom from the tomb of death, destruction, suffering, and public humiliation.
- Today, we celebrate that early morning miracle discovered by a trio of unlikely witnesses.
- Today, we remember that the stone that had entombed Jesus's dead body for three days was moved and Jesus was gone! The tomb that had held death became a passage for life—the resurrected life of Christ!

But wait a minute. Let's pause for a moment and realize something: None of us were there. None of us were physically present during the moment that stone was rolled away. None of us actually witnessed the moment when Christ's victory over death occurred, the moment when the light of truth prevailed over darkness, over all forms of violence, oppression, fear, and hostility, and even over death itself. We do not have any scientific proof of Jesus's resurrection. All we have is an empty tomb and the stories of faith that have prevailed for more than two thousand years. And yet, today, on this Easter Sunday, we are called to believe a trio of unlikely people who gave witness that morning. Their story has become our story.

The first among the witnesses was a woman, Mary Magdalene. We hear a lot about the disciples of Jesus and while most references seem to infer men, the first disciple at the empty tomb was a woman. Her reputation has been tarnished over the centuries. She's been labeled as a prostitute, without any scriptural or scientific evidence. Given that history, it is all the more amazing for her to be the first disciple—in every gospel account—to notify the other disciples about the empty tomb. Today, we hear her testimony once again, as we do every Easter Sunday, and we are called to believe her story.

The second disciple to arrive at the empty tomb is the "other disciple whom Jesus loved." No name is given, but scripture scholars agree this is most likely John, sometimes referenced as the "one whom Jesus loved the most" or "the beloved disciple." Perhaps it was the intention of the gospel writer to not mention his name so as to suggest that we are all beloved in the eyes of God, no matter our gender, no matter our sexual orientation, social class, or the color of our skin. Today, the story of the beloved disciple is heard once again and we are called to believe his story.

Last, but not least, Peter arrives at the tomb and immediately steps inside. There he sees the condition of the tomb: empty, no sign of any dead body, only a burial cloth for the body and a cloth for the head, neatly rolled up in a separate place. Where was all the suffering from three days earlier? "Where, O death, is your sting?" This enclosed tomb that once symbolized confinement and death had now become a place of freedom from all forms of hatred and inhumane conditions.

Peter didn't go back to being a fisherman. Instead, he went out on the road and told everyone who and what had changed his life so profoundly. As we hear in the First Reading from the Acts of the Apostles, he traveled throughout Judea, along the Mediterranean coast, and to Caesarea, where he recounts Jesus's life and ministry: how he was hung on a tree to die, and that God raised him up on the third day.

That same message needs to be proclaimed today, more than ever. Just as Mary Magdalene, the beloved disciple, and Peter witnessed and proclaimed the empty tomb two thousand years ago, so are we called to give witness to the tombs that remain in our world, those tombs that continue to confine and entrap us as a result of human darkness. And just like the three witnesses, we too have been empowered by the grace of God to witness, to testify, to proclaim, and to believe:

- When we witness institutional structures that prevent people from seeking freedom and liberty from their captivity, how may we break open these tombs today and, through the grace of God, proclaim that "Jesus Christ is risen TODAY"?

- When we witness any form of mistreatment toward other people, most especially the vulnerable, the women whose stories we have yet to believe, the young, and the elderly, how may we break open these tombs today and, through the grace of God, proclaim that "Jesus Christ is risen TODAY"?

- When we witness all forms of racism, most especially systemic racism, how may we break open these tombs today and, through the grace of God, proclaim that "Jesus Christ is risen TODAY"?

Yes, my friends: Tombs are everywhere, but the tombs of injustice that remain with us today need not be enclosed forever! For as long as we give witness to the Risen Christ and become animated by his presence; for as long as we live, breathe, and have our being in the power of the resurrection; and for as long as we pass on these stories from one generation to the next; then, one day, all of our sisters and brothers who remain entombed will be set free.

And on that fateful day, each of us will enter these tombs and, standing side-by-side with Mary Magdalene, the beloved disciple, and Peter, *together* we will proclaim:

"Jesus Christ is risen TODAY!"

2ND SUNDAY *of* EASTER

TIM SHRIVER

"My Lord and My God"

1ST READING:
ACTS 4:32-35

PSALM:
118:2-4, 13-15, 22-24

2ND READING:
1 JOHN 5:1-6

GOSPEL:
JOHN 20:19-31

LET'S BE HONEST: THOMAS GETS A BAD NAME. Earlier in John's gospel, he doesn't know the way: "Master, we do not know where you are going; how can we know the way?" In today's gospel, he doesn't believe the truth. Not a great resume for a role model of faith. He's clueless, cynical.

And maybe he's even a little irritating. He seems to pride himself on disrupting the flow of divine teaching, stopping Jesus in the middle of his great speech before his passion with an irritating, "Hey, wait a minute!! You're saying all this great stuff, but you're not making sense. Where the heck are you going? And how the heck are we supposed to get there when we don't know where it is? Stop the fancy talk; we can't possibly know the way!" And then, in today's gospel, his buddies are all drinking the Kool-Aid and thrilled and excited, and Thomas has a buzz-kill line: "You guys are nuts and I'll never believe you unless you prove it!"

Ok, those aren't direct scriptural quotes, but you get the point. Thomas asks the tough questions. And who of us really likes the tough questions? Be honest. This guy is the kind of guy who drives most of us crazy.

But not Jesus. He seems to thrive on the tough questions. In fact, he seeks them. Work on the sabbath? Tough question. Forgive a condemned criminal? Tough question. Waste a year's salary on an oil massage for a condemned man's feet? Tough question. Fight against an oppressive government? Tough question. Value the heart of a child over the mind of a religious leader? Tough question. In all these, there seems to be a pattern in Jesus's ministry: He seems to want to get right to the heart of the issue—to move beyond superficials and window dressing. All these questions seem to be about one big, tough question: "When all is said and done, what is the way to the heart of God?" That's a tough question, but it's the kind Jesus seems to like.

And that's why Thomas is our friend. It is his role, it seems, to ask the most powerful two questions on the road to the heart of God: "What is the way?" and, in today's gospel, "How can I believe?"

These are our questions too. If we had the strength to admit it, we're all struggling with these two monumental questions. Our country seems to have lost its purpose, its way. Our church is often in conflict, without a way forward. Our communities and even our families are divided. We live in a time of uncertainty and change—often change that seems to be happening too fast. I'm betting that any one of us would like to stand up in a kind of primal scream and echo Thomas: "Lord!!! Where are we going?? We don't know the way!" And, even more, "Lord! I can't believe you're alive in this mess of a world. Prove it to me!!!"

So, I invite you in this moment of confusion—and maybe, for some of us, despair—not to be afraid to awaken your inner Thomas. Don't brush off the questions in your heart. Jesus can handle them. Don't pretend like it's impolite to ask. I daresay, Jesus wants you to ask. The tougher the question, the better, because getting to the heart of things is the only way to learn how to get to the heart of God.

And consider finding a role model who helps you ask the questions of your deepest heart. I recently found my role model in a moment on a footbridge. I was riding my bike toward a beach path I'd never visited. I got off the bike to cross a narrow wooden bridge that stretched over a small marshy inlet to an open beach. Ahead of me were two women—moving very, very slowly. So, I slowed down and noticed they are mother and daughter—about fifty and seventy or so, a bit hunched, with baggy t-shirts and loose pants. And the daughter was struggling with movements and wanting to turn around. So, they turned and faced me, and I could see the weathered faces of love and compassion. I knew right away the two of them have travelled many roads together. The daughter, with her matted and unkempt hair, was living with a difference—limited language, limited analytic intelligence, halting movements. The mother was living with the child of her creation. Somehow, I knew they'd been together for all their lives.

They started toward me and the mother cautioned her daughter: "Stop, honey. Let the man go by." But I was in no mind to go by. "No," I said, "you come first. I'll wait here and you take your time."

A small smile inched across the daughter's face and the mother said something nice like, "Thank you." I stood my post, waiting for them to traverse the fifteen or so feet on the bridge to go by me. As they approached, the daughter, wearing a bright red and blue hat, looked up at me and her hat blew off into the marsh. She didn't even notice and kept walking. But her mother turned to her and said, "Honey! What happened to your hat?"

"Wait," I said, "I bet we can get the hat. It's just down below us in the tall marsh grass." I looked over and there it was, resting on the grass above the water level. Enter an old, worn-out salt fisherman, with a rod, who stepped onto the bridge to cross over to the beach. And the fisherman said, "Wait. I have a rod and a hook. Let me see if I can catch the hat."

So, we all watched the old salt dangle his hook above the hat and, with one easy motion, he hooked it and reeled it in. "Here you go, honey," he said. "I got your hat and you don't have to worry about a thing." The daughter, from under her uncombed and wild hair, smiled broadly. The mother helped her place her hat back on her head. "Say thank you to the man, darling." "Thaaaaannnnnnnk yoooooouuuuuuu," she said. And the old man could barely take it all in. He just looked at her with more love than a human knows what to do with. "Oh, don't worry. I'm so happy I got your hat. You look so beautiful in that hat."

Then the mother and daughter continued across the bridge, back to the land side, apparently foregoing their intended trip to the beach. And the old salt turned to me and said, "Sometimes, you know why you're alive. That was the best thing that's happened to me in a long time. My heart is bursting."

And I just looked at him and thanked him. "Yes," I said, "Sometimes we know why we're alive. My heart is bursting too."

And then he walked, ever so slowly, to the beach to fish as the mother and daughter walked onto the land, down the road to who knows where.

I don't know more than that, except that on that little bridge a mother of great love and a daughter of great struggle taught an old fisherman and me the first answer Jesus gave Thomas. *Love is the way.* Somehow, I knew they'd lived their whole lives making their minds and bodies and hearts one. And they passed through the question slowly, graciously, with many years of practice in the art of love, and fearless love at that—the kind that just holds the post when everyone and everything else has left you.

And the old fisherman gave Jesus's second answer too: Don't take it from someone else. Slow down. Stay awake. Put yourself in the wounds. Touch the hearts of those who've suffered. See how they live beyond the rules of this world and into the world of eternal love. And find yourself, like Thomas and the fisherman, declaring, "My Lord and My God!" "I know why I'm alive."

Thanks for asking, Thomas. And thanks for answering, Jesus, and all of you, too.

3RD SUNDAY *of* EASTER

MARGARET (MAGS) BLACKIE, PhD

"Why are you troubled?"

1ST READING:
ACTS 3:13-15, 17-19

2ND READING:
1 JOHN 2:1-5A

PSALM:
4:2, 4, 7-9

GOSPEL:
LUKE 24:35-48

IT IS NOT OFTEN THERE IS SUCH A CLEAR, consistent theme through all four texts: sin. In our obsession to appear righteous, it is easy to focus on this alone and ask the inevitable question: "How do we rid ourselves of our sinfulness?" Or, perhaps for some, the question is less introspective, and becomes a gentle tut-tutting as we look towards the licentious behaviour of those we deem as "other."

But if this is the message we take away from these readings, we have missed the point entirely. The much more powerful message inherent in all these texts is that the proximity of our Lord changes everything.

Later in 1 John (3:2–3), we are told, "we are God's children now . . . when it is revealed, we will be like him. . . . Everyone who has this hope based on him makes himself pure, as he is pure."

Gerry O'Mahoney, SJ, used to illustrate the idea of repentance in this way. Imagine you are walking down a road with the sun on your face. The sun symbolises God and our desire to be close to God. Sooner or later, we get distracted and turn a little. This happens again and again, until we reach a point where we discover that we are looking at our shadow on the ground in front of us. Of course, this means we are now headed in the wrong direction. But, at that point, all we have to do to reorient ourselves with respect to the sun is to turn around. We don't have to retrace our steps. We don't have to figure out where we got lost. We just have to turn around.

It embarrassingly simple. All we have to do is turn around. This is the good news infusing all the readings today. The sun is always shining. God is always present.

Of course, it is helpful to understand our own temptations and recognise where we are likely to stumble. But notice how Jesus deals with the disciples in the Gospel. He sees their fear, their confusion, their terror. Bear in mind that the text we have today is at the end of the story of the road to Emmaus. The disciples are gathered, talking about the various appearances of Jesus. And still, when he actually shows up, they don't immediately understand.

What is Jesus's response? He shows them his hands and his feet. He asks for some food to eat. He does normal things and waits for them to catch up. Only then does he explain what it is all about. The gentleness and patience Jesus shows to them on that day is available to us too.

The good news of the Gospel is that if we allow ourselves into the proximity of our Lord, we will find balm. His presence will gently allow us to lower our defences and tell the truth.

In the first reading, Peter is not shy about speaking the truth. He does not blur the truth with euphemism. He says explicitly, "The author of life you put to death." And then he says, "I know . . . you acted out of ignorance," and shows the way to God. But it is only those who own their part in the killing who will dare to turn their faces to God. Those who sit in self-defence and justification of their actions remain defended and inaccessible to the warm, gentle embrace.

Perhaps the greatest challenge in our journey of faith is to learn to tell the truth, to be completely honest, to own our part. It is profoundly difficult to do, because we find ourselves so hard to love when we face into the deep complexity of ourselves. To acknowledge that I am capable of wounding another is truly awful. I do not like to see that in myself. And yet, this is what is necessary.

Again though, notice that whilst sin may be the first thing that seems to link the four readings, it is the proximity of God that is the point. In proximity with God, as I let my heart slow to his rhythm, I begin to relax. I begin to breathe. I begin to tell my story. And there, in that place of being held, I can dare to speak the truth. There, in that place, the healing begins.

As John writes later in his letter (3:1), "See what love the Father has bestowed on us that we may be called the children of God. Yet so we are."

4TH SUNDAY *of* EASTER

PHYLLIS ZAGANO

"... in the name of Jesus Christ."

1ST READING:
ACT 4:8-12

2ND READING:
1 JOHN 3:1-2

PSALM:
118:1, 8-9, 21-23, 26-29

GOSPEL:
JOHN 10:11-18

THE THEME OF TODAY'S READINGS IS WHAT we do and how we are able to do it. That is, the theme of today's readings is vocation: who we are and who we are called to be.

Now, during the Easter Season we have readings from the Book of Acts, the fifth gospel book that tells us about how the Church developed in the first years after the death of Jesus. Today's first reading, from Acts, is plucked from the middle of a very exciting story. Peter and John have cured a forty-year-old man who had been lame from birth, a "cripple" well-known in the area. Some members of a particular Jewish sect called Sadducees take exception to Peter and John curing him, and so they bring these two apostles to trial before the Sanhedrin, a court made up of elders of the community. Listen to Peter's defense: "It was in the name of Jesus Christ the Nazorean whom you crucified, whom God raised from the dead; in his name this man stands before you healed."

In other words, the crippled man was healed by these apostles in the name of Jesus Christ.

How did the members of the Sanhedrin answer Peter? That comes later in Acts, but here it is: "When they saw the man who had been cured standing there with them, they could say nothing in reply" (Acts 4:14).

Today is Vocation Sunday. So, what does this story have to do with vocation?

Well, for starters, we can see in the story that these two apostles, Peter and John, are living the mandate given them by Jesus. They are curing the sick in the name of the risen Christ. And they say so, right there in the midst of the assembled Sanhedrin, probably at least two dozen older men. Their reply to the charges leaves the Sanhedrin silent. What would you think if you were one of the judges?

Wrapped up in this story is the promise of the gospel. In essence, Peter and John are called to be exactly who they are: apostles, preachers of the Good News, Christians, and witnesses to the words and actions of Jesus of Nazareth who, they remind the judges, is the one who rose from the dead. That is how they do what they do; that is how they did what they did.

We know from other parts of Scripture that it was not easy for people to accept the call of Jesus. Remember, it was Peter who denied Jesus three times. Here, he proclaims that his own life and abilities rest in Christ.

Now many years ago, today would be the day for the Vocation Talk. It was when vocations to celibate leadership in the Church were the only things anyone preached about: priesthood and religious life. These are wonderful calls. Our gospel today speaks about the "good shepherd [who] lays down his life for the sheep." The witness of priests, deacons, and religious through the centuries and today demonstrates the value of their own choices and sacrifices to serve the people of God. We know them, through books or reputation, or actually in person: the sister or deacon who founded the soup kitchen, the pastor who built the new church and gym, the bishop who preached against racism. They have all laid down their lives for the rest of the people of God, the Church. We know them and we remember them because they are who God called them to be, and they answered God's call with generosity and love.

There are many ways we can answer the call of God to be who we are intended to be. The idea of "vocation" applies to all of us in many different ways. Some of us have the vocation to priesthood, the diaconate, or religious life. Some are called to marriage or to the single life. In addition, married or single, religious or cleric, some of us have vocations to teaching, or medicine, or carpentry, or something else. The point is, Jesus has called us all to be Christians, and to be Christians within our specific vocations, both our states of life—married or single, religious or cleric—and the professional vocations we live within our states of life.

The bottom line is this: First, we are Christians.

So, place yourself in the shoes—or sandals—of the apostles Peter and John. You have done something that demonstrates your witness to Christ. Say you refused to participate in gossip, or you refused to take a monetary kickback at work, or you said you simply could not lie about something. And, in each of these incidents, you suffered: Your friends would not speak to you anymore if you would not gossip with them; your boss wants to know why you lost that account; you lost your job because you would not falsify a record. Your accusers are not the Sanhedrin of the dusty past. Your accusers are standing there, right before you.

Can you say, along with Peter and John, that because of who you are, you did what you did "in the name of Jesus Christ"? That, my friends, is what vocation means.

5TH SUNDAY *of* EASTER

RT. REV. V. GENE ROBINSON

"God is greater than our hearts and knows everything."

1ST READING:
ACTS 9:26-31

PSALM:
22:26-28, 30-32

2ND READING:
1 JOHN 3:18-24

GOSPEL:
JOHN 15:1-8

MOST EVERY CHRISTIAN KNOWS THE IMAGE and passage from John's Gospel, "I am the vine, you are the branches." It's a beautiful image, and its meaning is clear. Obviously, any version of the Christian faith would include the importance of staying connected to God through God's Son, Jesus Christ, and the Holy Spirit. That connection can be maintained in myriad ways.

Reading the scriptures prayerfully and thoughtfully keeps us connected to the reality of God, as experienced first by the Hebrews, and then by the early Christian community. The stories and words of Jesus especially bring us closer, not just to the historical Jesus, but also to the Christ who was present at the beginning of the world and sits at the right hand of God (see Ephesians 1:20).

Prayer itself is communion with God, and for many people it is a lifeline to the source of all that is. Prayer takes many forms, and there is no one right way or wrong way to do it, as long as it facilitates our mutual communication with God. Sometimes we have to remind ourselves that prayer is not just our opportunity to catch God up on what's going on in our lives. After all, God already knows. It is also an opportunity to listen—sometimes to wait and listen. Sometimes there is a still, small voice, as in days of old; more often, it's a tiny notion that begins somewhere in our heart and mind, and grows into what seems to be a message we need to hear *from* God. A good spiritual director can help us discern whether that small voice is God's voice, or our own ego doing a magnificent impression of God's voice! If the message is challenging us to do something hard, something we'd rather not do, it is more likely to be of God, and not of our own doing.

For some, meditation is a tool for maintaining communication, indeed communing with the divine, whether that be meditation techniques from the Christian tradition, or from Eastern faith traditions.

So, the most obvious meaning of this passage from John about Jesus being the "true vine," and the Father being the "vine grower," and our being branches connected to that true vine, might be, "Stay in touch!! If you want to be a follower of mine, we need to talk from time to time!!" And that's an important message. Nothing wrong with that!! But most everything in scripture operates on several levels at once. In order to go beyond this most obvious message, we need to dig a bit deeper.

This Gospel invites us to go deeper. Instead of limiting ourselves to this admittedly beautiful and comforting image of the vine and branches, let's ask these deeper questions: What is the fruit this vine should be producing? How do we know it when we see it? What does "remain in me as I remain in you" really mean?

Indeed, I would argue that the language used to describe this vine/branch relationship is tough going at best, and not all that helpful at worst. So, let's look at those two other lessons for some clues to its deeper meaning.

The first reading is taken from the Book of Acts. Written by Luke, this book covers the early years of the Church and the work of the disciples who are still trying to discern what it is that their friend (and now Savior) wants them to be doing. They are clearly building a faith community, but they keep running into snags (just like we do when *we* try to build community).

In today's reading, we hear of the reluctance of the community to accept Saul (Paul), as they were afraid of him, not believing he was now a disciple. But Paul continued to teach and preach and to speak "boldly in the name of the Lord," thereby setting this community on an ever-widening circle of inclusion, allowing the Spirit to grow within their numbers.

The 1st Letter of John is where we get "God is love." That's pretty standard fare, but today's passage is way deeper: "God is greater than our hearts and knows everything." And "we should . . . love one another just as he commanded us." Earlier on in John's letter (2:24), he reminds us, "If what you heard from the beginning remains in you, then you will remain in the Son and in the Father." Which seems to be saying that remaining in God means that, in God, we are surrounded, grounded, and enlivened by God's love, and God's love for us results in *our* love going outward from ourselves to others. When we see evidence of that outgoing love for others, "we know that he remains in us . . . from the Spirit that he gave us." Boundaries, separations, and gulfs which exist between us be damned!! *LOVE* dictates the response when it is *LOVE* that abides in us.

So this, then, is what it means for Jesus to be the "true vine," and for us to be branches, connected thoroughly and inextricably to the vine. What courses through the veins of the vine, courses through the veins of the branches. What Jesus is made of, we are made of. The vine imparts to the branches the divine love that was revealed in Jesus and which empowers us to love in Jesus's name.

Perhaps instead of "stay in touch," on a more profound level, this gospel message is, "The apple doesn't fall far from the tree." Let your branches be attached to the vine of Jesus Christ, and the love of God will both abide in you and guide your every choice. In the end, love wins, conquering even death—an Easter message if there ever was one!

6TH SUNDAY *of* EASTER

FR. RICHARD ROHR, OFM

"God is love."

1ST READING:
ACTS 10:25-26, 34-35, 44-48

PSALM:
98:1, 2-3A, 3B-4

2ND READING:
1 JOHN 4:7-10

GOSPEL:
JOHN 15:9-17

THESE READINGS ARE ALL ON THE ABSOLUTELY central theme of life and how we get there. We're told by moral psychologists that there's a staging to our growth in love. You have to start with self-love—respecting the self. If you don't respect yourself, you can't even know how to respect anybody else. Then, God has to move you to what I call group love, family love. This basically means to love people who are connected to you and like you, or who are like you. Now, a lot of people don't even get that far. They don't know how to love their family, or those close to them, or those in their group.

The third level is universal love, and I'm afraid it's an even smaller group of people who get there. As we see in our country and our politics, most people just get to the second stage of knowing how to love people who are like them: their race, their nationality, their religion, their political party. If you stay at that second stage of group love, you don't create a great or healthy society.

With that as a preface, let's look at these three readings. The first one, from the Acts of the Apostles, is very significant because we have Peter himself, the so-called first pope, being taught by the Holy Spirit how to grow up because he believes that God only loves the Jewish people.

Christianity hasn't emerged yet. They just think that what's happening is a reform of Judaism. And then this strange thing happens, where the Holy Spirit falls upon everybody. And Peter looks around and he says, "Oh my gosh! Well, God seems to be for everybody, and not just for the Jewish people. So, I guess it's okay to include them." And he does begin to include them in what we eventually call the church. Unfortunately, most of the church in history has not really imitated that. We've pulled back into groupthink and it's always about people who belong to our group.

Peter proceeds to speak. And he says, "In truth, I see that God shows no partiality. Rather, in every nation whoever fears God and acts uprightly is acceptable." Now, you've got to know, that's pretty amazing, to recognize that all we really need is goodwill—if we can call it that—and God is working with such people. So, all our distinctions between Jew and Christian and Hindu and Buddhist don't really mean that much. I'll take a good Buddhist or a good Jew, any day, over a bad or stupid Catholic. It's all about how much they have grown in love. And this is what Peter himself is beginning to recognize, but he had to be pushed there. He's the so-called conservative at the beginning. But, little by little, God leads him to universal love.

Now, in the second reading, we have that wonderful first letter of John, where John pretty much makes a perfect equation between God and law. "Love is of God; everyone who loves is begotten by God and knows God. Whoever is without love does not know God, for God is love." That's amazing, because it's moving us forward into a recognition that love and God are almost the same thing. So, you can see why it's quite amazing when you have people who are hateful in the name of religion: It doesn't make any sense.

Some time ago, a bunch of fraternity guys in upstate New York all took a pledge to hate. They pledged to hate Jews. They pledged to hate gays. They pledged to hate blacks. And I'll bet these were all nice, white, Christian boys, who apparently had never read John's letter. God is love. And those who love are in God. And those who do not love are not in God. It's pretty clear, pretty simple, because to grow into love is the supreme work of every one of our lives.

Then we have the gospel, from the magnificent Gospel of John, chapter 15, building on last week with the vine and the branches. Now, Jesus passes on this universal love to individual people: "As the father loves me, so I also love you. Remain in my love. If you keep my commandments, you will remain in my love." Then he defines what the commandment is. When we hear the word "commandment," we tend to think of the Ten Commandments, which is not what he is talking about. He says it very clearly at the end, "This I command you: love one another." All the Ten Commandments are summed up in love of God and love of neighbor. It's all ever-expanding circles of love, and that's the task of our life. You're on that journey. I'm on that journey. We all fail. We get it. We lose it. We get it. We lose it. But have no doubt: that's what our faith is all about. Because, as John and Jesus say here, God is love and without love, without living in love, we cannot know God.

7TH SUNDAY *of* EASTER

MEGAN McKENNA

"and the lot fell upon Matthias."

1ST READING:
ACTS 1:15-17, 20-26

PSALM:
103:1-2, 11-12, 19-20

2ND READING:
1 JOHN 4:11-16

GOSPEL:
JOHN 17:11B-19

TODAY WE ARE CAUGHT BETWEEN THE END of the season of Easter and the feast of the Ascension. This Sunday is a bridge between the presence of the Risen Lord, still with us in his resurrected body, and his leaving us so that he can remain with us in the energy and power of his Spirit. It's a hard time. None of us easily lets go of something precious that we love, and believing that something will be even better than what we cherish is harder still. But we have to lay aside something, empty our hands and hearts and minds, so that we can be given something else. Today we have to learn how to risk.

A story can perhaps help, or an image of an experience that many of us, if not all of us, have known at some time in our lives. When I was in high school, I lived to play basketball! In practice, we'd be divided off into teams and two people would be appointed the leaders. They, in turn, would choose who would be on their team. First, one leader would call out someone's name, then the other team leader would choose someone else. As the sides were made up, there was always this awful feeling: When was I going to be chosen? Would I be left until last, and they'd *have* to have me on the team? How terrible to be the one not chosen, waiting until you were the leftover one and they had to take you.

But, in reality, that is what the first reading from Acts is about today. There are eleven apostles. They are short one, since Judas has committed suicide, and it is time to replace him, to extend the leadership to twelve, which will reflect the tribes of Israel and all the nations of the world. The fledging community (about 120 persons, scholars think) gathers and prays to choose one person. The criteria were that they had been "with Jesus" from the beginning of his preaching, or from John's baptism, and that they were witnesses of his resurrection.

They are down to two people, two names: Barnabas (who also was known as Justus and as Joseph) and Matthias. And Matthias is chosen. This means Barnabas is not chosen. Yet, it is strange that we know absolutely nothing about the one chosen, Matthias. And Barnabas, the one not chosen, becomes the preacher, the missionary, the one who teaches Saul after his conversion, vouches for him, and then travels with him (and Mark). He is chosen to preach to the Gentiles and found churches. It seems, in Jesus's "game," if you're not immediately chosen for what seems to be a position of authority or a traditional role, God has other plans. You may be in the "wings" and will be called for even greater things when the time is fulfilled, according to God's ways.

Psalm 103 has us singing and blessing God for all his gifts to us. Everyone, from east to west, throughout heaven and earth, is forgiven and gifted. And we are not to forget these gifts that have been shared with us. We are to be obedient to his commands. Each of us has something of God that we are to learn to share with others.

John's first love letter to his community of the Beloved Disciples reminds us of Jesus's core command: "Beloved, if God so loved us, we also must love one another." A staggering command. None of us has seen God, yet, if we love one another, we begin to see as God sees, and catch glimpses of God in each person. "The first gift given to those who believe" [from the Eucharist Prayer], the Spirit, gives us the power to testify to the truth about our Father, who sent his beloved child Jesus to us—and has saved us, giving us resurrection life. Jesus and the Spirit remain in the Father and we remain in them, moving ever more deeply into them when we love as Jesus loves.

The gospel comes from Jesus's prayer for us to his beloved Father at the last supper, before he is arrested and handed over to torture and death. He calls God "Holy Father," and his underlying request is that we are one: one with each other, all of us, and one in them, as he and his Spirit are one with the Father. He protected us, guarded us, and shared his joy of being one with God with us. He gave us his Word to keep us company and consecrated himself for us, handing over his power, his spirit, his presence into our safekeeping now.

He speaks of the "world" and it is crucial to know that there are two very distinct understandings of this word. The first is found in John 3, where "God so loved the world that he . . . did not send his Son into the world to condemn the world, but that the world might be saved"—to bring it to fullness of life and complete it. This world is all peoples, nations, cultures, languages, genders, ages, places, arts, sciences, earth, air, waters, resources—in a word, all of creation, which is repeatedly described in Genesis 1 as "good," and ends with us, as "very good."

The other meaning of the word for world is what has developed in history and across the earth. It is based on the powers of evil, injustice, violence, hatred, dissension, fear, and insecurity that seek to destroy life: nations, groups, institutions, organizations, all made of people: individuals that resist the Word, the Good News of God to the Poor, and revile those who seek to live God's alternative of hope and abundant life. That's the "world" that hated Jesus. We live in that world, but we are to resist and live Jesus's truth in his Word and his Spirit among us.

Now, Jesus consecrates us to live for that world he created, following in his work of making holy all things and peoples. We don't belong to that "other" world that reeks of injustice, hate, violence, and despair, that beggars others and destroys life.

God is not going to take us out of the world. We are to stand our ground with Jesus's Word and Spirit, to live out our consecration to resist all that is evil, and to offer an alternative of hope, freedom, liberation, abundant life, and welcome to all, especially the poor, outsiders and outcasts, and the least among us that have been impacted by the world that seeks to undo God's creation and wreak destruction upon others, and the earth itself. Jesus prays for us! We need to remind ourselves of this, over and over again: Jesus prays for us. We pray with Jesus as we seek to love others as Jesus loves us and loves everyone.

One way of imaging these worlds is found among many poets and singers. There is an Irish saying: There is another world, but it is hidden in this one. There are places where the veil is thin, and this other world seeps out. This is the world of God's Spirit, the kin[g]dom of justice and abiding peace, where people are amazed and can exclaim: "See how these Christians love one another, there are no poor among them!" [As directed in the first-century *Didache.*] We are to be a place where God's world leaks out, and others can pass into God's domain and dwelling place.

Often, we can feel like Barnabas must have felt: not chosen. We sense or feel that we don't belong. We don't fit in the allotted places, or the way things are set up and run now. But that's okay. Barnabas went on to do things he would never have done as one of the twelve who were the figureheads and public leaders.

Today, and in these remaining days before the Ascension and Pentecost, is a time to think about what lies ahead, and what God has in store for us—what he has reserved for us to do and who he wants us to teach, preach to, stand up for, stand with, and draw deeper into his community of Beloved Disciples. It is a day for dreaming about all the things that Jesus is praying for us to do for and with him. Jesus today consecrates us to his service, his work, and being in his company as his friends.

Think of it: Jesus is choosing up who he wants for what lies ahead this year. It may have nothing to do with what we've been planning or want. But the Spirit is seeking to shift our base, where we stand in this world, and lead us into the great mystery of this wild world he has made and is making into his dwelling place for everyone. God dreams us in his Spirit. Don't let God dream alone these days. This is the way Thomas Merton put it:

> I was not sure where I was going, and I could not see what I would do when I got [there]. But you saw further and clearer than I, and you opened the seas before my ship, whose track led me across the waters to a place I had never dreamed of, and which you were even then preparing for me to be my rescue and my shelter and my home.[1]

Go forth from here, from this place, and dream, with your eyes wide open. And keep in mind that Jesus is praying for you always. AMEN.

1 Thomas Merton, *The Seven Storey Mountain* (New York: Harcourt, 1948), 143.

ASCENSION *of the* LORD

RICK MALLOY, SJ

"Go into the whole world and proclaim the gospel to every creature."

1ST READING:
ACTS 1:1-11

PSALM:
47:2-3, 6-7, 8-9

2ND READING:
EPH. 4:1-13

GOSPEL:
MARK 16:15-20

A JESUIT, A FRANCISCAN, AND A BENEDICTINE all get to heaven—yes, even the Jesuit! The Franciscan falls on his knees and begins singing praises with all the brother and sister angels. The Benedictine pulls out his Breviary, the Liturgy of the Hours, and starts chanting psalms. The Jesuit walks over to God and says, "I think you're sitting in my chair."

Ours is a wild, wacky, wonderful church. Even completely clueless Jesuits can hope to get to heaven. And ours is the only church in which you have to ask, "What time is Midnight Mass?" and "What day is Ascension Thursday?"

The mystery of the Ascension is all about what happens to Jesus as a result of the Resurrection, what it all means for us, and how we can access the meaning and truth of the Ascension. I will suggest we do so by entering the last frontier, the interior depths of ourselves in the community we encounter in silence.

The Ascension, significantly, means that Jesus is now accessible to all, to everyone, in every place, through all time and space. Jesus is now with God in the deepest depths of all reality. He is now "all up" in the mystery of all being. It is not that he flies "up" into a "galaxy far, far away." Jesus ascends the way one ascends to a throne, or gets a corner office, or goes up in the standings in a sports league. Jesus takes a position that places him in relation with all that exists or ever has existed, and all that will ever exist. Jesus has transcended all the limitations of human existence (see Philippians 2:6–11) and assumed his place at the right hand of the Father.

The letter to the Ephesians (1:21) tells us he is risen and seated at God's right hand, "not only in this age but also in the one to come." In the age to come. Think about that. Realize and relish what that means. Jesus is waiting for us in the future, ready to heal our hearts and love our lives into everlasting life forever! He is also here now, in the celebration of the Eucharist and all sacraments. He is in our service with one another to build the Reign of God, a social system of peace and progress, justice and joy, hope and healing, faith and freedom, life and love.

There is a potent theological idea that realizes we become ourselves in our relationship with the "other." To become who we really are, we must be transformed in and through our relationships with others. For example, parents become their deepest, truest selves in their children. Teachers become their true selves in their students. Karl Rahner articulates a theological vision of the mystery of God becoming God's real self in Jesus. Jesus becomes Jesus's real self in the church. The church becomes most real and true in the sacraments. And when we celebrate the sacraments, we see the chain relate in the other direction: sacraments to church to Jesus to God, who is always greater. The Ascension shows us Jesus becoming, ascending into, the truest, deepest reality. As Ephesians 1:18 tells us, he enters into "the riches of glory in his inheritance among the holy ones."

Much the same way we have faith in the mystery of the Ascension, we believe that "those who have gone before us marked with the sign of faith" are accessible to us when we pray, and especially when we celebrate the Eucharist.

The Resurrection means that the Reign of God has arrived on this earth. Heaven means we join the Ascended Jesus in his reign over the total outcome of creation. Jesus isn't in some retirement village, fishing and golfing until the Parousia. Through the Spirit, Jesus invites us to fashion the world according to the desires of God. Jesus is CEO of everything and everybody. He is the GOAT of GOATs (Greatest of All Time).

Jesus has ascended to all levels of reality, wherein and through which he is drawing all of human history, all of creation, all realities, to culmination and fulfillment. We await the new heavens and the new earth, where God will wipe away every tear (see Revelation 21:1–5).

Startlingly, the Ascension is so quiet. We don't even fight about it. We fight about so many things in the church these days, but we are curiously silent about the Ascension.

Maybe that's because it's in silence that Jesus is now accessible to everyone and everything, at all times and in all places. He has transcended this realm and is present in and through all realities, and that is done in silence. Jesus ascends in silence, into the silence.

I remember when I was sixteen years old, a big, tough, loud football player. For some stupid reason, I was mad about something and took my forearm and slammed it into a wall in my mother's house. The plasterboard gave way and created a huge 16x14-inch hole. I was really ashamed as I waited for her to get home from work.

She didn't say a word—just looked at it and walked away. My mother was absolutely silent (very unusual for a woman who could sit on the phone talking to her gal friends for hours). She ascended into silence. She put up a poster over the hole. She didn't even ground me, just kept silent. Never said a word about it. She just left me to figure it out.

It wasn't the silent treatment. It was her way of dealing with a recalcitrant teenager. Years later, when pious ladies would say, "Oh, you must be so proud that your son is a priest!" She'd reply, "I'm proud of all my children—and Ricky? I thought he'd be in jail or dead by the time he was 21." So, moms, there's hope for your kids!

In many ways, we come to know our silent God and our deepest selves in silence. There is a long tradition of silence in our church, from the desert mothers and fathers, to the Carthusians and Trappists, to the classic *Cloud of Unknowing*, to St. Ignatius's Spiritual Exercises on silent retreats.

Jon Sobrino, SJ, teaches that the poor are a privileged channel for an encounter with God, and he's correct. Another privileged channel is silence. One way we get in touch with our own poverty is to stop the endless chatter going on between our ears. Enter into the quiet. In the silence, we come to know our dependence on God; our inability to control our world or ourselves; the reality of our creaturehood and God's infinite power as creator. Compassion and mercy, hope and healing, life and love can be deeply experienced and relished in silence.

It is in silence that we enter the atrium, the threshold of the age to come. It is in silence that we can stop holding ourselves as the center of our consciousness and allow the still small whisper of God to slip into our hearts. From the prophet Elijah, to Jesus's times alone in prayer, to St. John of the Cross and Teresa of Avila, to Thomas Merton, the value of silence is heralded and held in high esteem.

So many are so afraid of silence these days. I invite and encourage young adults to think about a silent retreat, or encourage them to try the Trappists' simple but demanding Centering Prayer. And the reaction is intense. "Oh, I could never do that!" "I'd die without my cell phone." "I tried it once and hated it!" Yeah, when I was six, I took a sip of beer and hated it. Some tastes are cultivated!

God's response to the hatreds and horrors of humanity is to send the Son in the stillness of that silent night to work our transformation and redemption through the Holy Spirit. Grace, the power to do what we could not do before, is mediated to us in silence. Let's allow ourselves to enter the silence, the mystery, the awe-inspiring wonder, of the reality of Jesus the Christ's Ascension.

Silence and light are similar. We can't see light, but light makes it possible to see everything else. We can't hear silence. Still, silence enables us to hear truth and hope and love.

Let us ascend into the silence along with our church's contemplative orders like the Carthusians, the Trappists, and the Poor Clares who live in silence, alone with the alone, praying for us and our world. In silence, the false self fades. In that pregnant silence, we will meet Jesus and experience the birth of the transcendental realities of God's heart in our truest selves.

This connection to silence, and time spent alone with the alone, is crucial for the Church's mission. St. Ignatius teaches we must be contemplatives in action. The works of evangelization, preaching and teaching, administration, direct service to and with the poor: all are sustained and encouraged by the discipline of stepping back and resting in silence with God.

There's a line voiced these days: "No Money; No Mission." Actually, it's "No Contemplation; No Mission." Ascend into silent contemplation. You may like it!

And for all you little kids out there: I've got a joke for you! Why does God the Father always have to use his left hand? Answer: Jesus! Because Jesus is sitting on God's right hand!

Let us pray.

PENTECOST

PAT WENRICK

"Receive the holy Spirit."

1ST READING:
ACTS 2:1-11

PSALM:
104:1, 24, 29-30, 31, 34

2ND READING:
1 COR. 12:3-7

GOSPEL:
JOHN 20:19-23

ONE OF MY FAVORITE MOVIES OF ALL TIME was *Pay It Forward*. It was the story of an eleven-year-old boy, Trevor, whose social studies teacher presented his class with an opportunity to receive extra credit. Those that accepted the challenge were to look for a way to change the world and put it into action. Trevor was a latchkey kid, the son of a single mom who was a recovering alcoholic. She worked two jobs to make ends meet.

Most of the students in Trevor's social studies class paid more attention to the facial disfigurement of the new social studies teacher than to the fiery challenge he set forth for those who wanted extra credit. The challenge, if accepted, was to find a way to change the world and put it into action.

Trevor thought long and hard about the project. As the force of driving wind, he thought of a way to change the world, one person at a time. He would choose three people and do a significant favor for them. Then, in turn, he would ask those three people to choose three more and do favors for them. Paying it forward would create a chain reaction, much like collapsing dominoes falling after the first one is hit.

Trevor's first choice was to bring home a homeless man, allowing him a place to shower and get clean clothes and a meal, and then providing money for him. Second, he recognized that both his social studies teacher and his mom seemed to be a perfect couple and moved to get them together, despite their old tapes of fear and lack of self-esteem, and the resurgence of Trevor's abusive, alcoholic father. The third recipient of a favor was a classmate at school who was always being attacked by bullies.

Eventually, a reporter from Los Angeles is blown away when a lawyer gives him a Jaguar after seeing his Mustang totaled. Such kindness, the reporter discovered, was part of this pay-it-forward movement initiated by Trevor.

Today, we celebrate Pentecost or, as many refer to it, the birthday of the church. As we hear in the first reading and the gospel, the followers of Christ were gathered in one place, behind locked doors. Unlike the fear and isolation of Trevor, the latchkey movie character, the followers of Jesus isolated themselves from others because they feared that others were going to kill them like they did Jesus. They feared that their association with Jesus would bring the same fate as their teacher and friend. Lest we forget, they were still on an emotional rollercoaster, sometimes caught up in grief over the physical death of Jesus, but also wanting to believe in the presence of Christ risen.

As I write this reflection, I cannot help but think that we live in a world so divided. We fail to see the good in others and focus on the disfigurement. We would rather stay behind locked doors than venture out and change the world for the better. There seems to be a reluctance to let go of the disfigurement and tragedies of the past, as if it is better to hold onto the familiar than to let go of it and embrace a new way of experiencing life. We are afraid. We forget that God has never given up on us, even though we often give up on God. We hurt—the result of betrayal, abuse, and words spoken in anger.

Jesus, the Christ, broke through these same paralyzing emotions. Jesus broke through the greatest fear we all have, which is death. No tomb stone, no doubt, no wound, no disfigurement, no physical or psychological abuse, no betrayal, no lack of faith was or is powerful enough to keep his Spirit from penetrating our very being and our locked hearts. Jesus promised that the Father would send, in his name, the same Spirit that brought about his resurrection. Today, that same Spirit, that mighty wind that broke through the isolation of those latchkey disciples and gave them the courage and fire to move out into the world is challenging us to do the same. Jesus paid it forward for many during his earthly life, and then asked not only those gathered in that room, but all of us, to do the same.

The challenge is for each of us to choose someone we don't know and do a favor for them, then ask them, in turn, to do a favor for someone else. Keep that fire moving. It doesn't have to be a Jaguar. Be creative in passing it forward. The work of the Holy Spirit can bust us out of our isolation and end the divisive world in which we may find ourselves. The secret is connectivity. The followers of Christ emerged able to proclaim the Word of God and bring about actions of healing and forgiveness in many languages amongst many different cultures of people. They connected with others because they first connected with the Spirit of Jesus. All who heard the message of Christ listened to the same thing. Isn't it amazing that the Christian message keeps on moving forward after over two thousand years?

In paying it forward, let us remember the word from Paul's first letter to the Corinthians:

> For in one Spirit we were all baptized into one body, whether Jews or Greeks, slaves or free persons, and we were all given to drink of one Spirit.

Pay It Forward!

Ordinary Time

2ND SUNDAY *in* ORDINARY TIME

DEACON GREG KANDRA

"Behold, the Lamb of God."

1ST READING:
1 SAM. 3:3-10, 19

PSALM:
40:2,4, 7-10

2ND READING:
1 COR. 6:13-15, 17-20

GOSPEL:
JOHN 1:35-42

NOT LONG AGO, I CAME ACROSS THE remarkable story of a doctor who makes house calls to people who don't have houses.

His name is Dr. Jim Withers, of Pittsburgh. Most nights, you won't find him in the ER or in the operating room. You'll find him on the streets, a stethoscope around his neck, hunting the back alleys of downtown Pittsburgh. His waiting room is McDonald's, or a gutter, or a heating grate. His patients are the unemployed, the addicted, the elderly, the outcast. They include people suffering from depression and post-traumatic stress disorder; some are former prisoners and mental patients. They are people who can't afford to see a doctor. Many are just lost, needing to be found.

Dr. Withers practices in a growing field called Street Medicine through a group called Operation Safety Net, funded in part by the Sisters of Mercy in Pittsburgh. The work is hard and taxing. But, person by person, case by case, Dr. Withers gives the hopeless a reason for hope. He cares for the people no one else cares about.

Dr. Withers himself admits this is more than a job. It's a calling. It is, in fact, a mission. One of the most prominent items in his simple office is a framed picture of Mother Teresa.

Mother Teresa famously said that we need to see Christ in the distressing disguise of the poor. I think perhaps Dr. Withers does, too.

But I'd also suggest something else: I think the poor of Pittsburgh see in Dr. Withers the unexpected disguise of Christ.

Here is compassion. Mercy. Tenderness. Hope. Here is God using an ordinary man to do extraordinary good.

Behold, God at work in the world.

That, in many ways, is what John the Baptist was saying about another man, in another time, when he told anyone who would listen: "Behold, the Lamb of God."

John the Baptist spoke those words in an unlikely place, about an unlikely figure—but he pointed the way to a wondrous mystery: God isn't always where we expect.

He comes to us in a manger. He comes to us, here and now, in a piece of bread. He comes to us through one another.

He comes to us in a stranger with a stethoscope on the streets of Pittsburgh.

We've just completed the Christmas season, celebrating the Nativity and reliving, once again, the beauty of this miracle, God becoming man, an event recounted with great detail and eloquence in the gospels of Matthew and Luke.

But in John's gospel, which we just heard, there is no nativity story, no background about Jesus or his ancestry. Instead, there is this: "Behold, the Lamb of God." This is St. John's Annunciation. Here, God's entrance into human history isn't heralded by an angel. It is proclaimed, instead, by a prophet on the banks of a river. One solitary man sees another, and cannot help but bear witness—"testify"—and cry out for the world to look and to believe:

"Behold, the Lamb of God."

It's a bold challenge.

Do we see what John the Baptist sees?

And do any of us offer that kind of testimony?

How many of us act as heralds for Christ—not so much with the words we speak, but with the lives that we live?

We need to remember: Belief is more than the creed we profess, and faith is much more than the prayers we recite every Sunday at Mass.

It is a testimony, lived every day.

It is the testimony of missionaries, who offer their lives to people in broken and grieving places like Haiti and Syria and Ghana.

It is the testimony of the unnamed saints we encounter every day, in offices or at bus stops, on street corners and in supermarkets.

It is the testimony of doctors treating patients in alleyways and on muddy streets in places as varied as Pittsburgh or Palayur or Port-au-Prince, inspired by the love and compassion of a small nun in India—who was herself inspired by the love and compassion of God made flesh in Galilee.

It is the testimony of all who seek somehow to bring Christ to others and heal a wounded world.

All these examples and more testify to the Christian life. They speak of hope and belief in a world too often overcome by despair and doubt.

Look up, they say, and behold.

"Behold, the lamb of God."

This beautiful fact remains: The work of John the Baptist didn't end at the banks of the Jordan.

It goes on today.

All of us are called to proclaim God's presence in our world, just like John the Baptist.

It is the great work of our lives.

St. John's Gospel tells us, "In the beginning was the Word."

But, in fact, the Word was just the beginning.

I think the work of men like Dr. Jim Withers is a humbling reminder: The rest of it now is up to us.

3RD SUNDAY *in* ORDINARY TIME

BECKY ELDREDGE

"Then they abandoned their nets and followed him."

1ST READING:
JON. 3:1-5

PSALM
25:4-9

2ND READING:
1 COR. 7:29-31

GOSPEL:
MARK 1:14-20

AS A SPIRITUAL DIRECTOR, I AM ACCUSTOMED to being in the role of asking other people questions. I ask questions that invite people to explore the work of God in their lives, that help them unpack their experience of God, and that invite them to embrace the graces God is offering in their lives at that moment. Sometimes, I offer a suggestion here or there for them to take into prayer or into their discernment. My biggest role, though, is to simply listen. What a gift it is to listen to the sacred stories people share that connect to our larger salvation story. Each of our sacred stories begins with encountering Jesus in such a transforming way that we feel compelled at some point to drop our nets and follow Jesus. One of the ways we can strengthen our faith is by pausing, remembering, and celebrating our sacred stories of first encountering Jesus and being invited into relationship.

People I accompany in spiritual direction have come to expect that, from time to time, I will invite them to reflect on the fullness of their relationship with God: savoring when it all began, how it unfolded, and where it is now. It is an overwhelming gift to witness up close the uniqueness of God's movement in a person's life as they share their stories of how God invited them to enter into relationship and drop their nets. God's work in our lives is *profoundly* personal.

Coming out of the listener role is hard for me because of the number of hours I spend in this posture of accompaniment each week. It is why an encounter years ago with a young man at a coffee shop remains with me today. In an unexpected moment, he pulled me out of the role of listener to become the one sharing my sacred story of being encountered by Jesus and "dropping my nets."

I sat down at the rickety table at the coffee shop, trying not to spill my cup of coffee as the table swayed back and forth. I settled into my chair and looked across the table at the young man in his early twenties. I smiled and wondered why in the world he had reached out to me to meet. I could feel the posture of spiritual direction arise in me, preparing myself to listen deeply.

We exchanged pleasantries for a few minutes before he cleared his throat and asked me, "*Becky, when did you first encounter Christ? What was your net-dropping moment?*" Stunned not only by his question, but also by the role reversal his question spurred, I sat in silence, absorbing and reflecting on his questions. As I sat there, I could feel tears welling up in my eyes and catching in my throat as I went back to the moments where I felt I first encountered Christ during my junior year of high school.

I told him the stories of how I came to know Jesus was calling me into relationship through the welling up I felt inside me, in my inner chapel. It felt like someone had a string on my heart and was gently tugging me toward something or someone greater than myself. I also shared with him how the authentic witness of faith in my teachers and close friends ignited the search for God in my own life. I recalled how I wanted so badly what they had, a joy that seemed to rise above any of life's difficulties my friends and teachers experienced. The invitation within and their witness of faith helped me slowly but surely to drop my nets and follow Jesus.

As I continued to share with the young man my sacred story of relationship with God, I realized that it was more than just one net-dropping moment. There was a series of net-dropping moments throughout my journey of faith. Jesus inviting me, time and time again, to a *profoundly* personal encounter with him that simultaneously invited me to abandon my nets and follow him. Even that afternoon, as I reflected and shared with the young man, I sensed Jesus was yet again nudging me to let go of the current nets of security I was holding in order to step into even deeper waters of faith.

Simon, Andrew, James, and John experienced the *profoundly* personal moment of encounter with Jesus in the gospel today. Each was uniquely called. Each was invited to follow. Each was encouraged to drop their nets. As they stepped forward to follow Jesus, they experienced "the world in its present form passing away" (1 Corinthians 7:31). Their walk with Jesus immersed them in learning a new path to living—one that brought mercy, love, compassion, and mission into their lives.

Our own sacred stories of call invite us to remember how we are uniquely invited to follow Jesus, to drop our nets, and to walk a new path, letting the world as we once knew it to pass away. As Jesus teaches us his ways, we also learn the path that the disciples walked that brings us to an abundant life.

What this young man gave me that afternoon was a moment of grace. I could not remember the last time I reflected on where my faith journey actually began. It left me renewed and in awe of the *profoundly* personal way God continues to move in my life today.

After sharing my sacred story of call, I returned the question to the young man, asking him, "*When did you first encounter Christ? What was your net-dropping moment?*" I eagerly listened to his sacred story of call, all the while thanking God for this unexpected moment of encountering Jesus through the young man.

The question he posed to me that afternoon at the coffee shop I pose to you now. *What is your sacred story of being encountered by Jesus in a profoundly personal way that invited you to drop your nets and follow Jesus?* When is the last time you reflected on where your journey of faith began and how God unfolded it through the years? I invite you to remember and celebrate the moment Jesus encountered you and invited you to drop your nets and follow him.

4TH SUNDAY *in* ORDINARY TIME

FR. RICHARD ROHR, OFM

"He taught them as one having authority."

1ST READING:
DEUT. 18:15-20

2ND READING:
COR. 7:32-35

PSALM:
95:1-2, 6-9

GOSPEL:
MARK 1:21-28

LET'S LOOK AT A COUPLE OF THESE READINGS. The first reading from Deuteronomy is the text that begins the entire tradition of the prophets. Let me put this in context. There are two great strains of spiritual teachers in Judaism—and I think, if the truth be told, in all religions. The priestly strain holds the system together. They keep repeating the tradition. I'm sort of operating as a priest now. The strain that we're less familiar with is the prophetic strain, because that one hasn't been quite as well accepted. Prophets are critical of the very system that the priests maintain.

If you have both, you have a certain kind of wholeness or integrity. If you just have priest, priest, priest, you just keep repeating the party line and everything is about loyalty, conformity, and following the rules—and that looks like religion. But, if you have the priest *and* the prophet, you have the system constantly refining itself, correcting itself from within.

Now, that very seldom comes together. We see it in Moses himself, who both gathers Israel, yet is the most critical of his own people. We see it again in Jesus, who loves his people, but is lethally critical of hypocrisy, and illusion, and deceit. And we're living in a most amazing time, because we have it in Pope Francis right now. We very seldom have a pope who is also a prophet. He holds the tradition together, respects it, and, in that sense, is conservative—conserving the tradition. But, at the same time, with the things he's saying to the bishops and priests, he's often quite critical of us, as he should be. He's prophetic. But, of course, he's creating a lot of enemies in doing this.

With that as a background, you're prepared to understand the gospel.

This is the first exorcism, or recognizing of a demon or a dark spirit, and it's in a most amazing place. It's not in the marketplace. It's not with the prostitutes. It's not one of the tax collectors. The devil is *in the synagogue itself*. This is no small symbol. It would be like if I said, "Well, the big devil in the South Valley is right at Holy Family Parish." I don't think you would like that, right? That's the type of thing that prophets say.

So, Jesus enters the synagogue, in this first chapter of Mark's Gospel, and the evil ones, of course, he recognizes. They're exposed. You see, the only way evil can succeed is to disguise itself as good. And one of the best disguises for evil is religion. Just pretend to love God, just go to church every Sunday, just recite the creed, say all the right things, and you can be racist. You can be against the poor. You can hate immigrants. You can be totally concerned about making money and being a materialist, but you go to church each Sunday. Do you understand?

Those are the kinds of things that prophets point out. And so, prophets aren't nearly as popular as priests. Priests keep repeating the party line, so there's no reason to fight them. But, when you do both, when you put together—to use our contemporary language—the best of the conservative with the best of the liberal, no one likes them because they're neither Republican nor Democrat. They honor their tradition, but they say, "Here's what's phony about the tradition too." That's what a fully spiritually intelligent person can do. And I hope a gospel like this is respecting that.

One other point. You might not have noticed it in the reading of the gospel, but it says, twice, "He taught them as one having authority and not as the scribes." Then at the very end, we read, "All were amazed. . . . What is this? A new teaching with authority."

The normal way you proved you had authority was to quote the past. If you're Protestant, you quote the Scriptures. If you're Catholic, you quote the popes, or the saints, or the mystics. They both have their strengths and their weaknesses. But here's a man. Remember, Jesus is not a priest, he's not a formal prophet, and yet he's operating as both. He's a lay person, like all of you in this room. And he stands up and speaks with his own inner authority: "My experience says." That's daring. Who of you could do that? Here I am, standing before you in all my vestments, with my ordination, so I could get away with saying what I want to say. But if one of you came up here and said this, everybody would be grumbling, "Who is she? Who is he?" Well, that's what Jesus was doing. As a layman, he speaks, "This is how I see God." That's why it's difficult to be a prophet, because a prophet is never ordained as such.

Pope Francis is ordained, of course, but usually prophets just say, "This is my experience." Now, that can be true, or that can be false. And that's what Mark's Gospel is talking about here. If someone is speaking truth to power, they're always critiquing power: political power, economic power, governmental power. That's why all the prophets are killed—because they're not company men.

Do you see how we're trying to hold both sides together? How could you honor the tradition and yet, at the same time, recognize when it's telling lies? I think you know where this is leading. We have a great need for some prophets in our government right now. When untruth takes over and lies are told as a regular operation, you know we need prophets who speak truth to power. But you can be pretty sure they're never going to be popular. They'll probably be jailed and, often-times, at least in the Jewish tradition, they were killed. So, don't pray to be a prophet—but we still need them now.

5TH SUNDAY *in* ORDINARY TIME

DAVE DAVIS

"Let us go on to the nearby villages that I may preach there also."

1ST READING:
JOB 7:1-4, 6-7

PSALM:
147:1-6

2ND READING:
1 COR. 9:16-19, 22-23

GOSPEL:
MARK 1:29-39

IT WAS EVENING, JUST AS THE SUN WAS setting. Earlier in the day, Jesus had been teaching in the synagogue. After he left there, he went with James and John to the house of Simon and Andrew. There at the house, he healed Simon's mother-in-law. It was after that, after the teaching and the healing, just as the sun was setting, that they brought to Jesus all who were sick and those who were thought to possess a demon. As Mark records it, "the whole town was gathered at the door." The whole city was on the doorstep. Everyone was there at the house, including all who were sick. Capernaum turned out to see Jesus. He didn't need a key to the city; the whole city came to him.

Careful gospel readers might jot a note about how the text indicates that "he cured many" and "he drove out many." Many, not all. Matthew indicates early in his gospel that Jesus "went around all of Galilee, teaching in their synagogues, proclaiming the gospel of the kingdom, and curing every disease and illness among the people" (Matthew 4:23). Luke writes of how "all who had people sick with various diseases brought them to him. He laid his hands on each of them and cured them" (Luke 4:40). Here in Mark, the whole town was on the doorstep and he healed many, he cast out many, but not all.

The next day, "rising very early before dawn, he left." It was in the morning, but still very dark. This was something other than early rising. This wasn't just as dawn was breaking or just before sunrise. This was morning and still very dark. This was the kind of time of morning when babies wake up to nurse. This is the kind of time of morning when someone is up because sleep won't come, because the worry won't stop, because the mind and the heart keep racing. This was not the discipline of getting a start to the day. This was more like getting up so as to ease the torment of the night. Jesus got up in the morning, when it was still very dark.

And he "went off to a deserted place." One translation says that he went out to a solitary place. But the description of the place here in the text is stronger than that. The word in the Greek relates not just to a lonely place, but to a wilderness place. Like earlier in the first chapter of Mark when, right after his baptism, "at once the Spirit drove him out into the desert" to be tempted by Satan and to hang with wild beasts and to be waited on by angels. The place Jesus went to when it was morning, but still very dark, was a deserted, wilderness place. A place like he had been before.

In the region of Israel and Palestine, the wilderness areas refer to arid, desert-like, windswept mountainous regions below Jerusalem and to the south, toward the Dead Sea. In contrast, the landscape around the Sea of Galilee in the north is lush, fertile, and green. The area around Capernaum, spots within walking distance in the darkest part of the morning, are hardly what would be called "wilderness" by regional, topographical standards. So, this deserted, wilderness place of prayer, when it was still very dark, bears a deeper connotation. Jesus was not heading out for morning devotions, the first prayer office of the day. This was Jesus gutting it out in prayer, Jesus baring his soul. Like Jesus in the wilderness, being taunted by the devil. Like Jesus outside the garden, pleading for God to take the cup from him. Like Jesus weeping over Jerusalem: "If this day you only knew what makes for peace" (Luke 19:42). It was that kind of spiritual space for Jesus. There he went and prayed.

"Simon and those who were with him pursued him and on finding him said, 'Everyone is looking for you.'" They pursued him. No mention of someone waking up and realizing he was gone, or maybe someone who was responsible for standing watch by night. Just, they "pursued him." The King James softens it as the text indicates, "they followed him," almost like it was part of their discipleship, a following thing. But some scholars point out that the Greek word for pursued here is much stronger: hunted, chased, pursued. They didn't just follow him; they hunted for him.

They hunted for him in the way a parent goes looking for a child who is late coming home from a party. The parent has no trouble going to knock on the door of that house, knowing that if there is any adult in the house at all, they're probably asleep. The parent has absolutely no concern at all about embarrassing the seventeen-year-old in front of friends and everybody there—and God, for that matter. "Excuse me! Do you know what time it is? What are you doing here?! I have been looking all over for you. Do you know what it's like, driving around at this hour, not knowing where you are? I have been hunting for you."

The implication in Mark chapter 1 must be that they went after him with more intentionality than just looking for him. They went after him with a bit of attitude, determination, haste. They hunted him down. "Don't you know that everyone is searching for you? What are you doing here? What the heck? The whole town was on that doorstep, and there's more to do. You cured many, you cast out many—many, but not all. Come on, all of Capernaum is waiting!" They hunted for him, and when they found him, they gave him the "what for" about all the healing, all the need, all the brokenness, all the humanity waiting for him back in Capernaum.

Who knows? Maybe his struggle in prayer was about the magnitude of one day's accumulation of human suffering. Maybe what woke him up, kept him up, got him up, was the sheer amount of work that he was getting himself into, how much there was to do. Maybe his dark night of the soul was related to his own realization that they had to move on from there, even when there was more need to be met, more love to be shared, more kingdom work to do. Who knows?

What he said to Simon and the others who came hunting for him was, "Let us go on to the nearby villages that I may preach there also. For this purpose have I come." Here is where some would stress the importance of proclaiming the message—that Christ came to proclaim, to preach, to announce, to tell the Good News. The healings and miracles are all in service to, signs that point to, what Mark defines in 1:1 as "the gospel of Jesus Christ, the Son of God." This thread of an argument suggests that, rather than let miracles and healings become "*the thing*," Jesus moves on to affirm that the gospel, and proclaiming the gospel, is why he came. "For this purpose have I come," he told them as they headed out and, according to Mark, "he went into their synagogues, preaching and driving out demons throughout the whole of Galilee."

It makes sense, when you read it, that proclaiming the message is what he came out to do. Jesus says it. Mark repeats it. Proclaim the message. But, what if also, what if in addition, what if another way to read it is that what he came out to do was to go on to neighboring towns. "For this purpose have I come . . . to go on to neighboring towns, to not stay here, to go throughout Galilee, to proclaim the message to others, to not stay here, to preach not just to you, but to them. We have to go."

And the whole town of Capernaum that was on the doorstep? They were left in a huff that morning, what the Bible would describe as a whole lot of moaning and grumbling, because they were hunting for him. There was more healing to do. They wanted to keep Jesus for themselves. They wanted to hoard Jesus and he knew it. It kept him up that night. For the sake of the gospel, he had to go on.

Hoarding Jesus. The disciples were keeping Jesus to themselves. Like at the Mount of Transfiguration, when Peter wants to build the booths for Jesus, Moses, and Elijah, so they could all stay there and preserve the moment. Like when the mother of James and John asks Jesus to give them each a seat at his right and at his left in the kingdom. Like when the disciples were "astonished" that he would be speaking to a Samaritan woman. Like when they sternly told all those parents with children trying to get to Jesus to "go away, not now." Like those who told the blind beggar by the side of the road to be quiet. Like when the disciples were angry when the woman anointed Jesus with the expensive perfume. Like at the empty tomb, when the disciples held onto the feet of the Risen Christ, when they tried to cling to Jesus. That morning, when it was still really dark, somewhere near Capernaum, they hunted for Jesus. It wasn't a following thing. It was a "keeping Jesus for themselves" kind of thing.

Hoarding Jesus. When the followers of Jesus think the good news of the gospel is just for them, or is more important to them, or is, first and foremost, really about them. When those who use the name of Christian turn Jesus into a Christ of their own making, a Jesus who agrees with everything they already believe and a Jesus who will excuse or understand or rationalize, along with them, everything they do. Hunting down Jesus. In a time when public figures and political discourse and cable news and tax policy turn pretty much everything, reduce everything, bring everything back to "us vs. them," those who want to keep Jesus to themselves of course think Jesus is for them and no one else. They misconstrue the profound theological affirmation of "Christ is for us" into a sinful game of winners and losers that assumes Jesus is for us and not for them. But when it comes to the Jesus of the gospels, and the poor, and the stranger, and the foreigner, and the unclean, and the different, and the sick, it is clearly "Christ for them."

When you cling to Jesus, you head into interfaith relationships more concerned about pure doctrine than courageous love. You err on the side of judgement rather than grace because it's more important to be right than to be faithful. You yearn for a faith life, a church life, a religious life from the past rather than boldly looking to what God has in store in the days to come. You slip down that slope of thinking the world could be going down the drain in terms of justice and righteousness but as long as you and Jesus are good, as long as you're sure of your own salvation in him, it's all okay.

When you try to keep Jesus all for yourself, it's just too easy to make decisions, come to conclusions, form opinions—all in his name—that are hurtful to others. It's bound to happen, when you crave a Jesus of your own image, that you come off sounding and acting like that Pharisee who gave thanks that he was not like those others: the tax collectors, the sinners, the spiritual but not religious, the evangelical right, the liberal left, the new-agers, the atheists, the red-state voters, the liberal elites, on and on and on. When you try to cling to Jesus with both hands, you don't have to worry about patting yourself on the back, because you believe your Jesus is already doing that for you, thank you very much.

Here, in this sacrament, as you feast again on this love and grace and promise and presence, remember the holy words Jesus said. And remember, he never said, "Take, eat, this is my body broken . . . just for you."

6TH SUNDAY *in* ORDINARY TIME

FR. BILL BAUSCH

"Do everything for the glory of God."

1ST READING:
LEV. 13:1-2, 44-46

2ND READING:
1 COR. 10:31-11:1

PSALM:
32:1-2, 5, 11

GOSPEL:
MARK 1:40-45

I WILL PASS OVER THE GOSPEL FOR TODAY TO focus on St. Paul's short epistle, which you just heard. Recall these opening words: "*So whether you eat or drink, or whatever you do, do everything for the glory of God.*"

"Do everything for the glory of God." That sounds nice—but, to be honest, we would like to get some credit. I mean, it's nice to be self-effacing and do things from a high motive, deflecting attention away from oneself and doing deeds out of pure love of God and neighbor, without expecting anything in return. As I said, it's nice, but, deep down, we know we're not made of such lofty stuff. Surely one of the great joys in life is to have our good deeds found out and to try to act humble as the spotlight of praise is focused on us while a secret voice within whispers how good, noble, and powerful we are and that the world is a better place for our being here. Still, to counteract this bit of self-serving pride, there they are, Paul's words: "Do everything for the glory of God." And that's a directive found not only in Paul, but in all the spiritual masters throughout the ages. Listen, for example, to this ancient tale called the Holy Shadow.

As everybody knows (goes the story), the Angelic Council meets on Wednesday afternoons from 3:00 to 5:00 to consider earthly candidates for special gifts, rewards, and honors. The list of potential recipients is usually long and a lot of "weeding out" is necessary. Well, after one particularly tedious meeting, the potential recipient for the week was selected and the name was sent "upstairs." The Angelic Council, of course, is purely advisory to the Divine Source, who has to give the final OK to each nominee. This time, a memo came down that said, "Approved, but ask her first." The Angelic Council selected a subcommittee. They immediately flew to earth and found their potential recipient. In a formal and solemn presentation, they offered her a gift. "You have been found worthy," they said in unison. (With so much time spent in the angelic choir, angels always speak in unison.) "We are pleased to give you the gift of healing touch. Whomever you lay your hands upon will be healed."

The woman said that she was sure the gift of healing touch was very much needed in the world in which she lived, but she declined the honor. "Perhaps someone else would accept it," she said. The angels quickly caucused. Being superior beings, they adjusted their plans to meet the situation and returned with a new offer. "You have been found worthy," they said in unison. "We are pleased to give you the gift of conversion of hearts. Whenever you speak, people will be moved to change their lives for the better." "I am sure that the gift of conversion of hearts is very much needed in the world in which I live," replied the woman, "but someone else must accept that gift. I decline the honor."

Grumbling now, the angels caucused a second time. They returned with a new proposal. "You have been found worthy," they said in unison. "We are pleased to give you the gift of great virtue. People will see your deeds and be encouraged to live lives of high moral value." The woman agreed that the gift of great virtue was very much needed in the world in which she lived, but she insisted that someone else needed to receive it. She declined once again.

It was only after the woman's third refusal that the angels remembered what the divine memo had said: "Ask her first."

"So, if you don't want the healing touch, the gift of the conversion of hearts, or great virtue, what is it you do want?" the angels asked in frustrated unison. The woman answered quickly, for she always knew what she wanted. "I want the gift of doing good," she said, "but not knowing it."

The angels caucused. This was a new and unforeseen request. They were energized and buzzing with the challenge, their wings beating excitedly. After some time, they came upon the way that the "gift of doing good but not knowing it" could be bestowed. They made the woman's shadow a source of goodness. She would go about her life doing what had to be done, but whatever or whomever her shadow fell upon would be graced. As she walked by a withered brook and her shadow fell across it, for example, it would suddenly gurgle with sweet, clear, running water. If her shadow fell upon a sullen child, the child would suddenly smile contentedly. If she passed a world-weary man, he would reawaken to vital purpose and passion. And so the woman would live, going about doing good and not knowing it.

The people in her world respected the humility of the woman. They never told her of the healing effects of her shadow, although many tried to walk behind her. And since her good deeds were never explicitly attributed to her, her name has been forgotten: She is remembered only as the Holy Shadow.

This old Sufi story, as you can see, is a variation of Paul's words. It is a reminder to see oneself as a medium of grace and not the claimer and doer of good deeds. You see, the mystics like Paul rightly spy a danger in all human gifts and striving. The mystics fear we will not recognize and acknowledge the Divine Source, that the ego will step forward and pride will claim a place of honor. And we all know how often that can happen, and does happen, as Paul forewarns us.

But, of course, St. Paul was only repeating what Jesus taught. When Jesus told people they were the light of the world, he urged them to let their good works shine forth. What was the reason he gave? So that people would see them and "glorify your heavenly Father" (Matthew 5:16). In a similar vein, you may recall, when a man asks Jesus, "Teacher, what good must I do to gain eternal life?" Jesus shoots back, "Why do you ask me about the good? There is only One who is good" (Matthew 19:16–17). The retort is clear: Do not associate yourself with goodness.

Humans do not possess goodness; they only reflect the goodness of God. Again, Jesus claimed, "My food is to do the will of the one who sent me" and, on his death-cross, "Father, into your hands I commend my spirit." For Jesus, Abba—God—was all: the Beginning and the End, the Alpha and the Omega.

We have to ponder this for our spiritual lives. What St. Paul is teaching and what our experience shows is that the ego is forever insistent, and pride is our besetting sin. So, we must pray and strive and desire that, whatever we do, we do it for the glory of God who, after all, is the measure of all things. It is God from whom we came and to whom we shall return.

We Catholics, you know, are fond of litanies. We line up saints and plead with them to both influence God on our behalf and be models for our struggling lives:

> Holy Mary, pray for us.
> St. Joseph, pray for us.
> St. Michael, pray for us.
> St. Agnes, pray for us.

So we intone. I suggest that perhaps we should add another sentence to our public and private litanies, following St. Paul's injunction: one that is a plea for protection from vainglory and self-idolatry. I suggest that we add: "Holy Shadow, pray for us."

7TH SUNDAY *in* ORDINARY TIME

KEVIN AHERN

When Jesus saw their faith, he said to the paralytic, "Child, your sins are forgiven."

1ST READING:
ISA. 43:18-25

PSALM:
41:2-4

2ND READING:
2 COR. 1:18-22

GOSPEL:
MARK 2:1-12

THE HEALING OF THE PARALYTIC IN THE second chapter of St. Mark's Gospel presents us with one of the most memorable scenes from Jesus's ministry.

Whenever I think of this story, I am reminded of catechetical coloring books I had as a child. The scene is perfect to capture the imagination. A crowded room is filled with people clamoring to see Jesus, with faces peering in the windows and doorways. Then, suddenly, the roof opens up and a sick person is lowered down inside. And, to top it off, there is a group of grumpy scholars sitting in the front row.

As with many biblical stories, the healing of the paralytic is more profound and complex than the coloring book scenes many of us may remember as children. Here, Jesus is teaching in the town of Capernaum on the shores of the beautiful Sea of Galilee. The hometown of Simon Peter and Andrew becomes the base for Jesus's public ministry. It became a place where he was known.

We see this in the previous chapter of Mark's Gospel, when Jesus goes to St. Peter's house, after preaching in the synagogue, to visit Peter's mother-in-law, who is sick in bed. In healing the woman, he "approached, grasped her hand, and helped her up" (Mark 1:31). Word must have quickly spread in this fishing community, because later that evening, St. Mark describes how "the whole town was gathered at the door" as they "brought to him all who were ill or possessed by demons" (Mark 1:33, 32). So, it's no wonder that a large crowd would again gather to see Jesus and listen to him preach the word. So much so that today's Gospel tells us that "there was no longer room for them, not even around the door" (Mark 2:2).

The crowded setting reveals the momentum building in the early stages of the Jesus movement, while also setting the stage for the dramatic actions that would happen next as four men come carrying a paralytic on his mat.

The experience of paralysis or immobility of any kind, even in today's context, brings with it a tremendous amount of suffering, especially if you are economically poor. In a time before advanced scientific knowledge, the physical suffering of paralysis was often compounded by social and religious stigma that linked illness with sin. Yet, here we have four men bringing a person in need to see Jesus. Undaunted by the crowd in front of the door, the group rips open the thatched roof to lower the paralytic down. How did people inside react to this commotion? If this was Peter's house, as many believe, what did he or his wife think of the new skylight?

As Pope Francis points out in a 2016 homily on this gospel, the four men were not afraid to take risks in their determination to bring their companion to Jesus. They were not afraid because they had faith. This dramatic act of faith moves Jesus to respond. "Child," he says, "your sins are forgiven." A few moments later, he tells him to "rise, pick up your mat, and go home" (Mark 2:5, 11) and the man is miraculously healed.

In the Gospel of Mark, having the gift of faith is deeply related to healing. When people lack faith, as when Jesus is rejected in Nazareth, they are unable to receive the grace of his miraculous healing actions (6:5). Where such miracles do happen, as with the dramatic healing of the woman with the bleeding condition (5:25–34), the restoration of Bartimaeus's vision

(10:46–52), and the healing of a boy with a seizure condition (9:14–29), Jesus recognizes the faith of the sick person or their community.

In this scene in Capernaum, the faith embodied in the action of the four companions stands in tension with the doubt and discontent of the scribes comfortably seated in the room. Unlike the paralytic, the social position of these religious leaders likely meant they had no problem getting in to see Jesus. "Just how could Jesus," they grumble, "claim to forgive sins? What right does he have to do this?" As the first reading from the Prophet Isaiah points out, only God has the power to forgive sins. The scribes are thus correct to be wary of anyone who claims to do this, but sadly, they do not have the gift of faith to see the divine nature of the person right in front of them.

This tension and conflict between Jesus and certain religious leaders, as we know, will only grow, and ultimately will lead to his arrest and execution. Biblical scholars speak of this as the first of five "controversy stories" in the Gospel of Mark, where conflict arises as the Christological nature of Jesus's identity becomes known.

The courage and compassion of the four companions reveals at least three sets of questions for Christian discipleship today. First, the healing at Capernaum speaks to the power of God to transform creation and our deepest selves. Isaiah speaks of this in the way God does new and surprising things. Like the four companions, Christians are called to trust in the power of God to transform the world and our lives. The four men trusted in God, in Jesus, to heal their friend, to restore his dignity, and "wipe out" his sins (Isaiah 43:25). Do we trust in the power of God to transform our lives? Do we have faith to see the new things God is doing?

Second, the acts of the companions reveal the corporate nature of faith. Faith is not an individualistic reality. The grace or gift of faith is not something we can earn or do all on our own. We need to support each other and carry each other on our way to God. In our life as Christians, how do we carry each other on this pilgrim journey? Over the past few weeks, have we shared any of the burdens that others carry? Have we brought anyone to Jesus?

Finally, the faith of the companions inspires them to go beyond themselves and take risks. Here, they embody the teachings of St. James when he affirms the need for faith to manifest itself in action (2:17). The Psalm today reminds us of God's special concern for the poor and the rewards given to those who care for them (41:2). But how do we transform our faith into action today? When people share with us their struggles, do we respond, or do we just say, "I will pray for you," with little intention of actually doing that or, really, anything concrete? Do we see the suffering and injustice of people around us? If yes, do we take action?

As we take time to reflect on the gift of faith this week, let us imagine the scene at that crowded house. Are we more like the four companions, who trust in Jesus and bring those in need to him, or are we more like the religious leaders, who think they know everything about faith, yet ultimately are unable to see the presence of God in front of them?

8TH SUNDAY *in* ORDINARY TIME

KATHERINE CORDOVA

"New wine is poured into fresh wineskins."

1ST READING:
HOS. 2:16B, 17B, 21-22

PSALM:
103:1-4, 8, 10, 12-13

2ND READING:
2 COR. 3:1B-6

GOSPEL:
MARK 2:18-22

WHAT HAS YOUR EXPERIENCE BEEN IN THIS new reality of living with a viral plague? Have you had experience of living with other plagues? Have there been other times in your life when you have been isolated from people you know and care about? How have you experienced loneliness and loss in the last year?

We are all familiar with the salutation, "Peace be with you." It refers, of course, to God's peace, which is another way of talking about having God with you and wishing that for others. How do you feel when you think of being reconnected with those you love? How is that true in your relationship with God? How is that relationship? Is God sometimes a stranger? Perhaps you can take a moment now and consider your current relationship status with God.

Our readings today all reveal a part of what it is to be in relationship with God. They are particularly potent when we consider them as methods to test our own relationship with the Holy One. Where is the stranger in this relationship? Perhaps, at times, you have been a stranger to God. Perhaps God has been a stranger to you. Perhaps you have been so cozy in your relationship, there has been no room to welcome others. These are passages for our times and, given the current state of pandemic, we all have clear lived experience of having loved ones "with us and not with us" as we have had to quarantine, wear masks, stand at a distance, and stay home. Let us bring some of that together as we consider the Bible readings for today.

We first hear Hosea speaking about God's desire for relationship with the land and peoples in the personification of a bride and bridegroom. This is a very intimate relationship. The requirement is that people give up their other gods, just as in the marriage vow that demands the forsaking of all others. If that condition is met, God will shower the land with plenty. There is a give and take that is part of any relationship: the action and response of trust and exclusivity. What is our relationship to the land? What is the bond between God and the land? Do our actions cause larger-scale consequences? How might we engage with God in this way?

As if in response to any doubts that we might have that we could live up to the prophet Hosea's staggeringly large vision of our relationship to God and the land, the next portion of scripture is a song in praise of God's wondrous care and love. This is sung by someone who knows God as the good parent. Notice the repeated use of the phrase, "Bless the Lord, my soul." What does it mean to bless someone or something with the very essence of your being? Has that happened to you? Could you take a moment and put yourself in a place where you might give such a blessing—to God? To a loved one? To a stranger? It is a good exercise, especially if you are feeling cross with the world. I find it very helpful when I am frustrated in traffic. When do you find you most benefit from blessings?

Next, we read about a relationship being compared to a recommendation letter in Paul's second letter to the Corinthians. He begins by saying that his relationship with the Corinthians is so close that they do not need such a letter between them. He then goes on to suggest that the Corinthians are their own embodied letter of recommendation to the world for Christ, while, at the same time, telling us that God's glowing recommendation is the spirit of our actions. Let's consider for a moment what recommendation we are giving of our relationship with God. I am not asking these questions to shame you. Rather, it is often in asking such questions about any relationship that we can honestly consider how we can be our best selves.

What would a glowing recommendation for Christ feel like? What would it look like if you saw it in someone else? What steps could you take immediately to be a better recommendation for your relationship with the Beloved? How can you best indicate that you are a letter of Christ, "written not in ink but by the Spirit of the living God, not on tablets of stone but on tablets that are hearts of flesh"?

Lastly, we come to the Gospel reading from Mark. This passage comes in the midst of several examples of how Jesus, his ministry, and those around him are being scrutinized for behaving in ways out of the norm. In Mark's telling, the scribes and the Pharisees have just raised an eyebrow when Jesus feasted with tax collectors and sinners. We now learn that John's disciples and those of the Pharisees are fasting while Jesus's people are not. The verses following are about the Pharisees' complaints that Jesus is plucking grain from the field on the Sabbath. Jesus is changing our relationship to the laws of worship, religious practice, and the demonstration of relationship to God. In Jesus, there is welcome for people that the Pharisees won't acknowledge. The disciples celebrate his presence in their lives. Jesus then ignores long-held rules about honoring God on the Sabbath to instead honor God by feeding the hungry.

Mark uses this pattern of repeated examples to illustrate the changed relationship into which Jesus invites us. He uses the metaphor of new wine in new wineskins. He acts differently from the ways of the past. Old wineskins won't be flexible enough to hold the new wine. We also must make ourselves new to contain the new. Christ came to show us a different way to relate to both God and the stranger. If our relationship is to work with Christ, we need to be different too. We cannot maintain our old habits. There will be time for fasting later. Now there are outcasts to eat with and the hungry to be fed.

With Jesus's presence, we must rejoice like the psalmist. We need to remember, as Hosea told us, that God has loved and wanted us—and all the land and all the people—for a very long time. We have a responsibility to be the spirit of a recommendation for God and we must, like those first disciples, celebrate the Messiah in our midst.

9TH SUNDAY *in* ORDINARY TIME

FR. BILL BAUSCH

"Let light shine out of darkness."

1ST READING:
DEUT. 5:12-15

2ND READING:
2 COR. 4:6-11

PSALM:
81:3-11

GOSPEL:
MARK 2:23-3:6

ST. PAUL WRITES IN TODAY'S EPISTLE: "GOD who said, 'Let light shine out of darkness,' has shone in our hearts to bring to light the knowledge of the glory of God."

These words jumped to mind when I read a David Brooks column in a recent issue of the *New York Times.*[1] He was commenting on how an audience is brought to tears watching the new documentary, "Won't You Be My Neighbor?" It's about how the *Mr. Rogers' Neighborhood* show got started and how he used it for over thirty years to teach and accompany children. It describes the famous opening sequence—Mister Rogers going to the closet, putting on the sweater, changing his shoes. It describes how he gently gave children obvious and nonobvious advice: "You are special just the way you are." "No, children can't fall down drains in the bathtub!"

Sometimes a tiger puppet sang, "Sometimes I wonder if I'm a mistake," meaning "I'm so different; am I a mistake?" An adult character sang along and tried to reassure him that he was not a mistake. Sometimes Mr. Rogers

1 David Brooks, "Fred Rogers and the Loveliness of the Little Good," *The New York Times*, July 5, 2018, https://www.nytimes.com/2018/07/05/opinion/mister-fred-rogers-wont-you-be-my-neighbor.html.

would slow down time by being silent for long periods of time as he fed his fish. Occasionally, Mr. Rogers touched on politics. During the civil right era, when black kids were being thrown out of swimming pools, Rogers and a black character bathed their feet together in a tub. After Bobby Kennedy was killed, Rogers gently explained what an assassination was.

Once, a reporter wrote about how Rogers met a fourteen-year-old boy whose cerebral palsy left him sometimes unable to walk. Rogers, an ordained Presbyterian minister, asked the boy to pray for him. The boy was thunderstruck. He had been the object of prayers many times, but nobody had asked him to pray for another. He said he would try, since Mr. Rogers must be close to God and, if Mr. Rogers liked him, he must be O.K. The reporter, a man of his times, complimented Rogers on his cleverly boosting the boy's self-esteem, but Rogers didn't look at the situation like that at all: "Oh, heavens, no, Tom! I didn't ask him for his prayers for *him*, I asked for *me*. I asked him because I think that anyone who has gone through challenges like that must be very close to God. I asked him because I wanted his *intercession*."

And here, notes Brooks, is the gospel radicalism that infused the Mr. Rogers show: that the child is closer to God than the adult; the sick are closer than the healthy; the poor are closer than the rich; and the marginalized closer than the celebrated.

Another incident: In 1997, a teenage boy in Kentucky warned his classmates that "something big" was going to happen. The next day, he took a gun to school and shot eight classmates, killing three. Mr. Rogers' response was "Oh, wouldn't the world be a different place if he had said, 'I'm going to do something really little tomorrow.'" Rogers dedicated a week's worth of shows to the theme "Little and Big," on how little things can be done with great care. In his dealings with children, Rogers was drawing on a long moral tradition—the Jesus tradition—about which St. Paul wrote in today's epistle: "We are afflicted in every way, but not constrained."

What is obvious is that, over the decades, all the things Mr. Rogers taught have been reversed. Mr. Rogers seems to be an archaic voice. Today, new secular voices tell us that winners are better than losers, power is better than humility, being served is better than serving, making money is better than making friendships, greed is better than giving, the successful are better than the weak. "I" is not only better that "we," but "I" is the measurement of all things. This message is in every commercial, every graduation address: Follow your own passion. March to the beat of your own drummer. Listen to your own heart. You do you!

In another column, in June 2018,[2] Brooks reminded us that such destructive advice was extolled by Supreme Court Justice Anthony Kennedy, in his now famous "mystery of life" passage of 1992. At that time, Kennedy wrote, "At the heart of liberty is the right to define *one's own* concept of existence, of meaning, of the universe, and of the mystery of human life." There it is: no Mr. Rogers' concept of otherness at all, no acknowledgement that our Constitution begins with "*We* the people," that we were born as a nation, a collective, that we share common values and have a role to play to make them happen.

There is no sense that we are embedded in a social order or that we have inherited things we do not choose, such as bodies, family, and race, along with customs and values that were handed down by our common culture. Everyone privately defining his or her own concept of meaning is bound to make *public* kindness to the other not only scarce, but counterproductive, a danger to one's personal autonomy.

During the documentary, "Won't You Be My Neighbor?" the audience is often clearly moved, wiping moisture from their cheeks. The emotion, I think, is a nostalgic one: It provokes in the audience, and us, the question, "What happened?" How did we stray so far from the radical kindness that Mr. Rogers preached?

They weep because today's climate is so uncivil. Vulgar, crude name-calling is everywhere. Revenge and verbal and physical violence fill the atmosphere, the movies, the games. Kids are groomed to do well from day one—with no break from the pressure to get into the best schools, get the best job, the six-figure salary, the most toys.

The sad thing is that there is not always the counterbalancing injunction that says, "Yes, of course do well, but, even more—even more—do good, do good with your life." Be kind, and if there is ever a conflict, always choose to do the good, no matter what the cost. Choose kindness over

---

2 David Brooks, "Anthony Kennedy and the Personalization of Meaning," *The New York Times*, June 28, 2018, https://www.nytimes.com/2018/06/28/opinion/anthony-kennedy-individualism.html.

one-upmanship. Get an A+ in the kindness that lifts up the lowly and heals the broken.

Our children do need and deserve the best, cleverest teachers, but, above them all, they need a Mr. Rogers, a guiding, gentle friend who reminds them that, in the end, a successful life will be measured in the kindness they receive and the kindness they give. It's not what they have but who they are that matters. They are special just the way they are: sick, crippled, abused, disliked, sad, failed—they are special and they are loved. They need to hear that, and hear it often. In their race to achievement, do you tell them that today?

10TH SUNDAY *in* ORDINARY TIME

DAVE DAVIS

"Whoever does the will of God is my brother and sister and mother."

1ST READING:
GEN. 3:9-15

PSALM:
130:1-8

2ND READING:
2 COR. 4:13-5:1

GOSPEL:
MARK 3:20-35

VERSE 20 SEEMS LIKE AN ODD PLACE TO BEGIN the gospel lection for the day. Verse 20 begins in the middle of a sentence. The first part of the verse reads, "He came home." Jesus went home. Most would conclude that Jesus coming home brings an end to all that Mark describes early in the chapter. But it also has everything to do with the gospel reading for today. Jesus at home. I, for one, had never paid any attention to the phrase that dangles there in Mark, just after Jesus completes his disciple roster and before he teaches about Satan and a house divided against itself and the unforgiveable sin of blaspheming against the Holy Spirit. "He came home."

Just a chapter before, when Jesus returned to Capernaum, Mark writes that, "It became known that he was at home." It's the Greek word for house, home. One can try to dig a bit more; was he home, or just in the house? Was it his house, or Simon and Andrew's house? Is the use of the word here by Mark some sort of literary device intended to set up the teaching which is to come, which is about a house divided against itself? He came home. Was he in the house, or was he home? It is so Mark, so uniquely Mark; Jesus at home.

It seems pretty clear that, when it comes to Mark's gospel, and Capernaum, and Jesus proclaiming the Good News of God, this was Jesus's dwelling place, his abiding place. He came home. It's not just any house, not a random gathering place. No, the domestic connotation must be intended. Good News proclaimed. Unclean spirits sent packing. The sick healed. A leper made clean. Sins forgiven. A crippled man walking. Sinners and tax collectors at the table. Teaching and teaching and more teaching about the Kingdom of God. Jesus is in the house. Jesus is home.

So, when his family heard about it? It wasn't just a house so crowded that they couldn't break bread that bothered them. It was all of it: what he was saying, what he was doing, who he was with, where he felt so at home. Some Bible translations try to defend Jesus's relatives a bit here, distinguishing the attempt to stop him from the word spreading that he was out of his mind. Distinguishing his family as those who were stopping him and then other people saying he is out of his mind. But it's all just pronouns in the Greek. When his family heard it, they went out to apprehend him, to stop him, to restrain him, and they were saying he has gone out of his mind, he is not himself. He is beside himself. He is outside of himself. He is other than himself. When it came to Jesus and all that was going on, in and around Capernaum, his family was very clear: *This* is not our home!

His mother, Mary, and his brothers arrived outside the house and they stood there calling for Jesus, sending for him. The crowd said to Jesus, "Your mother and your brothers and your sisters are outside asking for you." Well, that's a polite way to put it. And Jesus replied to those who relayed the message from his family, "Who are my mother and my brothers?" Then Jesus looked around at the crowd that sat around him, the crowd that had been following him, the crowd that was in the house, a crowd that by then would have included sinners and tax collectors, and those crying out to be healed, and those who brought someone to be healed, and the disciples, and all who found themselves so taken with his teaching, so claimed by his authority, those who found themselves captive to his spirit—it was that same crowd.

Jesus looked at those who were around him and he said, "Here are my mother and my brothers!" In a move, in a quote, in an affirmation, that should have forever given pause to politicians and pundits and preachers who claim some higher ground on family values and the Bible, Jesus says, for every generation to hear, "Whoever does the will of God is my brother and sister and mother." To put it another way, Jesus looked at all those faces in the crowd gathered around him and he said, "This is my home."

"Whoever does the will of God is my brother and sister and mother." Whoever does—and somewhere in the Kingdom of Heaven James is shouting, "Amen!" You remember James, the Epistle of James: "Faith without works is dead." James, who always makes the Reformed, grace-alone hairs on our neck stand up: "Be doers of the word and not hearers only. . . . Demonstrate your faith to me without works, and I will demonstrate my faith to you from my works."

Jesus said, "Whoever does the will of God is my brother and sister and mother." Here in Mark, when it comes to kinship, and family, and home, it's not belief or faith that Jesus cites. It's doing the will of God, living the will of God, serving the will of God. "Whoever does the will of God is my brother and sister and mother." Our salvation in Christ comes by grace alone, the gift of faith and his righteousness. But our kinship, our family tie, comes through servanthood. A life of serving in God's Kingdom. The life to which we were ordained at our baptism.

I remember, on a trip to the Holy Land a long time ago, we went into church after church after church. Christians have been coming from around the world for centuries to visit the Church of the Annunciation, the Church of the Nativity, the Church of the Holy Sepulcher, and all the others. And it doesn't take long for folks to realize that the churches hire men to help with the crowd, to work the door, to make sure there is appropriate dress, and the holiness of the site is observed. Let's just say their primary role is not that of hospitality. Not a lot of smiling going on. Some even use long sticks to get the attention of a wayward pilgrim who is talking too much. When the psalmist wrote about being a "doorkeeper in the house of God," I don't think these bouncers were what the psalmist had in mind. At one particular church that wasn't crowded, our group was heading down a flight of stairs to see the tomb of St. Jerome. The church attendant just kept "shushing" us. He "shushed" us all the way down the flight of stairs. Taking his responsibility very seriously, he followed us all the way down and kept "shushing" us.

When it comes to Jesus and what Mark calls in his gospel the Good News of God, maybe it is obvious to all, but it is worth saying that there's a big difference between "shushing" and serving. There is no shortage of politicians and pundits and preachers and people who, with the most sincere yearning to be faithful, think the Christian calling is to "shush" the world. But when you look around—just in the first few chapters of Mark, when you look around—you can't help thinking about Jesus and the disciples and that crowd and the kingdom. When you find yourself so taken with his teaching, so claimed by his authority, and drawn to his spirit, when you are so moved, inspired, and transformed by what and who and where he considered home, you realize once again that Jesus of Nazareth, the man of Galilee, he calls you and I to serve the world, not to "shush" it.

The congregation I serve sits on a university campus. One day, the local police called my office to tell me that the next day there was going to be a protest. Folks would be protesting on the campus and entering the campus next to our parking lot, using the sidewalk just next door. They just wanted us to know. So, one day that week, I'm in my office and I'm suddenly aware of all this ruckus that is going on outside of the office. And I look out my office window and realize that the plaza outside of the church was the staging ground for the protest. I looked out and there were thirty, forty, fifty people, and they were making signs, getting ready for their protest. And then I read some of their signs. And then, in my office, looking out the window, my fear was that everyone walking by would think they were protesting the church! So, my first reaction was to walk out and "shush" them.

When the police called, they didn't tell me the nature of the demonstration. It was a group of differently abled folks who were gathering from all around the region to protest a professor who has repeatedly said provocative, disturbing things about the value of human life. And so I went out and talked to the folks who were gathered. It was then that I realized that most of them were in wheelchairs. Wheelchairs can't stage on the sidewalk; they were all over the plaza. And because of the afternoon sun, the front steps of the church were providing shade. There were ten to twenty other folks sitting on the steps of the church to get out of the sun. The plaza and the front steps of the church were just packed with folks, making signs, cheering, getting ready for their march on the university campus to proclaim the value of their lives.

A little while later, I went out to get lunch, and as I came back, I was on the other side of Palmer Square, looking back at the church. There were still forty, fifty, sixty folks filling the plaza: folks with disabilities, caregivers, family members. Still filling out signs. I looked above and there was our banner, "Serving God's Kingdom"—and I smiled to myself the rest of the way to my office.

Never, ever, has the front of Nassau Church looked more like the Kingdom of God. And I smiled because I'm pretty sure that somewhere, on the front steps of the church that day, I saw the face of Jesus.

11TH SUNDAY *in* ORDINARY TIME

DAN HORAN, OFM

"It is like a mustard seed...."

1ST READING:
EZEK. 17:22-24

PSALM:
92:2-3, 13-16

2ND READING:
2 COR. 5:6-10

GOSPEL:
MARK 4:26-34

THE OLDEST OF FOUR BOYS, I GREW UP IN the 1980s and 1990s watching the kinds of action shows that many young boys enjoyed. There were, of course, reruns of *The A-Team* and *Knight Rider*, new episodes of William Shatner's *Rescue 911*, but the show that most captured my adventurous and intellectually curious childhood imagination was *MacGyver*.

For those unfamiliar with this culturally iconic television program starring Richard Dean Anderson as the title character—Angus "Mac" MacGyver—let me give you some highlights. MacGyver was a character that was part secret agent, part handyman, and part savant. He worked for a sort of nongovernmental spy agency or think-tank (it was never totally clear), which deployed MacGyver's services in all sorts of social justice causes around the world. It was hard to place what exactly MacGyver's "deal" was, except that he had a big heart, an even bigger intellect, and could handle the most absurd and difficult situations. He was also very, very cool. So cool, in fact, that he is to this day one of the few people I know of who successfully pulled off wearing his hair in a "mullet" without looking simply terrible.

What has made MacGyver not only a household name but also a verb in modern colloquial English was his ability to solve seemingly impossible challenges with often the fewest resources imaginable. He had to rely on his knowledge and experience, creativity and educated risk, and he was almost always successful (he was the star of the show, after all). One of the interesting things about the character of MacGyver was, despite his regularly being thrown into violent and threatening contexts, a strict adherence to a personal code of nonviolence. Oh, he had no problem with destruction of property—blowing up cars and vaults and helicopters, oh my—but he went out of his way to avoid directly killing anybody and refused to carry a firearm. How many TV action heroes do you know that adamantly refused to use a gun?

On its face, this character's commitment to nonviolence would be laughable when presented alongside all the other action shows and movies of its time (or our own). MacGyver was perceived, especially within the world of the show and among his colleagues in this think-tank-meets-spy-agency operation, as, at times, foolish and illogical. Why rely on a pocket-knife and a roll of duct tape when you could use an automatic machine gun? And yet, despite the impossible circumstances he would find himself in every week and his odd commitment to nonviolence, given his notably violent line of work and what little he had in terms of resources, MacGyver always managed to save the day.

And it is this point that I thought about when thinking about today's readings from scripture.

For instance, take the parable of the mustard seed in today's gospel. Jesus has a great sense of humor. Mustard seeds are indeed very, very small, but the way he describes the grown plant is absurd! Fully grown mustard plants are, nevertheless, still scraggly, weak, tiny bushes. Those who would have heard the parable in Jesus's time would have been confused, maybe entertained, but certainly would have greeted his comments with a sense that he was foolish and illogical.

Nevertheless, Jesus is making an important point about what it means to have faith in God and to live in the world as if the Kingdom or Reign of God were breaking in at this very moment. God, in this setting, is sort of like MacGyver—God doesn't have much to work with in the beginning (only that mustard-seed-sized faith that all believers start with). Given the limitations of the resources, the thought that anything can be accomplished with so little seems impossible.

But even with our small, weak, unimpressive plants of faith, God can do some extraordinary things. The history of Christianity is replete with illustrations of exactly this point. Think of St. Francis of Assisi. He was basically a "nobody" from the Umbrian region of Italy and had his own share of struggles, and yet God accomplished through his little faith a tremendous revolution of reform and inspiration in the church. Or think of the modern saint Mother Teresa of Calcutta. After her death, we came to learn that she had struggled for decades with her own faith and belief in God, yet God was able to accomplish such tremendous charity and good work through her and her community of sisters.

Our faith is so often like a mustard seed. It starts out, and at times can return to, feeling like a small, insignificant speck. But we are reminded today that God can take the seemingly impossible, the weak, the ordinary, and the simple and make something magnificent with it. What we often think is weak and worthless can be used for tremendous things by God, not unlike some duct tape and a pocketknife in the hands of MacGyver.

Another thing we hear in today's gospel is that we cannot see exactly how God is working in the faith lives of all people. Like a farmer who has scattered seeds and then patiently waits for them to sprout and grow, God knows what has been planted in the hearts of women and men. Just because we, standing on the sidelines and late to the game, cannot see what is at work beneath the surface, does not mean that nothing is happening or could happen. I sometimes hear from people, especially parents of teenagers and young adults, that they are worried about their kids losing their faith. While well-intentioned, this is often a response to external realities or things that can be perceived by another person, rather than a deep assessment of what is happening internally.

What today's gospel shows us is that we need the patience and trust of a farmer who doesn't see everything that is unfolding beneath the surface of the soil. We simply do not know how God is working in the lives of others. Those who seem to us not to be people of faith at all might have a profound spirituality that governs their lives and choices, informing their whole existence in the world rather than merely conforming to our particular or personal understanding of what "real faith" should look like. What

God calls us to do is nurture and care for the field with love, gentleness, kindness, and—most importantly—patience.

This sense of our inability to fully know how God is working in the lives of others or beneath the surface of our awareness also comes through in today's first reading. Through the Prophet Ezekiel, God tells us that it is only God who governs all life and death, growing and withering, expansion and decline in the world; God raises up and lowers down. And, what's more, God is the one who knows and reveals what is in store for each plant. In God's field, the vast collection of seemingly insignificant mustard plants of faith may actually make up an exceptionally beautiful garden of believers whose faith inspires them to reveal the compassionate face of God to the whole world. This garden will blossom and the unexpected will take shape—the plants will become a safe haven, a shelter for all sorts of creatures.

The key theme here is that God's plan for a fully grown faith is not isolation or individual connection with God that leads to private spiritual success. Instead, God envisions the bringing together of all creation, all people together as one family, one divine garden of love and support.

Perhaps this week would be a good time for each of us to dedicate a few moments to reflecting on how God is working in our lives and in the lives of those around us in ways we might easily overlook, in ways that seem to be weak or simple to us. May we remember, as our readings today have reminded us, that it is God who is working behind the scenes, drawing near to each person, and planting the little seeds of our faith. And, like MacGyver, it is God who does amazing things with seemingly few resources in the midst of otherwise impossible situations.

12TH SUNDAY *in* ORDINARY TIME

RT. REV. V. GENE ROBINSON

"Do you not yet have faith?"

1ST READING:
JOB 38:1, 8-11

PSALM:
107:23-6, 28-29

2ND READING:
2 COR. 5:14-17

GOSPEL:
MARK 4:35-41

TWO MEMORABLE EVENTS HAPPEN IN THE life of Jesus out on the Sea of Galilee. In one, the disciples are in a boat out on the lake, and they see Jesus coming toward them, walking on the water. Peter, known for his brashness and his tendency to overreach, attempts to walk to Jesus, also on the water. In a detail most readers seem to miss, Peter actually *does* walk on water, which is remarkable, until he gets scared, loses faith, and begins to sink. Jesus pulls him up and they both get into the boat.

In the other event, which we explore today, Jesus is exhausted from all the preaching and teaching he's been doing, and frankly, needs a little rest. He suggests that they get in a boat and escape the crowds by going across the lake to the other side, rather than walking the long way around on the shore. Alas, they cannot fully escape, as some other boats come along with them. Jesus is asleep in the stern of the boat when a big storm comes up. Such storms come up quickly on an inland lake and can very rapidly become quite fierce. Indeed, Mark (who is usually short on details) tells us that indeed the "waves were breaking over the boat, so that it was already filling up." Fearing that the boat will be overcome by the waves, the disciples wake Jesus with the Aramaic version of "Do something!!" Jesus rebukes the wind, and to the sea says, "Quiet! Be still!" And it is so. The disciples are mightily impressed and wonder what sort of fellow they've latched onto.

Mark's telling of this story contains one very interesting and curious description. Mark's is the shortest of the gospels, and in the service of "nothin' but the facts, ma'am," Mark is very spare when it comes to the details of any story. And so, this descriptive phrase is all the more unusual. Most readers probably skip right over it, and I admit to having read this story in Mark's gospel countless times before ever noticing it!

"[Jesus] said to them, 'Let us cross to the other side.' Leaving the crowd, they took him with them in the boat just as he was." Doesn't that seem like an odd thing to say, that they took him "just as he was"?! Perhaps it was a "come as you are" sail! Maybe he didn't have time to change into a navy jacket, white pants, and a captain's cap. And besides, *how else* would they have taken him, other than "just as he was"?!

But seriously, what are we to make of this strange notation? At a minimum, when we go on a journey with Jesus, he comes along just as he is, and *not* as we might want him to be! The disciples were hoping for a peaceful and uneventful crossing of the lake, hoping that the exhausted rabbi could get some rest along the way. But what they got was a frightening and threatening storm.

They would soon learn that being on a journey with Jesus is full of storms, challenges, and threatening situations. Ultimately, every one of the disciples would die at the hands of the authorities because of their beliefs and their loyalty to Jesus and his memory. This journey was not what they thought it would be. Rather, it was harder and more dangerous than they ever dreamed. This particular crossing of the Sea of Galilee was an omen for what awaited all of them.

Here we can see a tie-in with the epistle reading from Paul's Second Letter to the Corinthians. We are reminded that not only did Paul find the congregations he had founded to be a real challenge, but also that he was ultimately executed in Rome while in prison for his faith in and allegiance to Jesus. You might think you're going for a sunset cruise on the lake, but there are storms ahead!!

You and I usually come to church, at least in part, seeking comfort and assurance and peace. But what we get is Jesus! Just as he is! We expect that our lives, for the most part, will be joyful and rewarding and quite marvelous. What we get is a child born with Down Syndrome or an abusive spouse or a nasty divorce or a debilitating disease. We expect the world to be fair, ordered, and constantly improving, little by little. Yet often, we experience the world as just the opposite. Racism and white supremacy, the vastly unequal distribution of resources, and countless forms of oppression are storms most of us have to weather. And those storms threaten to upend the tiny boats of our lives. The effects of climate change threaten to swamp "this fragile earth, our island home."[1]

As followers of Jesus, we too are called to "speak" a firm, but calming word to these storms which rage in our midst. Jesus demands justice for all—not just in the words we use in our founding documents, but in our lives. And fighting for that justice is always dangerous business. In our fear and frustration, we might cry out to God, "Do something!" But, in the end, God will only speak that word of calm and peace through *us*!

If we get in the boat with Jesus, he will be there "just as he is," not as the meek-and-mild, stained-glass version of a savior, but one who calls us to be our best, bravest, most risk-taking selves in his service. The storms will come, and Jesus will be with us. But being a follower of Jesus does not mean he will make all the storms go away.

When I was living through a difficult time in my life and ministry, receiving daily death threats and being the target of hatred from "good Christian people" around the world, someone gave me a small, calligraphed, framed saying: "Sometimes, God calms the storm. But sometimes, God lets the storm rage, and calms his child."

The Good News of this day is that we are not in this little boat alone. We have a brother, friend, and savior who knows exactly what it's like to be us, and to face these storms. The storms don't go away, but as a result of being in relationship with Jesus, *we* are changed. Like David facing Goliath, like Paul standing up for his faith to the Romans, and like Jesus laying down his life for us, God takes us into the boat "just as we are." And then God transforms *us*, making us just strong and courageous enough to face the storms that come our way. For that, thanks be to God!

---

1 The Episcopal Church, "Eucharistic Prayer C," *The Book Common Prayer* (New York: Oxford University Press, 1979), 370.

13TH SUNDAY *in* ORDINARY TIME

ROBERT ELLSBERG

"Your faith has saved you. Go in peace and be cured of your affliction."

1ST READING:
WIS. 1:13-15; 2:23-24

PSALM:
30:2, 4, 5-6, 11-13

2ND READING:
2 COR. 8:7, 9, 13-15

GOSPEL:
MARK 5:21-43

AS JESUS TRAVELED ABOUT THE COUNTRYSIDE, he often attracted a crowd that jostled and pressed against him. On the occasion described in today's gospel reading, Jesus suddenly perceives in himself "that power had gone out from him." It is one of the most mysterious lines in all of scripture. "Who has touched my clothes?" he asks. Even his disciples are puzzled, observing the crowd pressing all about him. "And he looked around to see who had done it."

There was no special saving power in physical proximity to Christ. Among those who heard him preach were the ones who plotted his death. Judas dipped his hand into the same bowl as Jesus before going out to betray him. It was not enough merely to touch him, for so did the many others who pressed against him in the crowd, and so did those others who later stripped and scourged him and nailed him to a cross.

And yet Christ was present in that crowd in all his love and power. As it turns out, it was the faith of a poor, frightened, sick, and untouchable woman who recognized that power, drew it forth with her touch, and brought it into full view. The last thing she wanted was to be recognized for her deed. But, in response to Jesus's question, she came forward "in fear and trembling" to confess her story.

As she relates, she had suffered for twelve years from a "flow of blood"—a condition that not only signified illness, but which consigned her to a status of social outcast. Her very touch had the power of defilement. In telling her story, she must have braced herself for the crowd's revulsion. Yet, by her action, she had understood in a way that the disciples as yet did not, that the power of Jesus was at the service of love; that his very touch could heal what the law divided.

"Daughter," he said to her, "your faith has saved you. Go in peace and be cured of your affliction."

As extraordinary as this story is, it is only the middle part of a larger story of faith and healing. The story of a woman with a flow of blood interrupts Jesus's response to an appeal from Jairus, one of the leaders of the synagogue, whose young daughter is at "the point of death." We don't learn the little girl's name; only that she is twelve (thus, at the age of puberty, her age is coinciding with the duration of the older woman's flow of blood). But by the time they arrive at Jairus's home, it is apparently too late. The house is surrounded by wailing mourners who bring the tragic news: The child is dead. Yet Jesus ignores them. He tells the father, "Do not be afraid; just have faith." The child, he says, is not dead, but only sleeping. And taking her by the hand, he speaks to her (the precious Aramaic words from Jesus's lips, lovingly remembered and passed along): *Talitha koum*; which means, "Little girl, arise."

I remember the day when Jesus came to my parish. There were many people in church that day to hear this gospel story and reflect on Jesus's words. But among them was a father whose young daughter was suffering from anorexia and who was steadily starving herself. Though she was in her teens, her illness had delayed her maturity and she had the appearance of a young child. The family had consulted many doctors and therapists, and though their daughter had been hospitalized three times, she seemed no better. But, in that moment, hearing this story, her father was overcome. Silently, he wished he could reach out and touch the hem of Jesus's clothes on his daughter's behalf. He longed to hear him say, "Why do you make a tumult and weep? The child is not dead, but only sleeping." He imagined Jesus taking her by the hand and lifting her up. He imagined her walking about, and hearing Jesus's words, "Give her something to eat."

Perhaps Jesus is always as close to us as that—not just when we're in church, or receiving Communion, or hearing the gospel read on Sundays. His loving mercy is always there, only a touch, a gesture, a prayer away. But it is only by faith—sometimes a faith born of desperation—that we dare to reach out and touch him.

Perhaps that day, when I wept during the gospel, I was as much in need of healing as my young daughter. I needed to trust in the healing work of professionals. I needed to let go of my desperate need to be in control. I needed to believe there was some place in my daughter that was waiting to be healed. And I needed to believe that my own faith was not dead, but merely sleeping, and that Jesus was as present to me as he was to Jairus, as he was to the woman with a flow of blood, and that the power of his healing love was available to all who asked.

It was too much for that father to hope that his daughter would arise and eat when he returned from church that Sunday—but eventually she did. Years would pass, and there would come a time when that long, fearsome ordeal would lie behind them. But he didn't want to forget what happened that day, when, through his tears, he had reached out to touch the hem of Jesus's clothes and heard his words: "Go in peace and be cured of your affliction."

14TH SUNDAY *in* ORDINARY TIME

BRIAN McLAREN

"And they took offense at him."

1ST READING:
EZEK. 2:2-5

PSALM:
123:1-2A, 2BC, 3-4

2ND READING:
2 COR. 12:7-10

GOSPEL:
MARK 6:1-6

JESUS WAS ON A WINNING STREAK. HE HAD performed healing after healing. People loved his sermons (on the mount, in homes and synagogues, and otherwise). His crowds were growing. His fame was growing. If he were alive today, we would say he was *trending*.

Then he came to his hometown and, for a while, he was popular there too. At first, people said, "Wow! What great miracles! Wow! What great wisdom! Wow! How eloquent and poetic!"

But then, it seems like a little rivalry or jealousy set in. "But wait a minute," they said. "We knew him when he was just a local handyman, working hard every day like the rest of us. We know his mom, his brothers and sisters... who does he think he is? Does he think he's better than us?"

Luke's gospel adds some additional detail. When he said, "God cares for the poor and oppressed," they praised him because they were poor and oppressed. But when he said, "God also cares for the Syrians like Naaman and Sidonians like the widow of Zarephath," that irked them.

"Hey," they thought, "we're of a superior religion. How dare Jesus put others on the same level as us?"

Of course, we see the same elitism and supremacy among people today. Religious supremacy, racial supremacy, nationalist supremacy—there seems to be something in many of us that can't relax unless we feel superior. We can't feel safe until we put someone else in danger. We can't feel good or well-off unless we compare ourselves with someone else who seems bad or worse-off.

Mark's diagnosis for their problem might surprise you. The problem, he says, is unbelief. Now, you might think that he means, "Ah, their problem is that they don't know the creeds. They don't hold to correct beliefs." But the creeds wouldn't be invented for a few more centuries, so that's one thing Mark could not possibly have meant.

We can better understand Mark's diagnosis if we translate unbelief as "distrust." If they trusted Jesus, they would have given his message a chance. But they refused to trust him.

It's a little sad, when you think about it: Today, there are lots of people who sincerely believe all the creeds, but they still suffer from unbelief, in the sense of distrust. They might believe that Jesus is the Savior or the Second Person of the Trinity, but if Jesus says something that contradicts their current opinions, they trust their opinions more than Jesus.

That's the essence of unbelief or distrust: You believe or trust your current assumptions and opinions so much that you distrust anything new that comes your way. Psychologists call this *confirmation bias*. They tell us that our brains are wired to only accept ideas that confirm what we already think, and to reject anything that challenges our assumptions.

In the gospels, the opposite of confirmation bias is *repentance*. It means a willingness to rethink our assumptions. (The word literally means "think again.")

What could make you rethink your own assumptions? One thing: trust. Trust that someone else knows something you don't. That's why Jesus constantly says, "Believe me. Trust me." He sees something you don't, and wants you to break free from your confirmation bias.

This is the job of all true prophets and teachers. It's why God says to Ezekiel (as God said to many other prophets too), "They might listen to you. They might not. Either way, speak the truth you have been given. That's your job, so do it—succeed or fail, popular or unpopular."

Paul feels this same tension. Some people love him and his message.

Others hate him and want to kill him. So he says, "Whether I feel strong or weak, I'm going to do my work. In fact, the weaker I feel, the more I feel Christ's strength flowing through me."

Mark tells us something shocking in this regard. We often speak of the power of faith, but Mark is also honest about the power of unbelief or distrust. Because of the distrust of the people of Jesus's hometown, there was little Jesus could do for them. Their unbelief kept them trapped in their confirmation bias, which meant they were stuck in their status quo of sickness, narrow-mindedness, and ignorance.

When you decide what to do based on a promise of popularity or a guarantee of success, you'll never do anything very revolutionary. Sure, you might get rich. You might be popular. But you won't challenge people's false assumptions. You'll just play within the little box of confirmation bias.

But if you're willing to step beyond conformity to the status quo, if you're willing to join Ezekiel and Paul and Jesus in challenging people to think some new thoughts and see things in a new way, prepare yourself to have some people listen and trust you while others reject and distrust you.

St. Francis was that kind of person. He dared to be different. For that reason, he was beloved by some and hated by others. In word and especially in deed, he modeled a radically different form of Christianity. One of his most important questions was one many of us today still ask ourselves on a regular basis: *What is mine to do?*

When you know what is yours to do, you don't give up when people criticize you. You don't back off when people distrust you. Like Jesus, you do what is yours to do, you say what is yours to say, and you move on.

Whether they listen or not, do your work.

Whether you feel weak or strong, do your work.

Whether others honor you or insult you, do your work.

And be on your guard against confirmation bias. Otherwise, you'll be a prisoner of your own assumptions; you'll distrust anyone who challenges what you currently think, and you'll never be any wiser than you are right now.

15TH SUNDAY *in* ORDINARY TIME

MARY SPERRY

"He summoned the Twelve and began to send them out two by two."

1ST READING:
AMOS 7:12-15

PSALM:
85:9-14

2ND READING:
EPH. 1:3-14

GOSPEL:
MARK 6:7-13

IMAGINE YOURSELF IN AMOS'S PLACE—at home in Tekoa, minding his sheep and his sycamores—when God sends him to prophesy at the royal sanctuary in Bethel. The sanctuary in Bethel was home to companies of court prophets who made their living telling the powerful what they wanted to hear, maintaining the status quo. At God's command, Amos leaves his comfortable, familiar life to walk into this toxic environment to share God's decidedly discomforting message. In today's first reading, we see the consequences of Amos's decision to respond positively to God's call. His message has disturbed the court prophets, leading to his expulsion from the sanctuary.

The gospel tells of another sending. Jesus sends the Twelve on their first mission. After all, the word *apostolos* means "one who is sent." Jesus sends the apostles out two by two to preach the good news of the healing and liberation that Jesus brings. But this mission is not easy. Jesus tells them to leave behind money and other necessities (except sandals and a walking stick) and to expect opposition and inhospitality. The apostles set out with faith and courage and return with joy, reporting on the success of their efforts: Demons have been driven out and people are healed.

In the second reading, St. Paul reminds us that God has chosen and called each of us as well. Like Amos, we are called to leave behind our own comfort and carry God's message to those on the peripheries. As we go out in response to God's call, we must be careful that we do not become like the court prophets who were Amos's adversaries. It is all too easy to put our energy behind the status quo, making sure that those in power are not challenged and our privilege is not disrupted. But God's message is always challenging and disruptive! The poor and humble are exalted, while the rich and powerful are cast down! The desperate have their needs met and those in pain receive healing! Death is no longer the end of the story!

Instead, we must take our cue from the apostles. Their mission is grounded in their encounter with Jesus. They followed Jesus in the days of his ministry, listening to his teaching, witnessing his mighty deeds, and coming to know him more fully. Having come to know God's liberation and healing in their own lives, they are able to go out and share these fruits with others. In the same way, our call to be missionary disciples begins in our own encounter with Jesus. We have come to know him in his Word, in the Church, in the Sacraments, in prayer, and in the faces of our sisters and brothers. We have allowed God's grace to begin to transform our lives, conforming them to his will.

Conformed to Jesus Christ, we follow the apostles' example and begin our mission. But where shall we go? Pope Francis has called the Church—that's us, you know—to go out to the peripheries. This doesn't mean that we need to pack our bags and board a plane for parts unknown. The peripheries are not necessarily a geographic reality. They may be closer than we think. Who is forgotten? Who is treated with disdain rather than dignity? Whose lives are not valued? Whose voices are not heard? The answers to these questions may point to the peripheries where we are called to share the healing and liberation that Jesus brings.

Jesus charged the apostles to take nothing with them. They were to leave behind money and other possessions, even food! They were not even to carry a bag, so that each day they had to begin anew, trusting in the kindness of others. What are we called to leave behind as we undertake our mission? Like Amos, we may have to give up the comfort of our familiar lives and stop measuring ourselves by the world's standards of success: status, influence, and wealth. We will have to die to ourselves so that Christ may live in us, allowing those we meet to encounter him.

But we must be clear about the nature of our task. God calls us to be missionary disciples. Missionary because we are sent, disciples because our primary identity is as followers of Christ. We are not sent to save those on the peripheries or to "fix" their lives. We are sent to invite those we meet to encounter Christ. We share with them the joy, hope, healing, and freedom that we have come to know with Christ. Then, we can work together to heal our world, bringing forth the justice, peace, and love that are the hallmarks of God's everlasting reign.

Our encounter with those on the peripheries and those closer to us will not—and should not—leave us unchanged. Amos was changed by the prophetic word he spoke. St. Paul's life changed radically after his encounter with the risen Lord. The apostles were changed as they went out to preach the kingdom. So, must we be changed by our efforts to help others encounter Christ and by the ways that we encounter Christ in them.

At the end of this liturgy, strengthened by the Eucharist, we will be sent forth to share the gospel. Take nothing with you, let nothing hold you back. Go!

16TH SUNDAY *in* ORDINARY TIME

MIKE JONCAS

"Woe to the shepherds who destroy and scatter the flock of my pasture."

1ST READING:
JER. 23:1-6

PSALM:
23:1-6

2ND READING:
EPH. 2:13-18

GOSPEL:
MARK 6:30-34

I WANT TO WARN YOU NOW: MANY OF YOU will not like this homily. I will be focusing on the First Reading from Jeremiah. First, I would like to explore the context in which Jeremiah pronounced this prophecy. Then I'd like to take a deep dive into the prophecy itself. Finally, I would like to suggest a way in which this prophecy might apply to life in the United States.

Jeremiah is known as a "gloom and doom" prophet, but his prophecies actually vary, based on the situation God called him to address. He was part of a prophetic triumvirate, with his cousin Huldah speaking to the women of Judah, Jeremiah speaking to the men in the street, while Jeremiah's teacher, Zephaniah, preached in the synagogue. Jeremiah began his prophetic career aligned with King Josiah on Judah's reforms, including destruction of idolatrous "high places" and the rebuilding of the Temple of Solomon, cleansing it of the worship of Baal and the "host of heaven." Jeremiah consistently called God's covenant people to conversion of heart and change of behavior, and he specifically warned King Josiah not to involve himself in Egypt's affairs. Josiah ignored his advice, however, and was killed in the battle of Megiddo. Josiah's religious reforms ceased with his death.

Eventually, Josiah's son Jehoiakim, an Egyptian vassal, succeeded him on the throne of the Kingdom of Judah. Jeremiah, meanwhile, earned Jehoiakim's wrath by continuing to preach against any alliance with Egypt. Jehoiakim tore up Jeremiah's dictated prophecies and instead welcomed "optimistic" prophets to his court who blessed the king's political maneuvers. The passage that we heard as the First Reading today is Jeremiah's response to these optimistic false prophets.

Speaking in God's name, Jeremiah thunders against the national leadership of the Kingdom of Judah. Because they have acted as false shepherds who destroy and scatter God's people, God will punish the kings of Judah. God promises that he will gather his people from the various exiles they have experienced and bring them back to their land, where they can live in peace and increase in number. Most importantly, God commits himself to raising up "a righteous branch . . . as king he shall reign and govern wisely, he shall do what is just and right in the land." Summarizing Jeremiah's message in this passage, John J. Pilch writes: "God's people need to know God's will. They do not need to hear feel-good messages that make the prophet popular. God's people need courageous leaders to face reality squarely rather than to engage in deception and false optimism."[1]

I warned you at the beginning of this homily that many of you may not like it. While I am personally tempted to join the "optimistic" prophets who served as lickspittles to those in power, just so that you will not be angry with me, I think the Word of God actually calls us to face reality squarely rather than to engage in deception and false optimism.

We have not been well served by our recent national leadership. "Deception and false optimism" seem a precise description of the messages we have been receiving from our highest executive leaders concerning the coronavirus pandemic. The consequences of this deception and false optimism are apparent in the appalling loss of life which has plagued our nation in comparison with the other nations of the world. In the face of

1 John J. Pilch, *The Cultural World of the Prophets* (Collegeville, MN: Liturgical Press, 2002), 93.

the greatest economic collapse since the 1930s, our legislative leaders seem paralyzed by partisan squabbles and unable to provide effective help to the unemployed and underemployed. By executive order, we turn masses of migrants seeking asylum in the land of the free and the home of the brave away from our borders, splitting up families and imprisoning children. Our eyes have been opened to the systemic racism that plagues our institutions of justice, while the just grievances of citizens exercising their rights of free speech are met by quasi-military force. We have lost a sense of common purpose and are tempted to retreat into scattered and selfish lives.

As Christians, we are not allowed the luxury of impotent despair. Jeremiah's terrifying prophecy may well be coming true in our age, but his words also convey hope. We recognize the vast difference in perspective and political engagement between the seventh century BCE and today. We do not look for a monarch "to reign and govern wisely" and "do what is just and right in the land." Rather, we look to ourselves, enlightened by the Holy Spirit, to volunteer for and elect political leaders who will attempt to do so. The seven themes of Catholic social thought (life and dignity of the human person; call to family, community, and participation; rights and responsibilities; option for the poor and vulnerable; the dignity of work and the rights of workers; solidarity; and care for God's creation) might serve as a framework to judge the practices and policies of those who would guide us. In any event, we are called to see what is going on in our nation and world, to judge it in the light of scripture and reason, and to act to prepare the way for the Kingdom of God, where we will "no longer fear or be terrified; none shall be missing," but all will be guests at the Banquet of Eternal Life.

17TH SUNDAY *in* ORDINARY TIME

GREG BOYLE, SJ

"You will eat and have some left over."

1ST READING:
2 KGS. 4: 42- 44

PSALM:
145: 10-11, 15-8

2ND READING:
EPH. 4:1-6

GOSPEL:
JOHN 6:1 -15

I GREW UP IN A FAMILY OF TEN AND NO ONE was thrilled by leftovers. There was no treat to it. It was the dregs of last night's dinner. In the miracle of Jesus feeding the thousands, it is about taking five barley loaves and two fish and filling everybody—and food was left over. It's a story about abundance and God's longing to fill us. We align our hearts with the vision of God when we believe scarcity, like separation, is an illusion. They say that when you have more than you need, you build a longer table rather than a higher wall.

I took Juan and Jermaine to Chicago with me to give a handful of talks. They were both gang members who were trainees at Homeboy Industries, the largest gang intervention and re-entry program on the planet. Located in Los Angeles, we offer a community of tenderness to engage "homies" in healing and transforming their pain. Combined, Jermaine and Juan had spent more than half a century in prison.

It wasn't until their stony silence in the car, on the way to the airport, that I realized these two were gang rivals. I braced myself for a very long five-day trip.

As we stood in line to board the plane, Juan, who the homies would say owns "a loud-ass voice," asks me, "CAN I USE AIRPLANE MODE?" I model a lower volume and tell him in a near whisper, "You're ok right now, but once on the plane, and when the doors close, you have to shift to airplane mode." Then, to a total stranger, a woman behind him, he says with outsized enthusiasm: "I'VE NEVER USED AIRPLANE MODE BEFORE." The woman looks startled and replies, "Oh . . . ok." Later, I reflected that Juan was inviting us both into the infinite moment of abundance in the now and we were occupied with propriety and volume-control. As the proverb goes, "Those who wish to sing . . . always find a song." Baskets overflowing.

After days of many talks and hugely moving presentations by both Juan and Jermaine, I gave them cash to bring gifts back to their womenfolk and kids. They went to Navy Pier. The following day, we were awaiting a cab to the airport, and Juan and Jermaine produced, from their duffel bags, Teddy Bears made to order from the "Build-A-Bear" store on Navy Pier. They'd taped their own voices into the bears, which are activated by pressing a paw. Juan's bear said this: "I love ya with all my heart, baby. Come here . . . give me a kiss." Juan is loud *and* excited. "Do you think my lady will like it?" "Oh, hell yeah," I tell him.

Predictably, as their bags went through the TSA machine, we heard, "I love ya with all my heart, baby." And as Juan forced and squeezed the bag into the overhead compartment: "Come here . . . give me a kiss." We found our song in the laughter.

We drove home from LAX and Juan, in the back seat, leans forward. "Hey, G—you know what the best part of this trip was?" Then he grabs Jermaine's arm, who is in the front passenger seat. "Getting to know him." I turn and watch Jermaine smile and nod. Baskets brimming with fragments.

Some days later, Juan steps into my office and announces that his father has just died. He had been deported many years before and Juan had not spoken to him in over twenty years—until, that is, five days ago, after someone alerted Juan that his father was dying of cancer.

Juan and his twin brother, when they were nine years old, made a pact. "When our dad comes home from work tonight, and he's drunk and starts to beat on our mom . . . let's defend her." They shook on it.

The twins' father came home, predictably drunk, and began to wail on the mom. The twins flew into action and leapt on the back of their dad like a couple of marsupials. They toppled their stunned father to the floor, until he awakened to a rage and flung the boys off of him. Then, he grabbed them by the backs of their shirts, opened the front door, and dragged them to the street, where he tossed them. He told them they were both dead to him now. They were never to enter the house again. And so they didn't.

They lived in a park down the block. "Every night, we'd pull a garbage bag out of the trash can," Juan told me, "then tip the can over and the two of us would slide in and sleep in each other's arms. Every night." They got into the local neighborhood gang, locked arms with other orphans, and sold drugs to survive. Juan's twin is still in prison, and Juan himself was released after twenty-four years.

"So . . . someone told me my dad was dying and I got his number. I needed to call him . . . to forgive him." Juan's eyes moisten in the telling of this. "Yeah. I just didn't want to carry this around anymore." He's patting his heart and composing himself. He pauses, then shifts gears. "You know something, G? In my six months here at Homeboy, I'm enjoying the man I've become . . . like I've never enjoyed anything before."

"Enjoy" is an odd word. It's not a "leftover" word, but an abundance word. It is soaked with the resurrection, God's longing to fill us. When the multitudes are fed in the wilderness, they enjoy what they have become. They are filled. Like ancient Israel, following the exodus from Egypt, they are fed by supernatural food. They are delivered by manna from the sky. Abundance—plenty for everyone. And anyone wishing to sing at this extended table will always find a song.

18TH SUNDAY *in* ORDINARY TIME

MEGAN McKENNA

"You are looking for me not because you saw signs but because you ate the loaves and were filled."

1ST READING:
EXOD. 16:2-4

PSALM:
PS 78: 3-4, 23-24, 25

2ND READING:
EPH. 4:17, 20-24

GOSPEL:
JOHN 6:24-35

WE ARE NOW MOVING EVER DEEPER INTO Ordinary Time. These many Sundays and weeks aren't "ordinary" in the sense of "nothing special"; the term comes from the Latin *ordinal* meaning "counting." We are counting out the last half of our liturgical year, when we seek to put into practice all we have learned of the wisdom and mystery of the Incarnation, life, death, and Resurrection of Jesus and the giving of his Risen Spirit to us to continue his presence and redeeming grace in the world through us. So, in that sense, this time is not ordinary at all!

And today, all the readings are about food, one of the daily necessities of life. Many of us eat three times a day, with a snack or two, while a good portion of the world is always hungry, food-deprived, and wondering where their next portion of nourishment will come from and what it will be. In our liturgy today, we look at food, beginning with manna in the desert of old, that physically sustained the people, yet was spiritual food that taught them trust and reliance on God. Then we look at how to eat and digest the food of the Spirit that has fed our life in God since baptism. And in the gospel, we look at the flesh and blood of Jesus, the flesh of God who became human among us and gave us himself as his Body and Blood in the food of Eucharist.

In the movie/play and book *Oliver Twist*, there is the image of the orphans being fed, when Oliver sings out: "MORE, please sir, MORE." And he is begging for gruel. But this pleading for "more" is embedded in all our readings and in our hungers, both for the food our bodies need to survive and grow, as well as what our souls, spirits, minds, and hearts hunger for in order to live and thrive as human beings, created to be fully alive as God's beloved children.

We begin in the desert, with the people hungry and exhausted and wanting to give up and go back to slavery in Egypt, where they at least had onions, meat, and their fill of bread. They *grumble* against Moses and Aaron; the word has overtones of violence, pent up frustration ready to break loose and be vented on others. They complain that God led them into the wilderness to die of famine. But we know that God feeds them, daily, and with a double portion the day before the Sabbath. The food they gather that appears as dew on the ground is not only sustenance, it's soul food.

Even food we eat with our mouths can be, and is, "soul food." It comes in at least two distinct categories. Any food can be soul food, depending on who you eat it with—and then there is "soul food." I learned about that when I learned how to really cook in New Orleans in my mid-twenties. I grew up in a large family, where my father did most of the cooking, which he learned from being in the Navy. There was a lot of it, filling (not always nutritious, as it needed to be rather inexpensive), and only on occasion would it fall into the "soul food" category. That would be anniversaries, birthdays, special feast days, or when someone had done something important—a reason to celebrate made the food (usually carefully chosen) into soul food.

But in New Orleans I learned how to eat, cook, prepare, and share "soul food." There is the saying that love is the first and most important ingredient in all food and it's true. Love of the food itself, whether crayfish or dirty rice, pralines, pecan pie, or oysters. Then comes how it is prepared, according to tradition and cherished recipes from others, everything from roux (gravies) to jambalaya, and food meant for two or huge gatherings, often outside. Sharing food made family, created community, afforded the setting for not only celebration but reconciliation and peacemaking.

This was the same at the time of Jesus. Anyone you ate with, shared food with, broke bread with, literally became family. In fact, if you ate together, stayed the night, and awoke in the morning to find your guests gone, and that they had become thieves overnight, you couldn't go after them to recover the stolen goods. They were family and you had to wait at least 72 hours, until the food you had shared together had been digested and had exited their bodies. Then you could go after them! This is important to keep in mind whenever we read about food, and meals that Jesus shared and initiated with others, whether his inner circle of friends or massive crowds on hillsides.

The letter to the Ephesians exhorts the new Christians to shift and change every area of their lives from how they lived before as unbelievers. They are to "learn" Christ and "put away" their old self in regard to their former practices, which often were corrupt. Instead, they are to put on their new self, "created in God's way in righteousness and holiness of truth." Every act, decision, or experience was to be renewed and infused with the life of the Spirit they received at baptism, and that included daily actions regarding sleep, exercise, food, economics, talk, and what they did both when alone and with others. Their example was to be a source of nourishment and expression of who they now were and who God is among us.

Jesus's words in the gospel are part of a long discourse to the crowds. It comes after he has fed the crowd of five thousand men (about 35,000 people) and he has slipped away, then walks on the water to get to his disciples in the boat at night. The crowd comes after, looking for him and wondering how he got where he is, on the other side of the water. But Jesus knows why they want to be with him. It has nothing to do with his preaching. They're interested in the free food. They still have the taste of the loaves in their mouths and the sense of being filled in their minds and hearts. So, Jesus begins to try to make them think about imperishable food and not just food for their bodies.

He tells them that he, the Son of Man, will himself feed them food that their Father gives them, food that God has set his seal on. But they balk and ask: "What can you do? What sign will you give so we can believe in you?" (They don't connect being fed as a crowd with anything of God or the Spirit.) He reminds them that Moses *did not* feed them; it was God that gave them the food. And the Father is trying to give them "bread from heaven," true bread that gives life to the world. They ask: "Sir, give us this bread always." But they have not made any connection between manna and God's sustaining grace, so they don't get it when Jesus replies: "*I am the bread of life*; whoever comes to me will never hunger, and whoever believes in me will never thirst." It is way *too much* for them—and still is for many of us.

Jesus is food for the body and soul food. His Word is food for the body, for life lived as Jesus lives, and food that both soul and body need to absorb so as to be able to live with Jesus and the Spirit in God, and live as his presence in the world. When we go to Eucharist, the bread or the cup is presented to us with the words: "The Body of Christ," but it is a piece of bread that has become the presence of the Risen Lord. But Jesus is trying to tell them, and us, that when we say "Amen" and take and eat that piece of his presence, we also say "Amen" to the Body of Christ, the people of God, all the people of the world. This "bread of life" is what gives us the strength to live and love others with Jesus's own power and presence.

In the early church, and at the last supper, Jesus tore off a piece of the bread and handed it to one of those at the table. That person took the large piece and tore off another, and passed it along, sharing it. Eucharist is best taken and shared by each of us, not taken from one person, to whom everyone goes to get it personally. Jesus's body and blood are for all, not meant so much to be eaten personally, one on one, but with others—all others.

This is the soul food that the whole community, the whole world needs to become the Body of Christ, his Risen Presence in the world. This is part of the reason why the Church gathered for liturgy has often been called the Sacrament of the Presence of the Risen Lord—his presence that's as strong and lasting in the people who do liturgy, and in the Word, as in the bread and wine consecrated as we are consecrated for God.

This is mystery, which means, the more we try to speak of it, the more we realize we know nothing and the more there is to say. The people wanted *more* manna. We want *more* Eucharist. The difference, though, is we can have *more*. The Word of the Scriptures is *more* soul food. (Hence the line in Matthew 4:4, "'One does not live by bread alone, but by every word that comes forth from the mouth of God'".) And there is The Other Eucharist (a phrase from Dom Helder Camara of Brazil), that is the men and women, especially the least and poorest among us, who are the Body of Christ on our streets, in the barrios, in our neighborhoods and cities, across the continents of the world. Our taking of them into our lives and hearts is *more* soul food, as nourishing and sustaining to our bodies and souls as Eucharist and Word. Our God, the Trinity, Three in One, stays with us and is *more* in bread and wine, in Word and in the flesh and blood of all human beings, all our sisters and brothers whom we are to share our life and our God with daily.

A short, marvelous story: Maurice Sendak used to get thousands of letters from children about his book, *Where the Wild Things Are*. One day, his assistant gave him a stack and said, "You have to see this one. Jimmy has sent his 'wild thing' drawing and a note saying he loved his wild thing." His note was all garbled; he hadn't learned to separate words, etc., so there was a translation from his mom. Sendak quickly sketched a Wild Thing on a piece of blotter-sized paper and off it went to Jimmy with a note sharing it with him. Two weeks later, another note arrived from Tommy's mother, saying how much it meant to him. He carried it around, slept with it, and then he *ate* it, telling his mother that's how much he loved the gift. (The going rate for one of those sketches at the time, signed by the author, was about $26,000, which could have paid for his education.)

Let us continue to chew on the Word, and to break and share our soul food, the Body and Blood of Christ, now, and then go forth from this place and be the Body of Christ for all the hungry people out there who are crying, "MORE, we want MORE," and God hopes we will feed them ourselves. Amen.

19TH SUNDAY *in* ORDINARY TIME

FR. RICHARD ROHR, OFM

"I am the bread that came down from heaven."

1ST READING:
1 KGS. 19:4-8

PSALM:
34:2-9

2ND READING:
EPH. 4:30-5:2

GOSPEL:
JOHN 6:41-51

FREQUENTLY, HERE AT THE ALTAR, I SAY THESE words: "We are what we eat. We are what we drink." That truth is very interesting to me, because Jesus so consistently presents himself, not as an idea, or a concept, or a theory that can be argued about, but as food. It's a very beautiful metaphor. You see, food can only be liked or disliked. It either tastes good or it doesn't. You digest it. You chew on it. You absorb it. It's a much bigger field than just an idea. And so Jesus presents himself as good food, good bread.

Now, I bet you older ones can remember this: Until I was middle-aged, we didn't have nutrition labels on the back of food packaging like we do now. We all pretty much ate meat and potatoes and one vegetable. I grew up in Kansas. We didn't have words for carbohydrates or fats or proteins or starches. We just ate, and food was to fill you up. Of course, most of my parents' generation died young, of heart attacks and cancers, because they weren't aware that there was a big difference between eating good food and eating bad food.

So, Jesus presents himself as living bread, as bread that comes down from heaven, as bread of eternal life—good food. Then, right in the middle of the text, he presents, or the text presents, people who apparently have eaten some bad food. He calls them murmurers, or complainers. They just always have to find something to argue about. "Is this not Jesus, the son of Joseph? Don't we know his mother and father? He came from the same town we did. He's from the South Valley. How can he know anything?"

That's a whole different level of people. I'm afraid it represents an awful lot of American people, who eat very bad food. Remember, what you eat is who you are. If you find yourself largely in negative circles of conversation, if you find yourself complaining like others are, if you find yourself attracted to conspiracy theories, if you find yourself always hating the president or always loving the president, that's a problem. That's bad food. You're letting someone else control your life.

And what you eat is what you are. If you only have one source of news, that's bad food. With only that food, you're going to become a very dualistic thinker—a very arbitrary, usually angry, thinker—because you can never balance yourself out. Jesus is good food. He's positive. He's upbeat. He's hopeful. He's living. He's the bread of life, not the bread of death.

We live in a culture, right now, that seems to have grown comfortable with bad food. It really doesn't mind being lied to, apparently. It doesn't mind having angry people around all day. Jesus is not angry. He's sad. He's disappointed. He's angry at evil, but never angry at people—that's very, very different. And I think, if we're going to grow up as a country, as a nation, we're going to have to eat a lot better food. And we're going to have to watch what we're already eating. If you find yourself talking negatively, or murmuring and complaining about things that usually don't matter anyway, you've probably been eating a lot of bad food. You are what you eat. You are what you drink.

In a few minutes, you're going to approach this table and we're going to offer you good food: food of life, food of love, food of communion, food of forgiveness, food of compassion. Make sure you don't just take it into your mouth. Make sure you take it into your body and your soul. Chew on it, digest it, absorb it, until it changes you, and you really know and believe that you are what you eat. You also are the body of Christ. And so is everybody else too.

20TH SUNDAY *in* ORDINARY TIME

MARGARET (MAGS) BLACKIE, PhD

"I am the living bread that came down from heaven."

1ST READING:
PROV. 9:1-6

PSALM:
34: 2-7

2ND READING:
EPH. 5:15-20

GOSPEL:
JOHN 6:51-58

AS A YOUNG ADULT, I FELT A CALL TO FULLTIME ministry. As a woman in the Roman Catholic Church, options are somewhat limited. I am a natural teacher and the desire to preach was certainly a part of that exploration. But that is simply not an option within this tradition, so why do I stay?

For me, the answer is the Eucharist. Sitting in mass one day, many years ago, it occurred to me that the molecules of the Eucharist become the molecules of my own body. By partaking in the Eucharist, the Body and Blood of Christ are quite literally becoming a part of my own body. I carry Christ within me as I leave the church.

But it is not just me who carries Christ. It is everyone who has stood around the communion table. We all emerge as bearers of Christ. We all emerge connected in a deeply physical manner.

The transformation achieved in the consecration is not just for the bread and the wine. The transformation is happening in me too.

Now, I am sure that understanding does not usually get taught in catechism class. To many, it may seem a rather radical proposition. And yet, this is consistent with the radical teaching of Jesus in the Gospel today: "Whoever eats my flesh and drinks my blood remains in me and I in him."

It is said that many who had gathered around Jesus fell away after hearing this message. It was too disturbing, too radical. And yet, Jesus doesn't need us to understand; he just needs us to risk partaking. As the reading from Proverbs says, "Let whoever is naïve turn in here; to any who lack sense I say, Come, eat of my food, and drink of the wine I have mixed!"

Denise Ackermann, who is a South African theologian, speaks of the power of the shared experience of the Eucharist under apartheid. It was the only space where all were equal, where white and black, male and female, rich and poor, all stood shoulder to shoulder, served in turn. It is hard to maintain a justification for the system of apartheid when you have shared the Eucharist together.

In a time of deep division across the world, where the "other" is so readily identified and called out, the "other" is often one who shares our faith. The "other" is one who is equally welcome at the table of the Lord. Imagine, for just a moment, standing at the communion rail next to someone who holds a radically different political position to your own. Imagine receiving alongside them. Imagine walking out of the church, each of you, a Christ bearer, each of you connected physically and spiritually through partaking in the one Body.

Take some time to talk to God about this experience.

21ST SUNDAY *in* ORDINARY TIME

DR. MASSIMO FAGGIOLI

"We have come to believe and are convinced that you are the Holy One of God."

1ST READING:
JOSH. 24:1-2, 15-17, 18

PSALM:
34: 2-3, 16-21

2ND READING:
EPH. 5:21-32

GOSPEL:
JOHN 6:60-69

IN THIS DAY AND AGE, THE BIGGEST CHALLENGE in commenting on the readings of this Sunday is probably the second reading, from Ephesians 5:21–32, which has become famous—or notorious—in the tradition as a way to justify a certain kind of gender relations: "Wives should be subordinate to their husbands as to the Lord. For the husband is head of his wife just as Christ is head of the church, he himself the savior of the body." In fact, the key to the readings of this Sunday is not about *subjection* to other humans, but about *faithfulness* to one another: Faithfulness as a consequence of the faithfulness to the God that led the people out of Egypt through the Exodus (Joshua 24:1–2, 15–17, 18); witness to the Lord's faithfulness, deliverance, and protection (Psalm 34); and faithfulness to Jesus Christ and the incarnation (John 6:60–69).

John's Gospel for this Sunday comes at the end of the long sixth chapter. After the multiplying of the loaves and fishes, Jesus explains the metaphor of the bread of life that the Father gives through the Son (vv. 25–35), a bread that is identified with Himself (37–40) and that is accessible to all the Father attracts to Him (41–51), being the bread given by Jesus as His own body and blood (51–58). In these last verses of the sixth chapter, we are faced with all the shock and the scandal that the words of Jesus caused, not only in the crowds of Jews, but also among his disciples.

This crisis in the relations between Jesus and his community is witnessed by all four gospels at the moment of a decisive word of Peter, who confessed the identity of Jesus as Messiah and as sent by the Father as His Son. The words of Jesus were sometimes harsh and even struck the ears of disciples who followed him with affection and attention, but could not accept that Jesus "came down from heaven" and that, in the flesh of a fragile and mortal human body, he narrated the living and true God. Jesus had said several times: "I am the living bread that came down from heaven," but it was precisely those who had acclaimed him as "the great prophet who comes into the world" and who had even wanted to proclaim him king—when faced with these words, they feel scandalized in their faith. Prophet yes, Messiah yes, but body given, and given up, to violent death, body to eat and blood to drink? No.

Jesus, who knows these murmurings of the disciples, is not afraid to tell the whole truth, at the cost of causing a division among his followers. We could say that he attacks the murmurers because he suffers for the unbelief, for the lack of understanding by those who for years had been following him and were assiduous to his word.

What is scandalous about Jesus is his very human condition, his surrender, in fragile flesh and in a mortal body, to fragile flesh and mortal bodies. How is it possible that God gives himself up in a man, "the son of Joseph," a human creature who can be betrayed and given into the hands of sinners, as will happen precisely because of one of the Twelve—Judas, a servant of the devil? Here, faith stumbles upon having to accept the image of a *reversed kind of Messiah*, who is fragile, poor, weak, and to whom men can do whatever they want. It's the scandal of the incarnation of God; a scandal not only in the eyes of non-Christians, but also, unconsciously, of many Christians.

The Gospel records that some disciples, scandalized by the words of Jesus's gestures, leave, whether out of fear or out of religious convictions or for other reasons. In any case, it's also a lack of faith. They had welcomed the calling from Jesus, they had perhaps followed Jesus with enthusiasm, but then, they stumbled into the misunderstanding of his words. Consequently, they embarked on a path of *de-vocation*, denying the path they had taken until they left. Among them, there is also Judas, one of the Twelve, personally chosen as a disciple by Jesus. It is possible that in the community of Jesus, and thus in the Christian community, there are those who become a minister of the devil, a disciple of the devil. Therefore, he can do nothing but betray.

This is a lesson for us, members of a church where often the measure is success instead of the quality of faith. As the constitution *Lumen Gentium* of Vatican II says:

> Just as Christ carried out the work of redemption in poverty and persecution, so the Church is called to follow the same route that it might communicate the fruits of salvation to men. Christ Jesus, "though He was by nature God... emptied Himself, taking the nature of a slave," and "being rich, became poor" for our sakes. Thus, the Church, although it needs human resources to carry out its mission, is not set up to seek earthly glory, but to proclaim, even by its own example, humility and self-sacrifice.[1]

This Gospel presents us not only with a case of crisis in Jesus's community. It also does not hide the danger of false success in the community, the danger of false unanimity and success because it avoids asking hard questions. Especially these days, the community of believers in Jesus Christ deserves more hope than optimism, and needs to accept the possibility of its own division and breakdown as risk entailed with the acceptance of the incarnation.

1 Second Vatican Council, *Lumen Gentium*, November 21, 1964, 8.

22ND SUNDAY *in* ORDINARY TIME

RORY COONEY

"You disregard God's commandment but cling to human tradition."

1ST READING:
DEUT. 4:1-2, 6-8

PSALM:
15:2-5

2ND READING:
JAS. 1:17-18, 21B-22, 27

GOSPEL:
MARK 7:1-8, 14-15, 21-23

WHENEVER JESUS TURNS HIS GAZE ON religious leaders and religious law, people like me should do some serious introspection. "People like me" is a group that includes bishops, priests, professional ministers, and church employees, among others. It also includes public servants, politicians, and law enforcement officers who, silently or ostentatiously, use the name "Christian" to describe themselves. Why? Because on days like today, when the readings are about the law and commandments, and about discerning what's important and not important, God's word is addressed to us personally. Making up little rules and giving them the importance of divine law isn't just an artifact of the history of Judaism. It's also part of the story of the church. It's the story of creating rules that divide and abuse, and allow us to attempt to be the sole mediators of the divine will and grace. It is a story of association with a god, with God, and it gives us a sense of self-importance, even narcissism. It is the story of how we play God, and playing God is a hard habit to break.

Jesus was a good Jew and, as we know from the Sermon on the Mount, had a great love for the law of Moses. But, to Jesus, even the Mosaic law needs interpretation and explanation. He seemed to know it was for a time and a place, and times and places change. As we walk through the Sermon on the Mount every three years or so on a Sunday, we hear Jesus reinterpret even some of the Ten Commandments. This is what a rabbi, a teacher, does.

At the time of the destruction of the Temple in 70 CE, shortly before the gospel of Mark was written, there was a division of opinion about how the Torah was to be interpreted—in fact, about how all of the Scripture was to be read. The rabbis descended from the Pharisees would have answered, "We read the Torah through the eyes of Moses, the meek." The teachers among the Jewish-Christian sect that was spreading through the Roman world would have said, "We read through the eyes of the Rabbi Jesus." They and we use Jesus's way of seeing the holy book. As we see in the Sermon on the Mount, Jesus was not afraid of saying, "You have heard it said . . . but I tell you . . . ," relativizing the accepted apparent meaning of the Scripture. He's even more dismissive of the *mishna*, the interpretations of the Scriptures that became little laws, laying even more burdens on God's people. His attitude seemed to be, "You were not led out of Egypt for this. You were not led out of Babylon for this. God made you for freedom, made you for one another and for mutual love. We have to be different from this."

At this point in Mark's gospel, Jesus is still trying to make room in the hearts of Galilean Jews for a God of freedom and healing, and not so much a God of rigorous adherence to law and purity. He needs to undermine the authority of those teaching a false or limited God in order to create a space for *metanoia*, that "repentance" he announces when he says, "Repent, and believe in the gospel." The scribes of the Pharisees keep the boundaries of the tribe and nation through the many rituals of diet and purity. These rituals functioned politically and socially, defining ethnic identity and status in the class hierarchy. What one ate and who one ate with were social markers. Simultaneously the legislators, gatekeepers, and judges, these religious leaders left little room for people to be arbiters of their own spiritual experience.

Some of us can relate to similar Catholic practice, such as abstaining from meat on Fridays, and how that became a social marker for Catholics, and how breaking the law of abstaining constituted (by virtue of "mortal sin") a breach with the community and God that could only be repaired by the action of a priest. The parallel is striking, especially to the extent that such laws and customs might overshadow other, more central biblical values like almsgiving, peacemaking, and love of neighbor, especially enemies and strangers.

And so, in today's gospel, Jesus attacks the table boundaries and purification laws that are made, interpreted, and enforced by the scribes and Pharisees. Note that they highlight "the tradition of the elders" about washing and purification, which allows Jesus to accuse them of disregarding God's commandments while clinging to human tradition. Jesus's point, drawn from Isaiah 29, is that an idolatry of law is not the same as true worship. Jesus goes on to say that it is what is inside of us, in our hearts, that makes us clean or unclean. Note that in the first reading, Deuteronomy itself says of the law, "In your observance of the commandments of the Lord, your God, which I am commanding you, you shall not add to what I command you nor subtract from it."

James, possibly "the brother of the Lord" and the head of the Jerusalem church, gives us a clear picture of exactly how we should welcome God's word: we are to be doers of the word, and not hearers only. In fact, with characteristic directness, he wants us to know that to do otherwise is to be deluding ourselves. James doesn't let us guess about what being doers of the word involves, and doesn't let us off the hook by allowing us to imagine that our belonging to Christ is merely something confessional, an act of the mind. In this short passage, James tells us that "religion that is pure and undefiled . . . is this: to care for orphans and widows in their affliction and to keep oneself unstained by the world." "The world" here is the empire, the value system of those who worship the god-emperor and rely on the legions to preserve a brutal peace that relies on fear and threats of violence.

Let us "humbly welcome the word that has been planted" in us, and let it grow in us and change us from rule-makers and rule-keepers into lovers of justice and mercy. Let us, as our psalm urges today, do justice in order to be seen as living in God's presence, visibly concerned that opportunity and resources are distributed so that everyone has enough. Our silence, closing our eyes to injustice and our ears to cries for help, has allowed racial discrimination and police brutality, violence against women and children, and gross inequalities in opportunity and distribution of resources to become systemic in our nation and our world.

In next week's gospel, Jesus heals a man with defective speech and hearing with a word and a touch. "*Ephphatha!*" He says. "*Open up!*" Let us be opened, too, to the word we hear today. Let our hearts be opened, changed by the gospel. To do so is its own reward, for those who *do* justice will live in the presence of God.

23RD SUNDAY *in* ORDINARY TIME

FR. JAMES MARTIN, SJ

"Be opened!"

1ST READING:
ISA. 35:4-7A

2ND READING:
JAS. 2:1-5

PSALM:
146:6-10

GOSPEL:
MARK 7:31-37

A FEW YEARS AGO, ON A PILGRIMAGE TO THE Holy Land with about a hundred other pilgrims, I got caught in a little rain shower in Jerusalem. We were on the Mount of Olives, which, as you'll remember from the Good Friday readings, is just outside the city walls.

Some in our group were taking photos of the Old City, which spreads out before you, or beneath you, as you stand on the Mount of Olives. Fortunately, I was inside our tour bus, talking to another pilgrim, so I wasn't getting wet. I remember the rain streaming down the big windows of the tour bus like tears.

Suddenly there was a knock on the closed door of the bus. It was our Israeli tour guide, Maher, who is a Catholic man from Galilee, not too far from Nazareth. Caught in the rain, he was trying to get the attention of the bus driver, and said, "*Ephphatha! Ephphatha!*" In response, the bus driver, named Tony, immediately opened the door.

It was an electric moment for me. I knew that Maher was an Aramaic-speaking Christian, and that Tony spoke Aramaic too. But I had never heard Aramaic used like that, as a living language. And, of course, I thought immediately of today's Gospel passage: "*Ephphatha!*" Be opened!

Now, before I studied theology, I used to wonder about the few foreign words that are sprinkled throughout the English-language version of the gospels, and which I had thought were Hebrew. And I wondered: Why do the English translations use a word like "*Ephphatha*"? Why don't they just translate it into English, like they do for all the rest of Jesus's words? Why is that word left untranslated?

Well, the reason is this: That word, an Aramaic word, is preserved in the original Greek manuscript that Mark wrote. In other words, in the middle of Mark's Greek narrative about the healing of the deaf and mute man, you come upon this one Aramaic word: "*Ephphatha!*"

Why is it there? Because the word itself, in Aramaic, the language that Jesus spoke, was so memorable that it became part of the story.

So, when you read or hear words in the gospels preserved in their original language like that, you're hearing Aramaic. That's why we hear Jesus say to Jairus's daughter, who is ill, "*Talitha koum,*" which means "Little Lamb, arise." That's why we hear Jesus say on the Cross, "*Eli, Eli, lema sabachthani,*" which means, "My God, My God, why have you forsaken me?" And that's why Mary Magdalene, when she sees the Risen Christ on Easter Sunday, says, "*Rabbouni,*" which means Rabbi.

In other words, when you hear these Aramaic words, you are hearing words directly from their lips. "*Ephphatha*" is the precise word that Jesus used, and that utterance so impressed itself on those present that the word was remembered and treasured by the eyewitnesses, was passed on to the early church, and became part of the story that Mark eventually wrote down, a few decades later.

Why am I mentioning all this? Why this excursion into New Testament criticism? To remind us all that Jesus Christ, fully human and fully divine, was a real person, who lived in a real time and who spoke a real language. He lived in the real world—our world. He understands us.

Jesus understands, in fact, everything about the human condition.

Further in the story, there is another telling word that reveals Jesus's humanity. Mark says that before Jesus healed the man, he "groaned." The Greek word is "*estenaxen.*"

Why is he groaning? Perhaps it took some physical effort to effect the healing; perhaps he was distressed about the man's condition; perhaps he was simply tired. My sense is the first possibility: It took effort. Remember when the woman with the hemorrhage touches the fringe of Jesus's garment, and he feels power go out of him? Perhaps healing drained him of some physical, emotional, or mental energy.

In our own lives, think of how tiring it can be to counsel someone who is struggling, to visit someone who is sick, or to engage in a conversation about an emotional topic, like one about a serious illness or death. It's a noble thing to do, but it takes a lot out of us. As apparently it did for Jesus.

So, Jesus fully understands the human condition. In his life on earth, he saw people who were ill; he saw people who were frustrated; he saw people who were angry. He saw life and death, good and evil, sin and even corruption.

Many of us have felt tremendous anger, frustration, and sadness over the stories of crimes and corruption that come from within our church. It is a terrible sickness that needs to be confronted, in the way that Jesus confronted illness in his time, as we just saw: head on.

Like Jesus, we are asked not to shrink before evil, not to falter in doing the right thing, and never to doubt that God has the power to heal, to cast out evil, and to change things utterly. Even with something that seems incurable, as this man's illnesses were in his time, we are not to despair.

My own sense now is that Jesus Christ, through his people, is groaning as he confronts the deaf and mute church—the church that has been for so long deaf to the cries of abuse victims and their families as well as mute about its own criminal activity. And my sense is that Jesus is asking us to bring it out into the open, so that it can be met, named, healed, and changed. So that the church can once again, as the deaf and mute man did, "speak plainly."

Jesus asks us, the church, now, I believe, to open up, including opening up our past—including our files and records—all our crimes, our sins, and our failings. Without fear. We need to bring the sick church before Jesus—just like the deaf and mute man's friends did for him, because they wanted him to be healed. And only if we are "opened" will we be able to see and hear again.

We need to let it all out, so that it can be confronted and changed and healed by Jesus. We need to hear Jesus, who is banging on the doors of the church, and shouting out, "*Ephphatha!*" Be opened!

24TH SUNDAY *in* ORDINARY TIME

DENNIS PLUMMER

"Go in peace; keep warm and eat your fill."

1ST READING:
ISA. 50:4-9

PSALM:
116:1-6, 8-9

2ND READING:
JAS. 2:14-18

GOSPEL:
MARK 8:27-35

IT WAS THE END OF A LONG DAY, AT THE END of a long week, at the end of a very long month. Some moments are like that—more exhausting than others—but, outwardly, everything seemed normal. The sky was blue, birds were singing, and traffic moved along just fine.

So, she could not have known—not known how deeply the customary greeting would pierce.

I was working seven odd jobs at the time, in an attempt to keep cash flowing as I tried to get my own business up and running. My day's agenda rested beside me on the seat of the car: 7 a.m., leaflet homes in the Northeast Heights; 9 a.m., sell washers and dryers at Costco; 1:30 p.m., secret shop a coffee bar; 2:30 p.m., pick up the elderly man with Alzheimer's from adult day care and provide care until he rested; 6 p.m., arrive late for four hours working at an emergency shelter. This had been my driving schedule for a month. I was hanging on, exhausted and facing an uncertain future.

Hungry, I pulled up to the fast food drive-through window and the cheery worker handed me my order. "Have a nice day," she extolled. If only she knew.

"Have a nice day." It's a phrase heard multiple times throughout the day. It has permeated our culture—so much in use by films, air traffic controllers, truckers, service employees, and others that it has certainly lost meaning. At worst, it is used as sarcasm; typically, it is meant to end a transaction; at best, the speaker may actually wish for you a good day.

Whatever the intent, it puts the onus on the hearer to have their own nice day. The speaker speaks it but does nothing to create it. The nice day has been wished, kindness has been spoken, and everyone is expected to move right along.

I imagine that it was the same in Jesus's time. Different words, different phrases, same meaning and result—or, rather, lack of result. "Go in peace; keep warm and eat your fill," one might have said. And yet, if they did not follow the words and supply the other's bodily needs, what was the good of that?

We Christians can be pretty good at words. We like to have the tongue of a teacher. We take a certain measure of comfort (pride?) in being in the know. It feels good to have the answer and we stand ready at any time to give a defense to anyone who asks for a reason for the hope that we have. The disciples knew the answer, and yet Jesus sternly told them not to tell anyone about him.

Why? Why would Jesus demand silence when so many needed the good news that he was bringing? Perhaps he knew from experience that words go only so far and, without accompanying action, they fall flat upon ears unable to hear. Speaking needs to be counterbalanced by action. Even today's emerging young authors are instructed, "Show. Don't tell." James certainly knew it. He went straight to the bottom line: Show me your works, then I shall see your faith.

During the COVID-19 pandemic that began to sweep the world in 2020, I was part of a consolidated effort to decrease population density in emergency shelters to reduce potential spread of the virus. One large shelter was split into multiple sites, moving 400+ people from one building into smaller groups among four sites. The move not only improved health safety measures; it also brought with it an ever-increasing calm. In smaller, quieter locations, women and men began to form community. They moved from living in survival mode on the streets, to sheltering en masse, to more peaceful resting in living accommodations that gave them security.

After some weeks in the new locations, one man reflected, "I have begun to have dreams again." The words chilled me. He had not dreamed for months! Nights of insecurity, of overcrowded conditions, of not knowing what threats would come next...these had so prevented him from deep sleep that dreams had eluded him. What this man needed was safety. He needed people to give actual shelter and care. He needed action, something that was a far cry from being told to "sleep tight."

But, "sleep tight" and "have a nice day" and "go in peace" are nice, easy words. They comfort the speaker. Saying them deludes us into thinking that we have done our work. Surely, these kind sentiments reflect our goodness and our compassionate caring. The transaction has been completed.

Too often, variants of "God helps those who help themselves" have crept into our thoughts, if not our actions. We love the story of someone who has pulled themselves up by their bootstraps. We favor "hand-ups" over "hand-outs." However, this proverb is *not* found in the Bible. By contrast, examples abound of God helping those who could not help themselves. Yet, the belief in first-come, first-served justice persists. We, with our homes and our clothing and our food, wish people well. We rest in our own good fortune and believe that others should find theirs. We send thoughts and prayers (more words) and expect that if everyone would just get a job and secure their own housing, then all would be well.

If only it were that easy. What of the woman who is severely disabled? How will she work again? What of the teenager who was born with an inherited predisposition to addiction? What of the man whose mental illness means that his "normal" will never look like your "normal"? Shall we say to them, "Go in peace," and believe that our work is done?

Jesus does not allow us this. He challenges our faith to go deeper than words. We must—not metaphorically—be our sisters' and brothers' keepers. We must house and clothe and feed and give care—in action. We cannot do all things at all times for all people. But, in the community of believers, we can do more than believe. We can find the one action that we, ourselves, can do today. By example, Jesus calls us to this faith in action. As St. Francis so poignantly said, "Preach the Gospel at all times. When necessary, use words."

And, as James reminds us this day, "if someone says he has faith but does not have works? Can that faith save him?"

25TH SUNDAY *in* ORDINARY TIME

SHIRIN McARTHUR

"Whoever receives one child such as this in my name, receives me."

1ST READING:
WIS. 2:12, 17-20

PSALM:
54: 3-8

2ND READING:
JAS. 3:16-4:3

GOSPEL:
MARK 9:30-37

AS I SIT TO WRITE THIS HOMILY, CITY STREETS and small-town squares across America are filled with protesters. George Floyd's murder has torn any slick veneer off the civil unrest which has been simmering around the country, mostly beneath the surface, for over 400 years. Viewed through the eyes, hearts, and experiences of indigenous and black peoples, the United States of America has never been the land of the free. All people have never been treated equally, even if the founding fathers dared to state that all men should be.

As a child of the American Southwest, I also know that civil unrest existed long before the arrival of Europeans. Recent analysis[1] of Native skeletal remains shows that most deaths eight centuries ago in the Mesa Verde area of southwestern Colorado were violent and traumatic. (That study in itself is a controversial subject. How would you feel about archae-

1 "The Most Violent Era in America Was Before Europeans Arrived," *Science 2.0*, August 3, 2014, https://www.science20.com/news_articles/the_most_violent_era_in_america_was_before_europeans_arrived-141847.

ologists digging up and studying your ancestors' graves?) Early European explorers also recorded discussions with Native peoples that referenced conflict and violence between neighboring tribes.

James is very forthright about conflict in his letter to the early Christians, writing, "Where jealousy and selfish ambition exist, there is disorder and every foul practice." He goes on to talk about covetousness—our desire to have what others have, which is often a key factor in the development of conflict. Even back as far as the Ten Commandments, we are told not to covet anything that belongs to our neighbor. Over the course of human history, that commandment has, as Shakespeare phrased it, been more honored in the breach than the observance.

Covetousness is at the root of most human conflict. Wars have been fought over territory, wealth, and power because those who had much were not willing to share equitably with those who had little. James's logic is clear. We covet, but do not possess. Our covetousness doesn't gain us anything. Instead, it makes us angrier and more frustrated. This leads us to wage war, to conquer and kill those who have what we desire to possess, in order that we may possess it by force.

Then comes the kicker: James writes that we do not possess because we do not ask. So, why do we not ask? It might be because when we asked in the past, we did not receive. It might be because we've heard from family members and friends that asking is a waste of time. It might be because we've been taught that those who possess are bad people who won't share; we've learned that only force will work.

How did we reach this point in human affairs? A worthy answer to that question could be another entire homily in itself, but a short response is that those who do possess have developed an attitude of scarcity which prevents them—prevents us—from being open to sharing.

We, who have much, believe that if we share, there will not be enough for us—for our tribe, for our kind or color of people. We, who have much, fear that sharing our possessions will not address the bigger issues of inequity. We, who have much, are accustomed to our privilege and position and don't want to end up trading places. We don't want to end up on the streets.

Because we, who have much, have refused to share, others are on the streets. Protesters are marching on the streets and the homeless are begging on the streets. Because too many of us view the world in terms of black and white, white and black—and we've lost the capacity to dream beyond dualistic limitations. Because we, who possess wealth and power, have refused to listen and share, passions prevail and peace becomes an unattainable mirage.

In today's gospel lesson, Jesus is teaching his disciples privately rather than addressing large crowds. Rather than the revolutionary hope of his public message, Jesus shares his realistic assessment about the very concrete consequences of his revolutionary teaching.

The wealthy and powerful of his day—the scribes and Pharisees, and religious leaders who colluded with Rome—also refused to share. They had very real, personal reasons for doing so. Colluding with Rome kept them in power and kept their families safe. It put food on the table. But it did not bring peace or justice for all peoples, which was why Jesus was out on the streets. It's why his message was such a threat. Jesus was teaching the people to ask. Jesus was encouraging his followers to speak up, to peacefully protest, to believe that possessions and power could be shared.

The religious leaders, who had much and refused to share, were jealous and fearful of Jesus's popularity. Those passions—fear and envy—led them into conflict with Jesus. James makes it clear that such "passions" are the root cause of conflicts and war. Whenever we react passionately, out of a mode of scarcity instead of God's abundance, disorder will arise, whether it be an ancient crucifixion or a modern protest movement.

Jesus's disciples didn't understand that even his death would be revolutionary. The religious leaders would kill Jesus, but he would rise again. He would prove, once for all, that scarcity always loses out to God's great abundance.

So, how do we respond out of a mode of abundance? James suggests cultivating a different set of passions. We are called to be peaceable, gentle, compliant, sincere, and full of mercy. We must faithfully and persistently sow peace and cultivate peace, rather than war.

For Jesus, the best response is to resist becoming powerful possessors. Rather than fighting over who is the greatest, we are to become like children. Children do not have any power or possessions of their own. (They may think they possess toys or food that come from the family, but they are perfectly powerless.) Children have little real control over their lives. Children therefore must ask for anything and everything they need.

If we all, like children, had to ask, then, at last, all people—of any ethnic background or social status or sexual orientation—would be equal. If anyone asked, anyone who possessed would be compelled to share.

If children of God are marching or begging on the streets, it's because we who possess are not listening and sharing. No one should have to protest or beg. A simple request, a straightforward ask, should be all that is required.

What would life look like if we all had to ask? How might the world be transformed if we all were willing to share? How can you begin to share from your abundance with those on the streets today?

26TH SUNDAY *in* ORDINARY TIME

DEACON JIM KNIPPER

"For whoever is not against us is for us."

1ST READING:
NUM. 11:25-29

PSALM:
19:8, 10, 12-13

2ND READING:
JAS. 5:1-6

GOSPEL:
MARK 9:38-43, 45, 47-48

A FEW YEARS AGO, THE POPE WAS IN IRELAND for the World Meeting of Families, where he reminded us to share the Gospel of the Family as a joy for the world—and for us to remember that love is our mission, so that our families can be fully alive. But, I guess, an obvious question is: What does that look like? What does it mean to be fully alive? And I think the gospels, and some of the recent wisdom of our pope, bring the answer to light.

Over the past few weeks, in our Sunday Gospels, we have been listening to this ongoing dialogue of Christ with his disciples and his patient efforts in trying to teach them what it means to be fully alive. Beginning a few weeks ago, after the disciples witnessed a number of miracles, Jesus asked them, "Who am I?" And, surprisingly, Peter gets it right away: "You are the Christ!" But once Jesus begins to foretell of the passion he will have to endure, Peter no longer gets it. He does not like it, and his rebuke to Christ is met with an even heavier scolding back at him. Christ is telling them that to be fully alive means you have to pick up your own crosses and follow him. Or, in the words of St. Francis de Sales: to be who you are and be that perfectly well.

Last week, the Gospel picks up this dialogue of Christ with his disciples as Jesus once again tells Peter, James, and John that it will be necessary for him to die and then, three days later, he will rise. But the disciples don't like any talk about suffering and, frankly, had no idea what he was talking about. Instead, once they rejoined the other disciples, Jesus found them arguing about who is the greatest among them. Clearly, the egos of the disciples were in full swing. So, Jesus responded by placing a child in front of them to make the point that to be fully alive means that life is not all about you—it is about serving others who are unable to care for themselves.

And as you just heard in this week's Gospel, the disciples continue to boost their egos by complaining that "people who are not following you, Jesus, are performing mighty deeds in your name. And how can that be? After all, we are the ones who are so special." So, it would seem that even before the Church has formed, even before Christ has died, the disciples are moving in the direction of exclusion, trying to define who is in and who is out, who is welcomed and who is not. And how does Jesus respond? "Whoever is not against us is for us." In other words, don't hinder others from doing good. Don't hinder others from being fully alive.

When preaching on this exact passage, Pope Francis reminded us that we are *all* created in God's image and likeness and we all have the commandment to do good—for, in doing so, *all* of us are redeemed—even atheists! And he went on to say, "it is [our] duty to build bridges and to help all men and women, in any way possible, to do the same."[1]

The second part of today's Gospel then speaks of what is translated as "sin"—although, in this setting, some scholars say the better translation would be "to stumble." Using graphic, metaphoric language, Jesus stresses the need to remove from your life that which causes you to stumble, which prevents you from being fully alive.

What does that look like for you? What is in your life that is causing you to stumble? Or, the flip side to that question: How could you be acting as a stumbling block to another person, just as the disciples were in this

1 "Transcript: Pope Francis's Speech to Congress," *The Washington Post*, September 24, 2015, https://www.washingtonpost.com/local/social-issues/transcript-pope-franciss-speech-to-congress/2015/09/24/6d7d7ac8-62bf-11e5-8e9e-dce8a2a2a679_story.html.

gospel story? In your life, within your family, who are you excluding or shunning? Do we go through the day focused more on what others are doing, versus on dealing with what we need to do?

Are we still wasting our time feeding our egos by spouting off to anyone who will listen about what we think is right, who we think is included, who we feel God loves, and measuring everyone by that standard? For, again, using the words of Pope Francis, "The yardstick we use for others will be the yardstick which time will use for us."[2] Do we live our life like the early years of the disciples, who wanted the glory and not the gore, who were more interested in the crown than the cross, who reveled in only joy and shunned the sorrow, who desired more of the comfort and less of the work?

Of all the words given to us by the pope at the World Meeting of Families, one of the messages that rang very clear is that if we want to be a Church which is renewed and fully alive, we need to go forth to build bridges, to break down walls, and to sow seeds of reconciliation and transformation. This work must take place in our society, in our towns, in our workplaces, and in our schools.

But this work must begin at home—within the family—where challenges and brokenness reside, where wounds linger, where pain is passed on (sometimes for generations), and where belief and healing and forgiveness and love are in desperate need. It is where brokenness connects with brokenness.

That is why the Holy Father reminds us that we are not called to judge; rather, we are called to be openly present. For all of us are equally loved by our God who works through all of us as we reach out to others. God's presence becomes manifested when each of us—young and old—use our gifts to enrich one another and not block how God is working through our lives and the lives of others. For the glory of all people lies within our capacity to love as God loves.

The words spoken by the pope at the US Congress have inspired, stimulated, and motivated people across all faiths—and with good reason. But do not get too comfortable, sitting back and just admiring his words—and thereby overlook the challenge he puts forth to all of us when he asks:

---

2 Ibid.

What about you? What are you going to do? Never underestimate what a call, a text, a note, a kind word can do for another.

For we all have a role in supporting the work of the Spirit—and, in doing so, living a life that is fully alive, a life that enables God to work through us, a life that implements a "culture of care," a life that feeds the hungry and clothes the naked, a life that is not focused on borders but rather breaks down the walls and the barriers—and thereby a life that is fully alive, to nurture what is good and restore dignity to every living person.

27TH SUNDAY *in* ORDINARY TIME

BRIAN McLAREN

"It is not good for the man to be alone. I will make a helper suited to him."

1ST READING:
GEN. 2:18-24

PSALM:
128: 1-6

2ND READING:
HEB. 2:9-11

GOSPEL:
MARK 10:2-16

SOME OF YOU WILL REMEMBER THE MUSIC of Joni Mitchell. In "Down to You," what she sang about one person is true of humanity as a whole: "You're a brute, you're an angel. You can crawl, you can fly too."[1]

Another great, but lesser-known, songwriter, Bruce Cockburn, said it this way in his song "Burden of the Angel/Beast": "From the lying mirror to the movement of stars/ Everybody's looking for who they are.... Could be the pusher/ Could be the priest/ Always ourselves we love the least/ That's the burden of the angel/beast."[2]

What is a human being? Long before contemporary singer-songwriters used guitars and microphones to answer this question, ancient Hebrew sages tried to answer it too, using ancient poetry and primal stories.

The book of Genesis begins with two such stories. It's clear that these stories were not meant as literal or scientific history because, for one thing,

1 Joni Mitchell, "Down to You," *Court and Spark*, Siquomb Music, 1974.

2 Bruce Cockburn, "Burden of the Angel/Beast," *Dart to the Heart*, Columbia, 1994.

they are so different from one another. Like a good song or poem or movie, each story gives one window or glimpse or perspective on what it means to be a human. Like our four gospels, each tells a key truth, but not the whole truth, so other stories, told from other perspectives, are needed.

In the first story, the words "God saw that it was good" resound again and again. In contrast, the second story begins with, "It was not good."

It was not good, and it is still not good today, for a human being to be alone. God remedies that loneliness with the creation of animals and birds. The original human names each creature. By naming it, the original human notices it, sees its uniqueness, sees its beauty, and acknowledges its belonging.

This is important for us to remember today. Many of us live in sterile, heated and air-conditioned boxes. We have little or no contact with our fellow creatures. If we see them at all, we see them through glass or on screens. Some of us walk out our doors every day for decades and hear birds singing, yet we don't know a single one of their names. We walk by streams filled with frogs and fish. We drive by fields full of amazing creatures. Even between and under our feet, life teems in the grass and soil. But we are alone, because we never notice and name our fellow creatures. That is unspeakably sad, but the good news is it can change. Today, tomorrow, the next day, you can begin to end your loneliness and isolation by noticing and naming your fellow creatures.

But even that rich companionship isn't enough. We humans need social companionship and sexual companionship with our fellow humans, the story tells us.

So, God creates woman. Some see this passage as reflecting ancient attitudes that are condescending and demeaning to women; women are just men's helpers. But others see this passage as presenting woman as an equal partner for the original man, taken not from his foot to rule over her, but from his side, near his heart, to stand as his beloved equal. The man leaves his parents and creates something new with her, a new family, a new shared identity. People who see the text this way note that God is called our helper, so the term isn't inherently demeaning.

So, what is a human being? A human being is a companion of animals, birds, and other living creatures. And a human being is a social and sexual being, an equal and companion of other humans, a member of a generation in human society, a bridge between parents and children—a link between the humans of the past and the humans of the future.

In today's Gospel, Jesus speaks to another related reality we must face: We humans easily abuse our power as human beings. Just as we humans are too often uncaring, cruel, and even abusive to animals, so we are too often uncaring, cruel, and abusive to one another.

In Jesus's day, men had nearly all the rights, and women were often seen as little more than property, as appendages to men. The same power imbalance is still too common today.

A man in Jesus's day might grow tired of his wife and discard her. He could even do it legally, "by the book." But that didn't change the fact that the woman, discarded by her husband, would face a future of terrible hardship. Jesus cared about women just as much as men.

In that context, the religious fundamentalists of his day tried to catch him in an error to discredit him. They came to him with the classic "gotcha" question: "What's your opinion on divorce?" However he answered, he would offend someone, and they would succeed in getting him into trouble, thus undermining his popularity.

In classic "Jesus style," he answers their question with a question. "You're Bible experts," he implies. "What does your Bible say?" They reply by affirming that men have a legal right to divorce their wives. (You'll notice they don't offer the same right to women.) They tried to expose Jesus to criticism, but he now exposes them: *They're concerned about their rights as men, but not the well-being of women. Even though they talk Bible, they're really motivated by power, pleasure, and self-interest.*

So, Jesus goes back, before the law, to the two original creation stories. He quotes from the first one, "God created them male and female," and then from the second, "The two of them become one body." He makes it clear that it's terribly dangerous to use a single Bible verse, just as it's dangerous to use a single story, to settle any matter. You have to see the bigger picture. You have to bring multiple stories to the table. You have to interpret those stories with a clear mind and a good heart.

Sadly, many people since that time have interpreted Jesus's words in exactly the same way as Jesus's fundamentalist critics interpreted their law: They use it to condemn those who get in their way or disagree with them. They use it to shame, control, and harm rather than to set free, heal, and make whole. Perhaps some of us have been shamed and harmed by people quoting this passage to us, if we've been divorced.

If we read this passage with a good heart, we see that Jesus is saying, "If you're trying to get away with as much as you can for yourself, if you're trying to use the Bible to justify your lust for power or pleasure or wealth, you've already forgotten what a human being really is. God's original dream is for men and women to be equals who care about one another and help one another be 'naked' and yet feel no shame, to be truly loved and not 'alone.' Let God's pure dream guide you, not your own polluted self-interest."

Yes, divorce happens, and laws regulating divorce are necessary because life is hard, and marriage is hard, and we humans can be so hardhearted that others need the legal protection divorce provides. But trying to get away with anything you can, as long as you find a legal justification for it—that's not fitting in with God's original dream for human beings.

As the passage in Hebrews says, Jesus sees every man as a beloved brother and every woman as a beloved sister. He doesn't give men or rich folks or people of a certain race or religion or nation any carte blanche to hurt or abuse others. To Jesus, all humans are equally precious, whether they're men or women or non-binary, whether they're single, married, or divorced.

As Jesus made clear to his critics, we would be wise to go back to the beginning and ask what God intends for us human beings to be. Do we want to be a brute or an angel? Do we want to crawl or fly? Do we want to be the pusher or the priest, the angel or the beast? The choice is ours.

That is one reason why we gather together each week, reading these ancient texts, celebrating the Eucharist, remembering Jesus and how he lived and taught. It's all too easy for us to stop flying and start crawling, to turn from priest to pusher. When we focus on Jesus as our model of compassionate, caring, mature humanity, we become our best selves.

And we can become Christ-like models for others as well.

28TH SUNDAY *in* ORDINARY TIME

MICHELLE FRANCL-DONNAY

"Children, how hard it is to enter the kingdom of God!"

1ST READING:
WIS. 7:7-11

PSALM:
90:12-17

1ST READING:
HEB. 4:12-13

GOSPEL:
MARK 10:17-30

MY KNIVES ARE THE WORKHORSES OF MY kitchen, their blades fine and sharp enough to slice a lemon paper thin or dice an onion without tears. They are an extension of my hands, almost alive. And when I'm not using them, I keep them safely cocooned in cork so that I don't inadvertently cut myself while reaching into the drawer.

The word of God, the author of Hebrews tells us, is like a sharp knife, alive in the hands of a skilled cook, able to separate the joint from the marrow. But, all too often, I find myself tempted to treat God's word—sharp, alive, and active—in the same way I treat my knives. I want to wrap it up, keep it from cutting me open, make it seem tractable and safe. The truth is that God's word is never safe. It can unexpectedly cut our lives open in a breath, as the rich young man in Mark's Gospel discovers.

The young man runs to Jesus, the question burning in his heart: "What must I do to have eternal life?" "Let go of everything you possess, give it to the poor, and then surrender yourself entirely into my hands," Jesus tells him. Discipleship on this scale seems impossible—to the young man and, frankly, to me, too, at times. So, I will admit to wanting to gloss over this gospel, seeking some way to sheathe its sharp blades. Perhaps, I tell myself, the needle's eye Jesus speaks of trying to get the camel through isn't really the eye of a sewing needle. I've heard it was actually an overly narrow gate in Jerusalem's walls that was known to be tough for an overladen camel to get through. So, it's not impossible; I wouldn't have to give away everything—just unload enough to squeeze through the gate and then I can reload my camel and be on my way to salvation.

But this blunting of the sharp edges is precisely what this gospel warns us against. Beware of doing just the minimum. Jesus reminds the young man what the basics of discipleship entail: Do not take what is not yours. Tell the truth. Honor your elders. But this isn't enough. The discipleship Christ is calling the young man—and us—toward is not about the basics, or even about what we have or don't have. It is about what God does.

Salvation isn't about me, a prize to be earned by my good works, for none of us can earn that. It is as impossible for me to do anything to merit salvation as it would be to squeeze a camel through the eye of a sewing needle. It's a gift for us all, earned by Christ, who put himself into our hands and let go of his breath. To grasp how great this gift is, I need to practice it myself: to let go of even the things that seem as necessary as breathing.

What is the wealth I cling to? There are obviously my material possessions, but there is also social privilege, my sense of accomplishment—I can make my own pasta, sew my own clothes, write a book, solve Schrödinger's equation. There are my seemingly innocent desires that are complicit with evil. When do I stop to wonder who has picked the bunch of flowers I buy at the grocery store? Are they paid enough to eat, do they have access to education, to a safe place to live, or clean water to drink?

It seems an impossible tangle, and like the young man in Mark's Gospel, I'm tempted to turn away, saddened at what I cannot separate myself from. But the author of Hebrews reminds us that the Scriptures are alive and can do this work in our lives, helping us separate out what we cling to for ourselves from what draws us closer to God.

In the Principle and Foundation of his *Spiritual Exercises*, St. Ignatius of Loyola reminds us that we must not fix our desires on poverty or wealth, success or failure, but desire instead what leads us to a deeper relationship with God. "Desire nothing but to live within me, and I within you," says Jesus. In the *Exercises*, St. Ignatius invites retreatants to pick up the Scriptures, the living Word of God, and let them come alive in their hearts. The *Exercises* use the Scriptures to strip away what we cling to and retain what draws us deeper into God's life.

I suspect we can do no better than to join in praying St. Vincent Pallotti's litany:

> Not the goods of the world, but God.
> Not riches, but God.
> Not honors, but God.
> Not distinction, but God. . . . God always and in everything.

Set down what you cling to, and pick up the Word—sharp edges and all.

29TH SUNDAY *in* ORDINARY TIME

DEACON JIM KNIPPER

"The Son of Man did not come to be served but to serve."

1ST READING:
ISA. 53:10-11

PSALM:
33:4-5, 18-20, 22

2ND READING:
HEB. 4:14-16

GOSPEL:
MARK 10:35-45

THIS LITURGICAL YEAR, THROUGH MOST OF Ordinary Time, we have been listening to Mark's Gospel—believed to have been the first gospel written. It is short, to the point, and thus, in order to realize some of the overarching themes of the Gospel, it really requires you to take a broader view so you can connect the dots of Mark's stories.

Case in point: Over the past few weeks, we have been given three gospel accounts where Jesus tells his disciples about his pending passion—about the need for suffering: that he will die, but, three days later, will rise. It would seem that Jesus is keen on teaching them about the pattern of life, death, and resurrection—a pattern that is ever-present in our lives.

But remember the responses? The first time Jesus tried to explain, Peter rebuked him. The second time, the disciples ignored what they heard and went on to argue about who was the greatest among them. And then, as they are walking to Jerusalem—to where Jesus knows he will die—he tells his disciples a third and final time of what is about to happen. And it is their response which is given to us in today's Gospel, with James and John asking if they can be the ones who will sit on his right and left—Can they have the special place of honor? Can they be the ones who will bask in the limelight?—which of course just irks the other ten disciples to no end.

Each time the disciples are faced with the reality that part of life is suffering and death, each time Jesus talks about the need to carry your cross to follow him, each time Jesus talks about serving others—the disciples focus on what is best for themselves: who is the greatest among them and how it is all about them gaining power and prestige. It is the first-century version of the "me" generation.

You see, when you tie these gospel stories together, they remind us of this paradox of life: that climbing the ladder of personal success really means learning to shed your ego and make your life all about others.

For centuries and throughout much of civilization, this lesson was learned through a prescribed form of initiation. While each culture had their own rites, the common characteristics usually involved a young teen boy (girls usually did not require such initiation) being taken by the elders into nature and taught how to face the dangers of being on his own in the wilderness—of facing his own life and his own death.

Our early Church had its own Rite of Initiation, whereby it would take a person 2–3 years of prayer and study before they were called catechumens—which comes from a Greek word meaning to "re-echo." It was during this time when the community strengthened and supported the catechumen by "re-echoing" their faith into the lives of those being initiated. Then, some eight months or so afterward, they were baptized by being fully immersed under water (symbolizing the death to oneself) and brought out of the waters, reborn into a life focused on discipleship. Many centuries later, much of this got watered down as the focus was on "making" the sacraments and the removal of original sin, and less about personal initiation and learning how to live this life in service as a disciple of Christ.

In general, most of civilization has walked away from the practice of initiating its young men, but just scan the news headlines and you will know that the need has only grown. And now, sociologists are saying that, due to changes in our society, some form of initiation is not just needed for young men, but also for young women . . . and that now, more than ever, our generations need to learn the following five core messages of initiation that had been universally taught throughout time:

- Life is hard.
- You are not that important.
- You are not in control.
- You are going to die.
- Life is not about you; you are about life and about serving others.

For these past months, we have been listening to the gospels as Jesus tries to open the eyes of his followers to these same messages—to initiate them on how to be human, on how suffering is part of life, and on how important it is to be servant first and to resist the desire to just feed the ego. But how much easier it is to be more like the disciples, who are looking for the seats of honor and glory, versus following what we heard in today's Gospel: that Christ is calling us to a role of servant, slave of all.

I think this is one of the main reasons there is so much universal love, across all faiths, for our Pope and his constant demonstration in reaching out and including all people. During his visit to the United States, we got to see, up close, his roles as a shepherd who tends to everyone and as a true pastor who is focused on being a servant leader. When addressing the Synod, he again reminded the bishops that those who exercise authority in the church are called "to serve" the people of God; and that he, as pope, is "the servant of the servants of God." His persistent plea to the entire Church—both laity and clergy—is to remember that our call to real discipleship must be rooted in love and mercy.

And during a month in which the Church has been so focused on the family, Pope Francis reminded us of how the love of the family must be mirrored in the Church when he said: "It is important that the Church in the United States also be a humble home, a family fire which attracts men and women through the attractive light and warmth of love. . . .

Only a Church which can gather around the family fire remains able to attract others."[1]

And it is this concept, of the fiery love within the family as being foundational to a healing, merciful Church, that Christ was attempting to teach the disciples, which is the same thing Pope Francis calls us to. But some may say, "How? Our family is so broken. How can it be the center of healing?"

Well, certainly, your presence here today is a gift in so many ways. More than ever, young men and women need healthy adult role models who, through their words and actions, will walk with them and mentor them, and teach them how to live and love and forgive and be present to others.

So, continue to stay connected to each other. Make it a priority to spend time together—time to truly listen to one another, whereby each of you will learn to live a life not focused on power, prestige, and possessions, or even where you sit, but focused on your baptismal commitment to truly live who you are in Christ—in a daily dance of life, death, and resurrection. For our ever-loving God calls us to become who you are. Become all that you are. For there is still so much more of you—more to be discovered, more to be forgiven, and much more to be loved.

---

1 Pope Francis, "Address of the Holy Father," Meeting with the Bishops of the United States of America, September 23, 2015, http://www.vatican.va/content/francesco/en/speeches/2015/september/documents/papa-francesco_20150923_usa-vescovi.html.

30TH SUNDAY *in* ORDINARY TIME

MIKE LEACH

"Let me see again!"

1ST READING:
JER. 31:7-9

2ND READING:
HEB. 5:1-6

PSALM:
126:1-6

GOSPEL:
MARK 10:46-52

ALL OF US—EACH OF US—IS BORN BLIND. WE spend our whole lives trying to see again, to regain what we lost sight of after paradise: that we live and move and have our being in God, and that nothing can change that, not even sin.

The story of the Garden of Eden is the story of how we got the crazy, sad idea that we can separate ourselves from the unconditional love of God. The story of Bartimaeus in today's gospel is the story of how our faith can restore our sight at any time—any old time at all—when we call upon Jesus, his son.

Eden wasn't just then. It is now.

We sin and we feel guilt and think that God wants to punish us, so we turn away from him in fear. We put fig leaves over our eyes and ears and cannot see the Father running out to meet us, his prodigal child, saying, "Come home! I have prepared a feast for you!" We think that our choice to leave home is unforgivable. We feel, not just naked and afraid, but alone and ashamed. We don't hear God's telling question, "Who told you that you were naked?" (Genesis 3:11)

We are lost.

This is half the story of our lives.

The other half is that now—right now, right here—God wants to return our sight. All we have to do is call out to him in Jesus's name.

That's what Bartimaeus did: "Jesus, have mercy on me! Let me see again!"

And when Bartimaeus saw the colors of life and love again, he laughed and shouted with joy, as the psalmist sings today.

Bartimaeus's miracle can be ours too. As we learn later in the epistle to the Hebrews (7:25), Jesus "is always able to save those who approach God through him, since he lives forever to make intercession for them."

We all need to ask Jesus for the gift to see again. We may have eyes, but we do not see what is really there. Jesus restores our vision so we can see what is real, what does not tarnish or fade away: forgiveness, love, beauty, goodness, gratitude, truth, peace, harmony, and joy. That is what brings laughter to our lips and joy to our hearts. "My peace I give to you. Not as the world gives do I give it to you. Do not let your hearts be troubled or afraid" (John 14:27).

When Jesus heals us, we no longer see with our eyes, but with our soul.

And the world comes alive again, as it was in Eden, as it became for Bartimaeus—at least for a little while.

Like a butterfly that alights in the palm of our hand, only to fly away moments later, our vision of Christ comes and goes many times in our lives. But we remember it always, just like the memory of Eden, implanted in our souls, and that's what keeps us going.

Was there ever a moment in your life when all seemed dark or even lost, and you begged God for mercy and a veil lifted and, sooner or later, your problems dissolved? You realized, as St. Julian of Norwich realized, that somehow, "all will be well and all will be well and every kind of thing shall be well." Was there ever a time when you were reading the Bible or a spiritual book and the book dropped to your lap because, suddenly, you understood: God is good. God loves me. God forgives me. I am all right.

These moments happen when we least expect them. But they surely will happen, sooner or later, after we cry out with all our heart to Jesus: "Let me see again!"

When Jesus encountered his first disciples on the shore of Galilee, they asked him what he was all about. He answered: "Come, and you will see" (John 1:39).

Our faith, writes Bishop Robert Barron in his book *And Now I See*, is all about seeing. "Holiness," wrote Origen of Alexandria, "is seeing with the eyes of Christ." The poet Gerard Manley Hopkins expressed this vision:

> Christ plays in ten thousand places,
> Lovely in limbs, and lovely in eyes not his
> To the Father through the features of men's faces.[1]

If Hopkins were alive today, he would have substituted the word "our" for "men's," but you get the point. There is a way of seeing that has nothing to do with the eyes, and everything to do with the soul. Jesus speaks of those who "may look and see but not perceive, and hear and listen but not understand" (Mark 4:12). Otherwise, they might turn back to God and, like the Prodigal Son, know forgiveness. To see again with the eyes of Christ is to know what the psalmist knew:

> "Where can I go from your spirit?
> From your presence, where can I flee?
> If I ascend to the heavens, you are there;
> if I lie down in Sheol, there you are.
> If I take the wings of dawn
> and dwell beyond the sea,
> even there your hand guides me,
> your right hand holds me fast." (Psalm 139:7–10)

The truth is, we never left Eden.

The truth is, God is with us still.

The truth is, "we have been consecrated through the offering of the body of Jesus Christ once for all" (Hebrews 10:10).

"Once for all" is always . . . and always is now. "Now is a very acceptable time" (2 Corinthians 6:2) to close our eyes, be like Bartimaeus, and, with our mind, speak his words: "Let me see again."

Go ahead. Close your eyes. Speak these words in your mind and heart:

---

1 Gerard Manley Hopkins, "As Kingfishers Catch Fire," *Poems* (London: Humphrey Milford, 1918); Bartleby.com, 1999. www.bartleby.com/122/.

Lord . . . let me see again.

Let me see you.

Let me see you in me and me in you.

Let me see you in everything and everyone, and everyone and everything in you.

We are, as you told us, one.

Just as a sunbeam can never be separated from the sun or from every other sunbeam, nothing can separate us from you or from each other.

Just as a wave is inseparable from the ocean, we are inseparable from you and from every creature, every star.

Lord, I am heartily sorry for my sins. You know that. Let me know that my original sin of turning my eyes away from you is totally forgiven. It is forgiven because you never turned your sight from me.

Let me know now what you assured Isaiah: "Though your sins be like scarlet, they may become white as snow" (Isaiah 1:18)!

Lord, let me see again.

Let me see you.

Be still now . . . .

Be still and know . . . .

(Silence)

31ST SUNDAY *in* ORDINARY TIME

REV. NADIA BOLZ-WEBER

"You shall love your neighbor as yourself."

1ST READING:
DEUT. 6:2-6

PSALM:
18:2-4, 47, 51

2ND READING:
HEB. 7:23-28

GOSPEL:
MARK 12:28B-34

"WHICH COMMANDMENT IS THE GREATEST?" they asked Jesus.

He answered, "Love God, Love your neighbor."

At first that seemed cool, but then they tried it for a while, and came back to Jesus saying, "Could you just say *go to church, be nice, and don't have sex before marriage* instead?"

See, the trap in what Jesus says in Mark 12 is that loving God and neighbor only seems easier than fulfilling the law until you actually give it a try. It only seems easier than obeying all the little rules until I make a fumbling attempt at loving someone with halitosis or who never pays me back or who just ate the banana I was saving for breakfast. So, I like to imagine that Jesus had that mischievous glint in his eye when he said the deceptively simple thing that all the law is summed up in love God and love the neighbor as yourself.

But sometimes loving the neighbor is really difficult, and that's when it's not just totally disappointing. I think the neighbor would be a lot easier to love were the neighbor an abstraction. Like if loving the neighbor meant little more than completing an online credit card transaction. But instead, the neighbor is always just hanging around. Sometimes they even share your apartment and leave dirty towels on the floor. Sometimes the neighbor takes the form of your teenage kid who just yelled at you for not giving them money. Sometimes the neighbor is restless and messy and inconsistent and never-ending in their ability to tap dance on your last nerve.

Sometimes loving that neighbor can feel impossible.

We've been brainwashed by endless hours of Hollywood and a thousand bad Hallmark cards to think that love means having feelings of warm affection toward someone we like or are attracted to. But human love is profoundly imperfect and almost always unreliable.

The reality of human love is that sometimes human love is a show-off. Love gets its feelings hurt. Love keeps getting those totally avoidable parking tickets. Love calls in the middle of the night from the train station and shows up when you still have rollers in your hair.

All the rom-coms in the world can't change the fact that human love is complicated—and that the issue of love is complicated for us because we so often are loved poorly, loved incompletely, loved conditionally. The subject of human love is a tricky one because *we* ourselves so often love poorly, incompletely, and conditionally. And, forgive the pop psychology, but my theory is that when we are loved poorly we begin, on some level, to assume that we are maybe undeserving of being loved well.

So, it can be hard to see a way forward—to see a way for loving the neighbor to mean anything but trying hard and falling short.

But the trying is so important.

Because Jesus knew the truth: *The only one who can really, really fulfill that commandment was the one who was speaking it.*

Because, on our own, even if we try our best, and day after day after day put the neighbor first, it only takes one fall-out, one misplaced word, one disappointing result to make the whole love Jenga collapse.

This is why, despite the impossibility of it, we must take this command to love God and love neighbor as ourselves seriously, if only because it is Christ who speaks it. Because Christ does not leave us on our own. For it is Christ who fills our imperfect, messy love with his. That's what makes our imperfect love holy to God—not us alone, but Christ working in us.

It's as though Christ takes our love and then crams it with his so that together it is enough.

Because if we *could* love perfectly on our own, then why, really, would we need Jesus? Our own perfect love could save us.

Yet Jesus gives this command, this hard, arduous, troubling command to love because *we* need it.

The thing to remember here is that Jesus knows who he's dealing with. Jesus knows our love is imperfect and self-centered and riddled with expectations and low blood sugar and regrets. He knows our love is conditional even when we tell ourselves it's not. And in his gracious response, he has chosen to fill our love with his. Watch how this command to love turns, like all things that Christ touches, and bears a promise. He does not give a command without a promise attached. And the promise that comes is this: It is not all dependent upon us. There is nothing that is.

See, if God desires that we be loved (and God does), then God will bless our little broken attempts to love each other and make them holy.

So, let us not discount our love for its imperfection.

Jesus leaves from this extended throwdown with the scribes and goes into the events of Holy Week as though he is saying *here is how far the love of God will go to claim you.* All he asks is that this love, given so indiscriminately, does not fall on fallow ground, but reproduces itself again and again in the love you have for both the neighbor and the enemy; an imperfect love made holy by a God who loves us madly.

It is enough. Amen.

32ND SUNDAY *in* ORDINARY TIME

PHYLLIS ZAGANO

"She... has contributed all she had, her whole livelihood."

1ST READING:
1 KGS. 17:10-16

2ND READING:
HEB. 9:24-28

PSALM:
146:6-10

GOSPEL:
MARK 12:38-44

TODAY'S READINGS TALK ABOUT SPECIAL people—you know, the "insiders." Every group has them. No matter what club or organization you belong to, there is always the "in crowd."

Church is supposed to be different. Church is not supposed to be about the "in crowd." Church is supposed to be about communion and community. Church is supposed to be about relationship, among us and with God.

Church is *not* supposed to be only about the "scribes, who like to go around in long robes and accept greetings in the marketplaces." That is, Church is not supposed to be about clerics, and it is certainly not supposed to be about clericalism.

Different times and different cultures have different practices. So, when we learn in today's reading from the Book of Hebrews that the high priest was the only one allowed in the sanctuary, perhaps we can understand, even appreciate the ways of the ancient world. But I wonder how those types of barriers might apply today. I mean, do they?

Am I the only one allowed near the sacred? No, of course not. We are all part of the liturgy and some of us play a special part in it, as altar servers, lectors, and cantors.

So, whose Church is it?

Let's go back to today's gospel. If Jesus was warning us about the scribes—the teachers of the law—what was Jesus saying about clericalism?

Recall that in today's reading from Mark's Gospel, Jesus warns us about those scribes who always took "seats of honor in synagogues, and places of honor at banquets." Somebody let those scribes sit up front. Somebody decided that what those scribes represented—the law—was most important in the community. Somebody ignored all sorts of biblical teaching to place the law and enforcers of the law above everybody else. Somebody said law was most important in the scheme of things.

And Jesus was not happy about it.

Then, Jesus explains: It wasn't really about what they were wearing, or maybe even about their professions. Jesus was really interested in something else. Mark tells us that, after speaking about the scribes, Jesus sat down opposite the treasury—the ancient collection box—watching some people put in a lot of money. Then, Mark relates, a poor widow came forward with "two small coins." She put in all she had. Mark tells us Jesus said that she "contributed all she had, her whole livelihood."

What is the connection? How do these two stories match up? We have three different sets of people: the scribes, the rich donors, and the poor widow. First, Jesus warns us about the scribes, the local big shots. Then, Jesus points out that the very rich give only from their surplus funds. Then, Jesus seems to say the poor widow is the person we should admire. But why?

Quite simply, the scribes have professional status, and the rich people have money, but the widow has no one to depend upon but God. And, she is not putting her two coins into the treasury to buy any sort of celestial insurance. She is putting her two coins in to share what little she has with the rest of her community. She is putting her share into the treasury because she belongs to the group, because she is part of the people of God.

I do not think it means you need, today, to put your last nickel into the collection basket. I do think it means that you need to understand and believe that, no matter how you participate in Church, you are a full member. You do not need to be a cleric or a teacher of the law or a millionaire to belong to the people of God. You *are* the people of God.

That is what I think. For sure, every group, every organization needs structure. Each creates for itself leaders, rules, and boundaries. And every organization depends on its supporters to carry on. But every organization needs to allow everyone the privilege of participation, in whatever way they can.

The Church, our Church, your Church, has leaders, rules, and boundaries. You are part of the people of God, and so am I. The difference with Church, I think, is that the leaders must continually learn from the others. Hierarchy—and I admit I am part of the hierarchy—hierarchy cannot cut itself off from the rest of the people of God. Hierarchy, from me to the bishop to the pope, is part of the people of God. And saying hierarchy is part of the people of God is not just another way of controlling the Church. It means we all belong.

If we mean that, if we mean that we are all part of the people of God, then we need to realize what today's reading from Hebrews teaches: Christ did not enter into a sanctuary made by hands, restricted and accessible only to special people. No, Christ came into our "sanctuary," the world, and his suffering and resurrection were for all. So, too, for all of us is access to Christ's redemptive grace—here, today, at this Mass.

And it will be the same again tomorrow, and the next day, and the next. We are all equal members of the Church.

33RD SUNDAY *in* ORDINARY TIME

FR. RICHARD ROHR, OFM

"Heaven and earth will pass away, but my words will not pass away."

1ST READING:
DAN. 12:1-3

PSALM:
15:5, 8-10

2ND READING:
HEB. 10:11-14, 18

GOSPEL:
MARK 13:24-32

AS WE COME TO THE END OF THE CHURCH year, we've grown used to these various readings about the end of time. It's a good opportunity to do a little Bible study. This is called "apocalyptic literature." Probably the closest comparison, for you and me, would be to science fiction. It uses very elaborate, exaggerated images and ideas to predict the falling apart, not just of the world, but of worlds. Like I'm sure many people in California have said, "My world fell apart when the fire came through." Or people in Florida would say, "My world fell apart when the hurricane came."

So, it's a description of the eternal pattern. If you think I'm exaggerating, he gives a way as he says, "This generation will not pass away until all these things have taken place," because it happens in every generation. Now, what's the spiritual message? The spiritual message is really quite simple, although it's a real hard one for us to learn. It's that nothing is permanent—not your house, not your car, and if you think you own your land, wait a few years. If you think you own anything, wait a few years. Your partner, your wife, your husband, your children. This isn't meant to be morbid, but it really isn't. It's just absolute realism. The real telling line is, "Heaven and earth will pass away, but my words will not."

I think all the religions of the world would agree that they're saying there's only one thing that lasts, and that's God. We are just here for a short time. We do our little dance on the stage of life—and remember, whatever we're doing or not doing, whatever we're learning or not learning, it's all a school of love.

I personally believe the Second Coming of Christ is you. You, the growing body of Christ through the ages, people who are growing in love and caring and commitment to the world: This is the Second Coming of Christ. And that's why it happens in every generation. There are always these fantastic people who emerge through the crisis of the hurricane or the wildfire, and who reveal themselves as larger than life. They give the rest of us hope that it all has meaning, that it's all going somewhere. So, the universal pattern is loss and renewal, loss and renewal, loss and renewal.

Now, our Christian metaphor for that is death and resurrection. That's why we use that language so much, because none of us want to believe it. We somehow foolishly believe that we're going to be an exception. Don't you? "I'm not going to die. I'm going to have this house forever." That's an illusion. We are being told, actually, a consoling truth: to be prepared for the passing away of everything.

Many wise people have said, if we knew we would live forever, we probably wouldn't grow up. We would always think we had another year, another year, another year. I'm in my seventy-sixth, and it's quite clear to me that I'm nearing the end. That isn't something that's scary for me, but it's realism. And I have to ask myself, every day—as you do too: What does it all mean? What are we here for? What is this building toward? Is it just to have a job? Is it just to get married? Is it just to have children? Yes, yes, yes. But no, it's more than that.

And once we've learned that, we won't be so afraid that our world also, like all worlds, is passing away, but that there's one thing we believe is eternal. It's God in whom we put our trust. It's God that we hope in. And that journey toward union with God shouldn't wait until we die. That's why we are here today: to be united to the real, to be united to the eternal.

Our Catholic phrase is to go to communion. It's a good phrase, really: to go to communion. But to be in communion with God is just shorthand for being in communion with everything. If you don't feel connected to the people in this room, you're not in communion. If you don't feel connected to the people in the caravan coming to the border, then you're not in communion. If you don't feel connected to black people, to white people, to gay people, to handicapped people, you're not in communion. Don't waste my time saying you love God. You don't. Be honest: You don't. To say you love God is quite simply to say you love everything.

Feast Days

TRINITY SUNDAY

FR. JAMES MARTIN, SJ

"And behold, I am with you always, until the end of the age."

1ST READING:
DUET. 4:32-34, 39-40

PSALM:
33:4-6, 9, 18-22

2ND READING:
ROM. 8:14-17

GOSPEL:
MATT. 28:16-20

IT PROBABLY DIDN'T ESCAPE YOUR NOTICE THAT the three readings this Sunday, Trinity Sunday, center on the Holy Trinity.

The first, from Deuteronomy, focuses on God the Father. Moses tells the People of Israel to follow the commands of the Creator, who made the heavens and the earth, and all that is in them, including humanity. If they do this, they will be granted long life in the land that the Lord has given them.

The second reading, from St. Paul's Letter to the Romans, focuses on the power of the Spirit. Paul reminds us that the Spirit, the power of the Risen Christ, is not in the possession of some elite group. Rather, the Spirit is for all of us.

And in the Gospel of Matthew, we hear the Trinitarian formula uttered by Jesus himself, the formula that began our Mass today, the formula used every time we pray, and the formula we still pronounce at baptisms: in the name of the Father and the Son and the Holy Spirit.

Now, when Catholics talk about their relationship to God, they mainly talk about their relationship either with the Father, which is what they often mean by "God," or with Jesus. At least in my experience, the Trinity per se does not figure heavily into the devotional life of most Catholics.

For example, I've rarely heard someone say, "When I pray to the Trinity, this is what happens," even though, whenever we pray, it's to the entire Trinity, since, as Catholic tradition teaches us, each person of the Trinity is always present in the others. That tradition is called "circumincession," by the way.

It's surprising that the Holy Spirit is the forgotten person of the Trinity, since this is the person in the Trinity to whom we relate most these days. That is, we relate to the Father and the Son through the Spirit.

What do I mean by that? Well, we are not Moses, and so we are not relating to the Father face to face. And even Moses wasn't granted that "access," if we can even use that word. Remember, God said to Moses, "You cannot see my face."

And, unlike the disciples, we are not seeing Jesus face to face either, and nor has anyone else since the Ascension. You could argue that various saints have had face-to-face encounters with Jesus through mystical experiences, like St. Francis of Assisi, to whom Jesus spoke from the Cross of San Damiano, or St. Margaret Mary, in her visions of the Sacred Heart. And, of course, we encounter Jesus in the Eucharist. But you know what I mean. We don't experience him face to face like people did in first-century Judea or Galilee.

Maybe it's our iconography that's responsible for this downplaying of the Spirit. The Father and the Son are pictured as people, but the Spirit usually is not. An exception is the famous Andrei Rublev icon of the three of them sitting at a table, as for a meal. But usually they are depicted—as someone once said to me on retreat—as "the old man, Jesus, and the bird." It's hard to pray to a bird.

But Jesus, as we've heard over the last few weeks in the gospel readings, tells the disciples not only that he will send the Advocate, or Paraclete, the interceder, after he goes, but also that they should rely on the Spirit, as they relied on him. As should we.

It's the Holy Spirit that encourages us, that builds us up, that inspires us, that consoles us. The Holy Spirit is also responsible for drawing us closer to God. You know that desire you have for a closer relationship to God? That's the Spirit. You know that wish to have a more contemplative life? That's the Spirit. You know that feeling that moves you when you hear a beautiful hymn, or when someone says something that gets you out of your depression, or when you see an inspiring movie? That's the Spirit.

Moreover, you know that voice in your head that says it's wrong to walk past a homeless person, or ignore the poor, or treat people like animals? That's the Holy Spirit, at work in your conscience. The Spirit is a regular participant in your spiritual life. In fact, the Spirit is your spiritual life.

How do you cultivate a deeper relationship with the Spirit? First, by trusting that the Spirit is with you all the time, present to you, inspiring you—and by noticing that. Second, by remembering that this is the way that we encounter the Father and the Son. And third, by actively praying to the Spirit. Saying, "God, help me," or "Jesus, be with me," is great, and I say them all the time.

But so is another prayer: "Come, Holy Spirit."

The MOST HOLY BODY *and* BLOOD *of* CHRIST

DAN HORAN, OFM

"We will do everything that the Lord has told us."

1ST READING:
EXOD. 24:3-8

PSALM:
116:12-13, 15-18

2ND READING:
HEB. 9:11-15

GOSPEL:
MARK 14:12-16, 22-26

MORE THAN SIXTEEN HUNDRED YEARS AGO, St. Augustine of Hippo addressed a group of catechumens whom he was instructing on the faith in anticipation of their baptism and reception into the church. In what has become known as Augustine's "Sermon 272," the great doctor of the church unpacked the theology of the *Corpus Christi*—the Body of Christ—in a strikingly profound and still-timely manner. He affirms that what appears in the elements as bread and wine to the senses of the body are recognized as the sacramental presence of Christ to the senses of faith. As he puts it, "My friends, these realities are called sacraments because in them one thing is seen, while another is grasped."[1]

But he does not stop at an explication of the Eucharistic species of bread and wine as the only reality of Christ's presence in the Eucharist. Drawing on the letters of St. Paul, he explains:

1 "Augustine on the Nature of the Sacrament of the Eucharist," Sermon 272, *Early Church Texts*, https://earlychurchtexts.com/public/augustine_sermon_272_eucharist.htm.

> So now, if you want to understand the body of Christ, listen to the Apostle Paul speaking to the faithful: "You are the body of Christ, member for member" (1 Cor. 12:27). If you, therefore, are Christ's body and members, it is your own mystery that is placed on the Lord's table! It is your own mystery that you are receiving! You are saying "Amen" to what you are: your response is a personal signature, affirming your faith. When you hear "The body of Christ," you reply "Amen." Therefore, be a member of Christ's body so that your "Amen" may ring true![2]

Augustine recognized that in addition to the sacramental presence of Christ in bread and wine, the Body of Christ is made present in the world in its members—you and me. When we celebrate the Eucharist and proclaim "amen" at communion, it is not merely an affirmation of what we grasp in faith present before us, but it is also—and, in many ways, more importantly—an affirmation that we recognize Christ made present in the assembly of the faithful. In this way, Augustine reminds his hearers that we are meant to "be what you see; receive what you are"[3] at the Eucharist.

As we celebrate the Solemnity of the Body and Blood of Christ, how do we think about Christ's presence among us? The Second Vatican Council, in its constitution on the liturgy, *Sacrosanctum Concilium*, reiterates Augustine's theological insights, reminding the church that Christ is made present in the Eucharistic species, the Word of God, and in the assembly, including the presider.[4] It's this last form—the entire people of God—that is most often overlooked in general and on this feast day in particular.

If we look to the first reading, we are reminded of the initial fervor with which the people of God responded to Moses's announcement of "all the words and ordinances of the Lord." They cried out: "We will do everything that the Lord has told us." The sprinkling of the sacrificial blood served as a seal for the renewed covenantal relationship God established with the chosen people. The church includes this passage on this day in the litur-

2 Ibid.

3 Ibid.

4 Vatican II, Sacrosanctum Concilium, 7.

gical cycle in order to call to mind what is sealed—that is, *confirmed*—for Christians with the blood of Christ and the gift of his body in the Eucharist. Like Augustine, who draws our attention to the gospel mandate to put into practice what we say we believe, we are called to take our "amen," our "we will do everything that the Lord has told us," seriously.

Too many of us are comfortable saying "amen" to the abstract notion of the sacramental presence of Christ in the Eucharistic species or to the philosophical theory of transubstantiation that is often used to express what happens at the Mass, but remain uncomfortable that our reception of the Blessed Sacrament demands anything of us beyond an assent of faith. In this spirit, I am reminded of another passage of scripture that challenges us to rethink what it means to say we have "faith" in the Eucharist.

> What good is it, my brothers [and sisters], if someone says he has faith but does not have works? Can that faith save him? If a brother or sister has nothing to wear and has no food for the day, and one of you says to them, "Go in peace, keep warm, and eat well," but you do not give them the necessities of the body, what good is it? So also faith of itself, if it does not have works, is dead. (James 2:14–17)

Today's gospel passage from Mark spends a fair amount of time on the instructions Jesus lays out to his followers for the manner in which they are to prepare what would become known as the Lord's Supper. The fact that so much time is spent focused on the preparation can easily be missed by modern hearers of the passage because we "know where the story is going," and we jump in our minds right to the meal. And yet, with a sense of the importance of reflecting on what the fuller meaning of the Eucharist is, what we are saying "amen" to, and what is demanded of us in light of our baptismal vocation, we would do well to take note of *the need for preparation.*

Indeed, we receive the sacramental presence of Christ and hear the Word of God proclaimed, and we should do our best to cultivate a sense of presence and attention. But we should also dedicate some of our energy to preparing ourselves to become the Body of Christ that we claim to be in baptism.

"Be what you see; receive what you are."

The celebration of the Eucharist is not an end in itself, nor is the Eucharist a reward for the perfect. We gather at the Lord's Table to hear the Word and break the bread in order to be renewed in our relationships with God and one another. As John's Gospel recounts in the washing of the feet, we are not meant to stay at the table (or in the pew), but to move outward in a spirit of service and solidarity.

Christ gives himself to us in the Eucharist, but also in his body, which is the church made up of all the baptized. If we really are to become what we receive, we must keep this in mind and put that "amen!" we proclaim at Mass into action the other six days and twenty-three hours of the week. Only then, as Augustine exhorted the catechumens centuries ago, will our "amen" ring true!

The FEAST *of* ALL SAINTS

MARTY HAUGEN

"Blessed are the merciful."

1ST READING:
REV. 7:2-4, 9-14

PSALM:
24:1-6

2ND READING:
1 JOHN 3:1-3

GOSPEL:
MATT. 5:1-12A

A CHILD IS ASKED, "WHO IS A SAINT?" THE child, looking up at a stained-glass image of a saint, replies, "A saint is someone the light shines through."

Each of us is a child of God. Created in God's image, we share, for a brief time, the holy breath of life with all of creation. In baptism, we are visibly signed and publicly named as belonging to God for the entire arc of our life. When we are given the great gift of life, we are also given the blessed opportunity to bear the light of God's love to others through our words and deeds.

Today we celebrate spiritual heroes, individuals whose lives manifested God's presence and light in the world. We name them and remember stories of their faithfulness and their love. Throughout the year, there are specific days assigned for the celebration of individual saints. On this day, we celebrate all of those people, and we also remember the millions of spiritual heroes known only to God.

The vast majority of holy people who have walked this earth are strangers to us. Millions of Christians and non-Christians have lived lives of quiet holiness and sacrifice, unrecognized and unremembered except by their closest friends and family. It is easy to celebrate a Saint Francis of Assisi or a St. Teresa of Avila; it is something else again to acknowledge that we are constantly encountering holy strangers in our everyday life. On this day, we are challenged to open our eyes and hearts to encountering the presence of Christ in each interaction with another, whether easy or awkward, joy-filled or contentious.

Scripture is filled with stories of how the holiness—the light—of God shines through encounters with the stranger and the marginalized. In Genesis, Abraham offers hospitality to strangers standing out in the desert heat and so welcomes God.[1] Elijah (as a stranger) is welcomed and sustained by a poor widow and they both experience God's grace.[2] Two of Jesus's disciples meet a stranger on the road at the darkest point of their lives and, inviting him in to break bread, they recognize Jesus.

In his first sermon in the Gospel of Matthew, Jesus defines the "blessed" as those who are passionately engaged in human life—mourning for and with others, hungering and thirsting for righteousness, showing mercy and making peace. In his final sermon, he identifies those same "blessed" as those who discover him present as they feed the hungry, provide comfort and clothing, and welcome in the stranger. In each case, *blessedness* or *saintliness* is not determined by an institution or a bureaucratic process of canonization; it is manifested by how the light shines through one's words and actions. As Dorothy Day said, "Don't call me a saint. I don't want to be dismissed so easily."[3]

The radical welcome to the stranger that Jesus proclaims is perhaps the greatest challenge to a predictable and safe faith journey. When we open our hearts, our home, our faith communities to the stranger, we will often discover the unknown and unexpected holy presence of God, but we will also occasionally encounter evil in an abusive or manipulative person, or even death in a deranged killer in our church. The dilemma is that we cannot offer an unconditional welcome without that risk. Regardless of the outcome, we are changed by our invitation to the stranger, and, in that process of change, God's Spirit can enter in and give us eyes to see the risen Christ present in each of us.

---

1 Genesis 18:1–2; Hebrews 13:2.

2 1 Kings 17:10–24.

3 Robert Ellsberg, "All Are Called to Be Saints," *The Catholic Worker*, May 2015, 1, 5.

A number of years ago, I was asked to give a presentation at a worship conference. Before my presentation, a local parish music group led a prayer service that included my hymn, "All Are Welcome." During the Q and A at the end of my talk, a young man came up to the microphone and asked me, "Everywhere I go, I see the words 'All are welcome' on signs in front of churches. But when I come in and the community finds out I am gay, I am not welcome. How could you have written such a hypocritical song for people to sing?"

As much as we would like to define exactly what sort of "stranger" we will welcome, Jesus's words (especially when he extends his welcome to "the least of these") require that our welcome be unconditional and without limitations. There is a very real risk in this kind of welcome. At the very least, it will often inconvenience and disturb our complacency. Beyond that, it can (and perhaps should at times) challenge our basic assumptions of where we find Christ and how we must respond to the cries and needs of others.

In his homily announcing the Jubilee Year of Mercy, Pope Francis said,

> The call of Jesus pushes each of us never to stop at the surface of things, especially when we are dealing with a person. We are called to look beyond, to focus on the heart to see how much generosity everyone is capable [of]. No one can be excluded from the mercy of God; everyone knows the way to access it and the Church is *the house that welcomes all and refuses no one.* [emphasis his][4]

"'Teach me thy ways, O Lord' is, like all prayers, a rash one,"[5] says Annie Dillard. And yet, that is the rash, blessed, saintly way that Jesus asks us to take—the risky, holy path of truly welcoming the stranger into our lives. Only in this way can we know the presence of Christ alive and working for God's Reign in this world.

---

4 From Pope Francis's homily announcing the Year of Mercy, St. Peter's Basilica, Rome, March 13, 2015.

5 Annie Dillard, *The Annie Dillard Reader* (New York: Harper Perennial, 1994), 430.

SOLEMNITY *of the* SACRED HEART *of* JESUS

DONNA L. CIANGIO, OP

"... to know the love of Christ that surpasses knowledge."

1ST READING:
HOS. 11:1, 3-4, 8C-9

PSALM:
ISA. 12:2-6

2ND READING:
EPH. 3:8-12, 14-19

GOSPEL:
JOHN 19:31-37

WHEN I THINK OF THE FEAST OF THE SACRED Heart of Jesus, the Beatles song, "Love, love, love... All you need is love," comes to mind. That is what it's all about. The Sacred Heart of Jesus, generally depicted in famous paintings, does not inspire me. Jesus is often depicted very statically and stoically, pointing to his heart. There is no motion or emotion captured in the portraits.

My meditations on his sacred, loving heart come through artistic representations of Jesus in action: Jesus washing Peter's feet, conversing with the Samaritan woman, healing the blind man, raising the son of the widow of Nain, feeding the five thousand, speaking Mary Magdalene's name lovingly at the tomb, caring for his mother, and, of course, the great act of giving his life on the cross.

All of these actions of Jesus go into the making of his sacred heart: a heart of love, compassion, vision, and commitment. In reflecting on the

Feast of the Sacred Heart, we need to ask ourselves how *we* are loving, compassionate, visionary, and committed in our call to ministry as parents, guardians, teachers, friends, clergy and religious, parish leaders, or whatever God calls us to. We need to reflect on how Jesus calls each of us, through our baptism, to act in his name the many ways that he did—to preach, to bless, to heal, to serve.

In the reading from Hosea, God is clearly disappointed in the chosen ones. They are stubborn and won't repent, but God remembers teaching them to walk, feeding them, and bending down to lift them up and hold them in love. As the parent, God's heart is stirred and he smiles and loves them, despite their faults and limitations. How often has that happened to you as a parent or a teacher? I am sure, over and over again. Frustration gives way to a smile and love.

In Ephesians, Paul is writing to those he loves dearly. He prays that God will give them the deepest insight into the heart of God. Paul prays that these faith-filled communities of Ephesus will know God deeply, be grounded in the love of Christ, and go out among all people with that kind of surety and energy for the gospel. Paul's prayer is one that each of us could pray often for each other and meditate on for ourselves, that we may be "rooted and grounded in love, [and] may have strength to comprehend with all the holy ones what is the breadth and length and height and depth, and to know the love of Christ that surpasses knowledge, so that you may be filled with all the fullness of God."

In the Gospel of John, the love of Jesus is poured out. The action of piercing his side is symbolic of his giving all. The very lifeblood of Jesus rushes out. It is not a drip, but a great flow of the two basic needs for life: blood and water. There is great symbolism here in the very life of Jesus being emptied for us. Jesus gives his all so that we live in the love of God. That love is what we concentrate on today in this feast—great love being poured out that we may recognize it and live.

Here's just a little history of the Feast of the Sacred Heart. It is centuries old in the Church. In 1856, Pope Pius IX established the Feast of the Sacred Heart for the whole Church. Even earlier, a devotion of the great love of God, symbolized by the heart of Jesus, is found in the writings of early church fathers, including Origen, St. Ambrose, St. Jerome, St. Augustine, and more.

Many women saints wrote about their mystical visions of the heart of Christ, including St. Catherine of Siena, St. Therese the Little Flower, St. Teresa of Avila, St. Margaret Mary Alacoque, and more. In our contemporary time, we see the Sacred Heart represented in the Divine Mercy image and prayer as experienced by St. Faustina. Recent popes have written about the Sacred Heart, all emphasizing the need to have a relationship with Jesus and experience his love through prayer and contemplation, and by living out our faith in the way we welcome and help our neighbors.

Throughout the centuries, this feast has captured the imagination and devotion of so many. We need the love and mercy of Jesus and we need to extend that love and mercy to others. Jesus's love reaches out to all. Can we do any less?

So, the Beatles' words, "Love is all you need," is something we can all hum, all day today, as a reminder of what we are called to do in celebrating this feast.

I would like to pray for you with this prayer of St. Paul to the Ephesians:

> For this reason I kneel before the Father,
> from whom every family in heaven and on earth is named,
> that he may grant you in accord with the riches of
> his glory
> to be strengthened with power through his Spirit in the
> inner self,
> and that Christ may dwell in your hearts through faith;
> that you, rooted and grounded in love,
> may have strength to comprehend with all the holy ones
> what is the breadth and length and height and depth,
> and to know the love of Christ that surpasses knowledge,
> so that you may be filled with all the fullness of God.
>
> Amen.

FEAST *of the* IMMACULATE CONCEPTION

DEACON GREG KANDRA

"May it be done to me according to your word."

1ST READING:
GEN. 3:9-15,20

PSALM:
98:1, 2-3, 3-4

2ND READING:
EPH. 1:3-6, 11-12

GOSPEL:
LUKE 1:26-38

IT PROBABLY BEGAN LIKE ANY OTHER DAY.

There were prayers to be said. Chores to do. Bread to bake. Clothes to clean or sew. Water to draw from the well.

We don't know what the weather was like. Nobody knows if a storm might have persuaded her to stay indoors, or if the sun was so warm that she wanted to go outside for a walk.

But at some point in an otherwise forgettable day in an ordinary town in an overlooked corner of an empire . . . a Jewish girl we call Mary made history. Nothing after that has ever been quite the same.

She did it with just a few words: "May it be done to me according to your word."

Put another way, she said, "Yes."

And here we are, twenty centuries later, remembering this moment, honoring the young woman who is at the center of it, and celebrating God's extravagant wisdom, generosity, and love.

And we do it because this moment didn't just happen. This feast we celebrate, the Immaculate Conception, commemorates a great mystery and a miracle: that God so loved the world that not only did he send us his son, but he also gave us Mary.

He planned for Mary to be his son's perfect vessel, conceived in her own mother's womb as sinless and pure, untouched by what happened in Eden.

That miracle of creation brought us to another miracle of creation—the Annunciation we just heard in Luke's Gospel.

But, for a moment, I want to go back to that key phrase at the heart of this Gospel—which is also at the heart of this feast: *May it be done to me according to your word.*

This is where everything began. Here is a complete and selfless desire to do the will of God, offered with humility and a sense of purpose.

I have to ask myself: Could I say anything like that?

Could any of us say that today?

Could any of us be so willing to surrender to God so eagerly, so completely, so beautifully?

In an age when personal freedom is prized above all else, when the culture tells us you don't have to do anything that is uncomfortable or inconvenient, this girl named Mary says something most modern people would find altogether shocking.

To an angel of the Lord, and to the God who created her, she says, "If you want it, I'll do it."

Her son would later put it another way, in a prayer that is known by every Christian: "Thy will be done."

But Mary's words carry the added weight of history being written.

Think of what came about because of that: Bethlehem. Egypt. Calvary.

Easter came about because of these words.

Our salvation came about because of these words.

Because of that moment, we are here this day, hearing God's word proclaimed, receiving the Eucharist, worshipping the Lord in faith and hope and love.

It all began with that one "Yes."

And yet, this feast of the Immaculate Conception also reminds us it began even before that, when Mary *herself* first began.

What a wonder in this season of wonders.

The life and sacrifice and love of Mary serves as a model for every one of us—and a bold challenge. Because the beautiful reality is, like her, each of us is called to be a vessel for Christ.

Each of us is called to bring Jesus into the world. To take him to others. To announce him.

To sacrifice for him. To surrender for him. To love for him.

To live our lives in such a way that we can, as Mary did, "proclaim the greatness of the Lord."

Know this: God had a plan for Mary before she was born—as he has a plan for everyone in this church.

Shortly before my ordination, Bishop Frank Caggiano put it beautifully. He told my diaconate class: "God has a dream for you. Your job is to discover what it is and to make that dream come true."

So, this day, overwhelmed once again by the humility and trust of Mary—her ability to say "Yes" to what God had planned from the first moment of her immaculate conception—we carry these questions in our hearts:

How can we be more like her?

What is God asking of us?

What is God's dream for us?

What is his dream for you? What particular gift has he given you? What plan does he want you to fulfill?

How can we make God's dream for us come true?

My friends, I would submit that it begins as it did for Mary—with a response that, on an otherwise ordinary day, changed everything.

"*May it be done to me according to your word.*"

FEAST *of* CHRIST *the* KING

THE REV. DR. MARGARET BULLITT-JONAS

"My kingdom does not belong to this world."

1ST READING:
DAN. 7:13-14

PSALM:
93:1-2, 5

2ND READING:
REV. 1:5-8

GOSPEL:
JOHN 18:33B-37

MY SON SAM GREW UP IN METROPOLITAN Boston, and as a kid he followed with devotion the progress of his favorite teams. Over the summer, whenever the Red Sox won, he would joyfully chant, "The Red Sox *rule!*" Over the winter, because Sam's father grew up in Wisconsin, our house would ring out sometimes with the delighted cry, "The Packers *rule!*" I'm not much of a sports fan, but I always smiled when I heard the exuberance in Sam's voice. There is something in the human spirit that is set free when we proclaim what we care about more than anything else.

This is the last Sunday of the church year, the grand finale. The great sweep of the liturgical year that begins in Advent and moves from Christ's birth through his ministry, passion, death, resurrection, and ascension, to the coming of his Spirit and the birth of the Church—this whole narrative reaches its conclusion and climax today, the Feast Day of Christ the King. To put it in terms that even a child would understand, today's the day when, around the world, the Church gathers to proclaim with joy, "Christ rules!"

What does it mean to say that Christ rules, that Christ is King? It means that our ultimate loyalty is to a loving God. Our deepest commitment is to love. Love is what called us into being and sent us into the world. Love is what sustains us throughout our lives and love is the embrace into which we will be welcomed at our journey's end. Love is what gives order and meaning to our days and what forms our true selves. Love is what impels us to cast off selfishness and self-centeredness and to help other beings thrive. Love is our home, our vocation, and our destiny. When we say that Christ is King, we honor the deepest truth we know. We bow to the One through whom all things were made, toward whom all things converge, and in whom all things hold together (c.f. John 1:3, Colossians 1:16–17, Revelation 1:8).

The language of poetry can help us here, when prosaic words fall short. Take, for instance, the ecstatic "night visions" recorded in the book of Daniel, in which the prophet sees Christ coming in glory to reconcile and unite all things, to gather up all things in love, things in heaven and things on earth: "He received dominion, splendor, and kingship; all nations, peoples and tongues will serve him. His dominion is an everlasting dominion that shall not pass away, his kingship, one that shall not be destroyed" (Daniel 7:14). In a vision as poetic as Daniel's, the author of the book of Revelation speaks of Christ as "the ruler of the kings of the earth" who is already "coming amid the clouds" (Revelation 1:5, 7). Before long, "every eye will see him" and his reign will last forever. Our Christian hope looks forward to the day when, in the fullness of time, God has "subjected everything" under Christ's feet (1 Corinthians 15:27).

Still, let's be honest here. Naming Christ as "king" may not appeal to most Americans. The word "king" can sound hopelessly patriarchal or conjure up images of despots lording it over their helpless subjects. After all, we formed ourselves as a nation by rejecting the whole idea of allegiance to a king. But, if Christ is King, he is unlike any earthly king. As Jesus says during his encounter with Pilate, "My kingdom does not belong to this world" (John 18:36). Jesus's authority does not reside in threats, violence, or weapons, as authority so often does in this world, but rather in the power of truth and the presence of love. "For this I was born," says Jesus, "and for this I came into the world, to testify to the truth" (John 18:37). The one whom Christians call "king" came among us not to dominate but to serve, not to exploit but to heal, not to force but to set free. Christ is no monarch who dominates with cruelty or indifference, but the One who pours himself out for us, who suffered and died for us, and whose loving arms sustain the world.

I wonder if God's heart breaks whenever Christians willfully or inadvertently interpret the kingship of Christ to mean that we have license to dominate and divide. When Christianity is wielded like a weapon and spread through force, when it is used to justify one group's superiority over another—including the supposed superiority of Christians over people of other faiths, when it is used to justify the domination of men over women or of white people over people of other races, when Christianity is coopted to enforce injustice and inequality, then we betray the kingship of Christ. From the Doctrine of Discovery to the ongoing legacy of white supremacy, Christianity has too often been hijacked by forces that have nothing to do with Christ's witness to the supremacy of self-giving, sacrificial love.

Yet the Holy Spirit within us and among us keeps goading us to enlarge the circle of love—to reach out to the last, the least, and the lost, to welcome the stranger, and to resist and transform unjust systems of privilege and rank that divide us from each other. The love that we know in Christ also extends beyond human communities; it embraces all beings on Earth, our other-than-human kin. God proclaimed the whole web of life "very good" (Genesis 1:31) and entrusted the world into our care. Too many Christians have conveniently (and tragically) interpreted the "dominion" (Genesis 1:26) that God gave humanity over the rest of the created world as permission to assault and destroy.

What would happen if we instead interpreted "dominion" as loving God's Creation as our Lord (*Dominus*) loves it—to love it without reserve, to care for and protect it as if our lives depended on it? For they do. At this late hour, when the extinction of species is accelerating, the global climate is rapidly warming, and in the very near future we risk ecological collapse—now is the time to claim the deep truth of what it means to call Christ King: we serve a God of love who calls us to bless and heal human communities and Earth communities alike.

How is God calling you today to open your heart to a wider, deeper love? What would change if you claimed love as your deepest value and deepest truth? For the sake of God's all-embracing, all-inclusive love, what are you willing to fight for, to defend, and to protect? With the joy of a kid whose sports team just won, today we affirm "Christ rules." Christ rules. Love is who we are and what we are made for. And—as the old hymn says—"If Love is lord of heaven and earth, how can I keep from singing?"

Funerals

FUNERAL HOMILY

FR. BILL BAUSCH

"You have faith in God."

READING:
JOHN 14:1–6

I BEGIN WITH A STORY AS I SHALL END with one.

A professional storyteller by the name of Dan Yashinsky was telling stories at a downtown arts center when a restless group of kids stomped in. They were ten-year-olds from a Catholic school in a new housing development. In they came, munching potato chips and blowing bubble gum, clearly not in a listening mood. Since it was close to Halloween, Yashinsky wisely lit a candle, turned off the lights, and started telling ghost stories. It wasn't long before they were hooked.

He wound up telling them one of those summer camp scary stories where, you know, the narrator's voice gets quieter and quieter until the moment when the ghost grabs the poor victim, then he raises his voice loudly and says something like "I gotcha!" and the kids scream and jump into one another's laps. That's exactly what happened.

Well, when the lights came on, the children lined up to leave, talking excitedly about their shocking experience. Yashinsky noticed one girl standing quietly, holding something suspended from around her neck.

He asked her if she liked the stories and she said, "Oh, yes, but when you told the last one, I didn't jump."

"I noticed," he said. "How come?"

"Because when I knew it was going to be scary, I held the Blessed Virgin Mary."

She showed him the medal she was still holding. "You should get one, too."

"I'm not sure I should," he answered. "I'm Jewish."

"That's okay," she said sagely. "Get a Jewish one."

Then he makes this telling comment: "Writing [my] book about storytelling as an art and a way of life, I have often remembered the girl's good counsel. When you know something scary is coming, you must find and hold on to your own source of reassurance and wisdom."[1] You must have a steady beacon to guide you through perilous waters.

That story tells us everything we need to know about Lillian Riley because the one thing, the one summary truth, we can say about her is that her life was unerringly guided by three steady beacons that defined and supported her, those three enduring "Fs" of a successful life: family, friends, and faith.

Family. This South Jersey, Camden-Catholic High school girl met the love of her life, Carl, in college and they were married in 1975. She and Carl lived simply and traveled extensively. It was a truly good, really dedicated, and loving sixty-year marriage. People noticed the deep love between them. They had three children, seven grandchildren, and two great-grandchildren. They were always there for the family. When their daughter Lillian became seriously ill, they traveled out West and stayed with her until she died. Family meant everything to her.

Friends. She had so many of these, so many lifelong friendships. I have to guess that it was her many and considerable gifts that brought her into constant contact with friends, because she excelled at so many things: bowling and bocce—she won several tournaments. She was an avid reader and charter member of the Book Club at Four Seasons, a formidable bridge player, and a writer for their monthly newsletter. Along with Carl, she ran the Friday Night movies at the clubhouse there. She was a member of

1 Dan Yashinsky, *Suddenly They Heard Footsteps: Storytelling for the Twenty-First Century* (Jackson, MS: University Press of Mississippi, 2004), xiii–xiv.

St. Mary's women's group and, on top of all that, a knowledgeable bird watcher. She cherished her friends and vice-versa.

Faith. It was as strong as her values and opinions. She and Carl lived their faith. It wasn't just a Sunday affair. They were longtime and contributing members at St. Mary's, where I first met them. She belonged to a faith-sharing group for more years than I can remember, until the day she died—and even when some of them crossed the Delaware and moved to Pennsylvania, they continued to meet. For some seventeen years, she went with certain other couples to the Weston Priory monastery in Vermont on retreat.

In times of trouble—she had her share, like the girl in our story—Lillian held on to her faith to steady and guide her.

It was only natural then, that when she found out the startling news of her terminal cancer, she would ask to see me. I remember she was comfortable, alert, and even looked good. Before I anointed her, we chatted. I remember asking her if she was old enough to recall the old, old days when, at the Easter Vigil Mass late on Holy Saturday night, the choir chanted the Litany of the Saints in Latin and the congregation responded. I remember it well because, for years as an altar boy, I struggled with my peers to stay awake—not always successfully.

The choir would sing names like *Sancta Theresa, Sanctus Michael, Sanctus Johannis,* and so on, and we would all reply, "*Ora pro nobis,*" "Pray for us." "*Sanctus Petrus, Sanctus Thomas, Sancta Agatha, Ora pro nobis.*" It went on forever. Then, when the list of saints—and ourselves—was exhausted, the Litany switched gears and went on with many heartfelt petitions like: "from fire, storm, and flood" and we would all sing in reply, "*Libera nos, O Domine.*" "Deliver us, O Lord." "From pestilence, disease, and war, *Libera nos, O Domine.*" Deliver us, O Lord. For some reason, out of all the petitions, I always remembered this one: "From a sudden and unprovided death, *Libera nos, O Domine.*" Deliver us, O Lord. That petition—"from a sudden and unprovided death"—was, I think, heard in Lillian's case.

It's a mixed bag. Dying suddenly relieves the mind and avoids the agony of a long vigil. Knowing one is slowly dying does concentrate one's fears. Knowing, however, also provides the blessings of time: the poignant goodbyes; the reconciling words; the reminders, signals, and silent gestures of deep affection; the golden memories; the shared tears; the ministrations of neighbors and hospice; the pilgrimage of relatives, near and distant, like the ones who came from Montana, Colorado, and Japan; the bequeathing of gifts: jewelry, mementoes, and so on; the planning of the liturgy. I think Lillian appreciated the gift of time and made the most of it.

I also like to think that, in her silent moments, perhaps moments of apprehension and fear, with eyes closed, Lillian fell into the role of the person of my second story—a brief one. It's a story about a long-ago celebrity of his time, a well-known playboy, wit, and editor of the famous British publication *Punch*. His name was Malcolm Muggeridge and one day, this skeptic, at quite an old age, "got religion." Because he was so famous, the elite, the sophisticates, who felt betrayed by him, couldn't ignore him. They allowed him his fifteen minutes of fame and then dropped him. He had committed the unpardonable sin: Not only did he get religion, he got the worst possible kind—he became a Catholic. He did so because he was inspired by the presence and work of Mother Teresa. Anyway, he wrote many lovely things after his conversion. Among them are these words, which could have been, might have been, Lillian's—words that I can hear her saying:

> As I approach my end, I find Jesus' outrageous claim ever more captivating and meaningful. Quite often, waking up in the night as the old do, I feel myself to be half out of my body, hovering between life and death, with eternity rising in the distance. I see my ancient carcass, prone between the sheets, stained and worn like a scrap of paper dropped in the gutter, and, hovering over it, myself, like a butterfly released from its chrysalis stage and ready to fly away.
>
> Are caterpillars told of their impending resurrection? How in dying they will be transformed from poor earth crawlers into creatures of the air with exquisitely painted wings? If told, do they believe it? I imagine the wise old caterpillars shaking their heads—no, it can't be; it's a fantasy.
>
> Yet, in the limbo between living and dying, as the night clocks tick remorselessly on, and the black sky implacably shows not one single scratch of gray, I hear those words:

> **"I am the resurrection" and then I feel myself to be carried along on a great tide of joy and peace.[2]**

I firmly believe that it was so with Lillian. With her peaceful death and Easter chrysalis stage now completed, we can say this of Lillian Riley: with her steady, rock-bottom beacons of family, friends, and faith, she

made a life,
made a marriage,
made a family,
made a community,
made a church
—made a difference.

Thank you. May you rest in peace.

2 I write about Muggeridge and share this quote in my book, *Once Upon a Gospel: Inspiring Homilies and Insightful Reflections* (New London, CT: Twenty-Third Publications, 2008), 520–521.

HOMILY *for* MY BROTHER'S FUNERAL

RICK MALLOY, SJ

"Rejoice with me because I have found my lost sheep."

1ST READING:
ISA. 55: 1-3, 8-11

PSALM:
143

2ND READING:
ROM. 8:18-27

GOSPEL:
LUKE 15:1-7

The homilist here preaches at the funeral of his brother who died by suicide.

NONE OF US WANT TO BE HERE TODAY—LEAST of all Tim. He's probably looking down on us right now, saying, "Darn! I can't believe I've given Ricky the chance to have the last word!"

But the last word is really the word we all have for Tim: love. We loved him. He was lovable. He was funny and fun. But he was also tortured and hurting, much more than we ever knew. To read the notes he left reveals a soul in searing pain.

At the University of Scranton, a freshman's dad committed suicide. I had to break the news to the kid. His mother was out on the West Coast for business, and they hadn't been able to contact her. The police in his home-town didn't want the young man getting the news via text or Facebook. A few days later, the priest who preached at the man's funeral sculpted an image that so helped me understand a bit about those who take their own lives. That priest said, "Think of 9/11 and the people atop the towers. They had the choice to be fatally burned by the fires climbing up the building or to jump to their death. People who take their own lives have fires burning inside them, flames we can't see. And sometimes they jump, rather than continue to suffer their internal torture."

I take some consolation in the fact that the church clearly teaches that, "We should not despair of the eternal salvation of persons who have taken their own lives."[1] By ways known only to God, they can be helped and healed. We cannot give up hope for Tim. As the Gospel today attests, God searches out and saves the lost.

Part of me, part of all of us, is hurting and angry and confused and wishing we could have done something to prevent the need for our being here today. But, in my more prayerful moments, I hear how much hurt was howling in my big brother. And I realize there is nothing anyone could have done to stop this.

I think my mother and Jesus are sitting with him at this moment, saying, "Tim, we're surprised you were able to hold on as long as you did. We love you. Come on, let's heal you now."

In life, some of us get lucky. I got lucky—very lucky. It took dozens of Jesuits to make me who I am. Without them, I'd have made an unimaginable mess of my life.

Timmy was always a harder worker than I was. As little boys, we delivered the *Inquirer* every morning. He delivered fifty papers a day. My route had twenty-five, and I didn't work too hard to increase subscriptions. During high school, we bussed tables at a local restaurant, and all through college, he was a hard worker at the ACME. He paid his own way through St. Joe's. He was the guitar player in Foundation and Empire. He was successful in those early years after college.

And one of his great successes was fostering friendships. He's been a friend to so many, especially his great life-long friends Barry O'Reilly and Bob Staub.

And he did something with his life that is much more commendable, valuable, and courageous than anything I ever did. He was a good father, a great father, to three wonderful young men. There's nothing he could have

---

1 *Catechism of the Catholic Church*, 2283.

done that will ever wipe out that great achievement of being a fearless and fun parent. I used to call you three Huey, Dewey, and Louie. He used to dangle you by your ankles and swing you around. You'd laugh and laugh. He never dropped you. I stand in awe of parents. I don't know how you do what you do. And I certainly cannot fathom how he did what he did with you three. Maybe your mother deserves the credit.

The problem was, Tim wasn't lucky. Yes, he made some mistakes. And he was lucky enough to marry into the Purtell clan. He had the support of so many friends and family. He often had the help of our Uncle Terry. And he had our mother, the best luck a guy could ever have.

But, in some aspects of life, he wasn't lucky. He never recovered from the blows life dealt him. In many ways, he was a gentle guy—too gentle. He didn't want to fight and claw and beat others to get ahead. Not on the hard, black asphalt recess yards here at our parish grade school, nor in the hard, stressful, competitive economic climate of our times. He survived time in jail, but, frankly, was terrified of being sent back to prison. Of all the triggers, he was haunted by the thought of being behind bars again. Few of us have ever had to face such a terrifying possibility.

As much as I'm shocked, stunned, angry, hurt, and sad at how he ended his life, as much as we all are shocked, stunned, angry, hurt, and sad that we are here today, to put ourselves in his skin provides another perspective. Fires burned within him. Searing flames scorched his soul.

He was in deep distress, long-term psychic pain. Years of struggling with feelings of failure. Nights and nights, and days and days, in the depths of depression. What many of us saw in public were the highs. Maureen and my mom were witness to his lows. The notes he left reveal the depths of his agony.

Maureen stood by him through so much and has been more than gracious and welcoming and supportive to all of us these days. She's been a wonderful mother to her boys. She's borne the brunt of dealing with the aftermath of Tim's death.

So many friends have come forth: Longtime family friends. The whole fraternity of Devon Prep is here. The good Piarist fathers, who generously did so much for Tim and his sons, were here for my mother's funeral so very few days ago, and they are here again today. Many friends, especially Gabby, tried to see him through these past months. We thank you all.

We all loved Tim, but we couldn't save him. Now we must depend on God to save him, heal him, transform him, and make him happy and healthy and holy and free. That's the promise of our faith: that God can and will transform us.

Most importantly, let's not let the last six minutes of his life make us forget the previous almost sixty years. Keep your favorite images and memories of Tim present in your mind and heart.

My favorite image of Tim is of him fishing. I understand his golfing was not much to brag about. But, a truth I am reluctant to admit is that he was a better fisherman than me. He'd catch fish when I caught none. If I caught a nice one, he'd get a bigger one. In October of 2002, he wrote in his fishing journal, "Well, my brother emailed me, and we were able to get out and fly fish together. Up to the Little Lehigh [River]. For Ricky, it was his best day fly fishing, he claims. For me, very slow. Only got two and a half fish. Rain hit about 2:00 PM, so we went to lunch." In 2008, he talks about our being up on the Beaverkill River. He caught a 24-inch trout and he says I was ecstatic about his catch. He forgets to mention I lost a big fish. May 5, 2006: "This is one for the books. Timmy [his eldest son] and I to the Little Lehigh." He describes catching a lot of fish. And then he writes, "Being with Timmy, my lucky charm. Wow did that feel great."

This doesn't feel so great. We lost a big fish. Today hurts. This pains us. But our faith shows that transformation comes through the crosses of life. There is no resurrection without the cross, which means there is no cross in life that does not contain within it the seeds of resurrection.

We are here at the cross today, but we won't be here forever. We will see Tim again. I want to fish with him again. We hope God will achieve in the next life what was not able to be achieved in this one. Jesus finds and saves the lost sheep. We hope and wait with endurance for God's saving grace and mercy in our lives. This is our hope. This is our faith.

Let us turn to the Lord to find mercy; to our God, who is generous and forgiving. For God's thoughts are not our thoughts, nor are our ways God's ways. Thanks be to God.

FUNERAL HOMILY

FR. BILL BAUSCH

"I go and prepare a place for you."

READING:
JOHN 14:1–3

The focus for the homilist here is the wonderful story by Arthur Gordon and its connection to the gospel. It's a great and comforting story and can be used in many configurations for a funeral.

I NOTICED IN HIS OFFICIAL OBITUARY THAT Michael Capenegro—Colonel Michael Capenegro—had a distinguished career. He was an infantry officer for twenty-five years, a professor of military science, and, after military retirement, he taught at St. John's school of business, not to mention that he was also mayor of this township for more than ten years. Impressive. I picture this talented man in these challenging roles, imagining him—both in and out of uniform—as straightforward, competent, undertaking his various duties with confidence, doing his tasks with level-headed integrity. I am indeed taken with his bio, am in awe of his achievements, and appreciate them dearly. His was an admirable and useful life.

But I have to confess that this marvelous resume I try so hard to keep in mind keeps dissolving into the wellsprings of my emotions, perhaps because I did not know him as a colonel or professor or politician. The fact is, whatever his achievements, I knew him simply as a man. I loved, not the colonel, nor the professor, nor the politician, but Mike. Just as, I know, his family knew and loved him as husband, father, brother, cousin, grandfather. These levels, these heart connections, these poignant memories, each one cherished to the point of tears, each one turned over, examined, held tightly, and traded these past few days, no obituary can capture.

As for me, we met casually and respectfully in his post-military days, when I first came to St. Mary's. We drew closer over the years as I sensed something special and honorable about him. When his lovely wife, Ramona, died, I presided at her Mass—as I am, sadly, doing at his—and I got to know him better, bound by a common event.

Then, in the course of time, a widow from Middletown, Peg Boyle, caught his eye. This was another link, because I had previously known Peg and her husband and family when, as a young priest—alas, a long time ago—I was stationed at St. Mary's in Middletown. A good woman from my past and a good man from my present built a new life, a good life—as they should have—and I was a part of it. But I think the bond was cemented because of two things. First, Mike was a faith-filled man. I admired that. He was true to his religion, loyal to his parish, and regular in his worship—and that's no small thing, no small witness. Secondly, most of all, as far as I was selfishly concerned, he liked me.

Mike was very supportive. He backed my efforts, praised my homilies, volunteered, like so many, for parish projects. He, like Peg, was simply there and, being there, like Woody Allen's "showing up," is the stuff of life and a badge of honor.

But I tell you, what remains in my memory occurred after I left St. Mary's. On occasions, unfortunately usually funerals, I would come back. Mike, who always attended daily Mass, would intercept me afterward. The routine was always the same; I can picture it now. Silently, in the back of church, with that manly grin on his face, he would stand directly in front of me, extend his right hand to my right hand to hold, take his left hand and place it on my shoulder, look me straight in the eye, and say sincerely, "How are you? It's good to see you." He meant every word.

I mention this because he, in fact, like some others have done, said to me after one of those funerals, "Father, I liked that story. When I die, I want you to come back and tell it to my family." I replied casually, "OK, Mike, it's a deal. And if I go before you, I hereby give you permission to read it at *my* funeral." And we both laughed. And afterward, whenever I came back for a funeral, he would point his finger at me and say, "Remember!" and I would give him thumbs up.

And here I am, unexpectedly, with a heavy heart, redeeming my promise.

Ironically, as some of you will recall, the story he wanted is one I shared here precisely a week ago, in this same church, in connection with a Lenten series I was giving. The story is a variation on the gospel I read. You may recall, Jesus, likely with his own next-day death in mind—knowing what abandonment and fear were like, as he would experience them in the garden of Gethsemane—wanted to give some comfort to his soon-to-be bereaved disciples. So, as you heard, he said, "Do not let your hearts be troubled. . . . In my Father's house there are many dwelling places. . . . I go and prepare a place for you, I will come back again and take you to myself, so that where I am you also may be."

So here, for Mike and his family, is that gospel, dressed up in the story he wanted.

A long time ago, there lived a little boy whose parents had died. He was taken in by an aunt who raised him as her own child. Years later, after he had grown up and left his aunt, he received a letter from her. She was in terminal illness and, from the tone of her letter, he knew she was afraid of death. This man, whom she had raised and touched, wrote her a letter in which he said:

> It is now thirty-five years since I, a little boy of six, was left quite alone in the world. You sent me word that you would give me a home and be a mother to me. I've never forgotten the day when I made the long journey of ten miles to your house. I can still recall my disappointment when, instead of coming for me yourself, you sent your servant, Caesar, a dark man, to fetch me. I well remember my tears and my anxiety as, perched high on your horse and clinging tight to Caesar, I rode off to my new home.

> Night fell before we finished the journey and, as it grew dark, I became even more afraid. "Do you think she'll go to bed before I get there?" I asked Caesar anxiously.
>
> "Oh, no," said Caesar, "she'll be sure to stay up for you. When we get out of these woods, you'll see her light shining in the window."
>
> Presently, we did ride out into the clearing and there was your light. I remember that you were waiting at the door; that you put your arms tight around me; that you lifted me—a tired, frightened little boy—down from the horse. You had a fire burning on the hearth; a hot supper waiting on the stove. After supper, you took me to my new room. You heard me say my prayers. Then you sat with me until I fell asleep.
>
> You probably realize why I am trying to recall this to your memory now. Very soon, God is going to send for you, and take you to a new home. I'm trying to tell you that you needn't be afraid of the summons or of the strange journey or of the dark messenger of death. God can be trusted. God can be trusted to do as much for you as you did for me so many years ago.
>
> At the end of the road you'll find love and a welcome waiting. And you'll be safe in God's care. I'm going to watch and pray for you until you're out of sight. And I shall wait for the day when I make the same journey myself and find you waiting at the end of the road to greet me.[1]

Notice the metaphors and symbols: Caesar, the dark figure, is death; the light at the end of the journey is Jesus, the light of the world. The house is the "many rooms" in the Father's house that Jesus promised. The

1 As recounted in William Bausch, *Once Upon a Gospel: Inspiring Homilies and Insightful Reflections* (New London, CT: Twenty-Third Publications, 2008), 107–108.

supper is the heavenly banquet. God is the loving aunt. It's a homecoming story. It is gospel.

Well, I hope you are pleased, Mike, not only that I kept my promise, but that you have found the story to be true and have arrived safely at your Father's house. And as for you, Peg—and also for you, his children and in-laws and grandchildren—I hope the comfort this thoughtful man wanted me to convey to you has found its mark in your hearts.

What more can I say? Be sad that he's gone. Be glad that he's home.

MEMORIAL MASS *for* JULIAN TAO KNIPPER

DEACON JIM KNIPPER

"Unless you change and become like little children, you will never enter the kingdom of heaven."

1ST READING:
ECCL. 3:4-14

PSALM:
23:1-6

2ND READING:
1 JOHN 3:1-2

GOSPEL:
MATT. 18:1-5

The following is the homily/eulogy given for my grandson.

OVER THE PAST FOUR YEARS, I HAVE BEGUN to realize the depth of love we can have for our grandchildren. I have four sons, who are all married to wonderful spouses and all of whom I love a great deal. But my grandchildren are different, as I can sense and feel the Divine Flow move between us when we hold onto each other. Given the nickname Buelo by my eldest grandson, I enjoy watching, with awe and wonder, my four young grandchildren grow—and feel the deepest love I could ever imagine.

But what I soon found out is deep love and deep grief are woven together from the beginning.

It was on the morning of August 31st, as I was watching the sun rise in Cape May, that I received the first text from my son in France that there had been an accident on his family farm, that my grandson Julian was seriously injured, and to say prayers as they rushed him to the hospital. It was not even an hour later that the next text I received simply said, "He's gone." And with that, our lives were turned upside down. A void opened up in my heart and soul that frankly will never fully mend.

Numerous calls were made, family notified, and heart-wrenching conversations shared with my son and his wife as we all tried to wrap ourselves around the loss of Julian. Wanton neglect on the part of a local French contractor led to the senseless death of a beautiful boy . . . leaving us with the deepest grief any of us have ever experienced.

Through a petition filed with the French consulate, my wife and I were granted permission to fly to France in the midst of COVID-19 pandemic so that we could be present for Julian's funeral. While there, we also were able to celebrate the first birthday of Julian's younger sister, Bloom . . . who spent a good part of the day looking around for her brother, who was now gone. No one should ever experience burying their own young child, or grandchild—and yet, unfortunately, this is an event that has happened before in our family. So, we know all too well that it is a loss that you never get over, or move on from, nor one that heals with time . . . although many well-intentioned people, looking for something to say, have told us so.

This death of an innocent three-year-old son and grandson is a death that changes you for the rest of your life, for there will be empty spaces at the tables of family gatherings, and holidays, and birthdays. Empty spaces in our family pictures. Empty spaces at graduations, weddings, and other celebrations. This is the kind of emptiness that lasts a lifetime—a ripple effect that seems endless. So now, nearing three months since his death, many of us in the family still wake each day wondering, "How will I live this day? How do I attempt to mend my heart and my soul? How will I interact with others?"

Perhaps some answers can be found in today's Gospel, where, as we hear so often, Jesus invites a child to come forward and reminds his followers that to enter the kingdom of heaven, we must change ourselves. We must be transformed, so we will be like a child. It is a necessary reminder for all of us that it is the children who know what it is to love another without any strings attached, with no expectation for anything in return. It reminds me of one of my favorite Fr. Richard Rohr quotes, where he writes: "We are not human beings trying to become spiritual. We're already spiritual beings—our job is learning how to be a good human."[1]

Even at his young age, Julian already had both the spiritual and the human aspects of life figured out. All you had to do was watch him with his mom and dad, or his baby sister, or his maternal grandparents (who lived next door to him), or even the short times he had with my wife and me—for you found yourself a recipient of an endless amount of his love, laughter, and kindness. Julian knew how to love, better than most adults I know—for he lived a life filled with much joy, which was expressed in so many ways.

This joy was really evident when his two cousins, who live nearby, would come over and visit. Even though they're a few years older than Julian, they would spend hours playing with him. It would not take long before the three boys were down to their underwear, dancing around the room to one of Julian's favorite songs, "Despacito." There they would be, just laughing, singing, dancing, and enjoying life and loving each other.

Because of the pandemic, the last time my wife and I saw Julian was Thanksgiving of last year, when our entire family gathered for a week at our Florida home. Then, barely two and a half years old, he announced upon his arrival that he would be sleeping by my bedside. So, every morning, about 45 minutes before the sun would rise, he would call out to me to come and cuddle with him. Soon after, we would go out on the porch and hold onto each other as we would wait for the sun to rise.

At the end of that week, on the last day he was with us, hours before he had to go, he was in the pool with my wife and me, sandwiching himself between us, with his arms wrapped around us and telling us that we needed to relax . . . just relax.

Then, this past summer, Julian's family, due to COVID-19, vacationed near to home, along the western shores of France. During their stay, I received a few videos of Julian. In one, he was looking out across the sea,

1 Richard Rohr (@RichardRohrOFM), "We are not human beings," Twitter, January 9, 2018, https://twitter.com/richardrohrofm/status/950729021830189056?lang=en.

just calling my name . . . knowing that I was somewhere on the other side of the ocean, and that I would hear his voice. In another, he let a feather go into the strong winds, watching it carry itself out over the ocean, confident that it would end up on my lap.

So, in turn, I sent him a video back, holding onto a feather and thanking him for sending me the gift, and reminding him how much I love him and always will. It wasn't long before his mom sent me a video of him watching my video (for the twelfth time!) and beaming with joy over our connection, then telling me that he loves me, "So much, forever time." Little did I know that it would be the last video I would receive from him.

When we arrived at the family farm in France for the funeral, it did not take long before we started sharing stories about Julian. Many were told, but there was one in particular that reminded me what an old soul Julian was—is—and how he knew what love and even resurrection were all about. For Julian had a deep connection with his maternal grandfather—Papé—who lives right on the farm, next door to my son's family. The two were inseparable, every single day. But, a short time before Julian died, his conversation with Papé went something like this:

> *Julian:* Papé, you are very old!
> *Papé:* Oh Julian, I am not as old as I look!
> *Julian:* So, Papé, what will happen when you die?
> *Papé:* What did you ask, Julian?
> *Julian:* What will happen when you die?
> *Papé:* Oh Julian . . . well, I will no longer be here with you, but I will be up in the stars and shining down and watching over you.
> *Julian:* Well Papé, not to worry, because when I am old enough, I will reach up to the stars and bring you back to myself.

Not even three and half years old and, somehow, Julian already knew what death and rebirth were all about.

So, we are reminded this day—and every day—of the great love Julian had for all of us—and also reminded of the Gospel call for all of us to become like little children, which requires a change of heart. That is what conversion is truly all about. Such a change of heart will transform the way we live and love—a gift that Julian gave us each day of his short life.

In his book, *The Wild Edge of Sorrow: Rituals of Renewal and the Sacred Work of Grief*, Francis Weller writes, "Grief and love are sisters, woven together from the beginning. Their kinship reminds us that there is no love that does not contain loss and no loss that is not a reminder of the love we carry for what we once held close."[2]

The depth of our collective grief will allow us, one day, to experience joy like no other joy, for our love for Julian will never die, nor will his spiritual presence in our lives ever diminish. Grief and love are indeed interwoven, but it is we who are blessed to have had Julian in our lives for 1,220 days and to have learned from him what Divine Love looks and feels and sounds like.

Julian was cremated wearing one of his favorite shirts that read, "Live Simply." So, I encourage all of you to take the time to do just that: to be more like a child . . . to live simply . . . to dance in your underwear to your favorite song . . . to send a loved one a wish over the breeze by the ocean . . . and to hug someone you love and tell them to relax.

Our days will never be the same, but we will always carry Julian's love, a love we are called to share with each other, this day and always, "So much, forever time."

---

2 Francis Weller, *The Wild Edge of Sorrow: Rituals of Renewal and the Sacred Work of Grief* (Berkeley, CA: North Atlantic, 2015) xvi.

HOMILIST BIOGRAPHIES

KEVIN AHERN is Assistant Professor of Religious Studies at Manhattan College. He received his doctorate in Theological Ethics at Boston College with a dissertation entitled "Structures of Grace: Catholic NGOs and the Church's Mission in a Globalized World." Prior to his graduate studies, Kevin served for four years as the President of the International Movement of Catholic Students (IMCS-Pax Romana), an international network of students in over eighty countries. In 2008, Kevin published The Radical Bible with Orbis Books. He continues to be active in several national and international networks, including as a Vice President of the ICMICA-Pax Romana and as a board member of the Catholic Common Ground Initiative and America Press. When not teaching, writing, or going to international meetings, Kevin enjoys hiking, the beach, and spending time with his wife.

WILLIAM J. BAUSCH is a retired parish priest of the diocese of Trenton, New Jersey. He is the award-winning author of numerous books on church life, parish ministry, storytelling, and several books of homiletics. He has lectured widely in the United States and abroad. Before COVID-19, he helped out at local parishes and gave seasonal lectures and holy hours. Post-COVID-19, confined to his senior residence, he celebrates Mass, lectures in house and, looking in a mirror, wonders who that old man is. Being locked down for sixty-seven straight days spawned his most recent book, to be published by Clear Faith Publishing in late 2020. This newest book may be one of the good or deplorable side effects of the pandemic, depending on how you look at it.

MARGARET BLACKIE, PhD is on faculty in the Department of Chemistry and Polymer Science at Stellenbosch University in South Africa. She is a trained spiritual director and the author of *Rooted in Love: Integrating Ignatian Spirituality into Daily Life* and *The Grace of Forgiveness*. Her vocation is to hold science, spirituality, and education in conversation.

REV. NADIA BOLZ-WEBER is an ordained Lutheran Pastor, founder of House for All Sinners & Saints in Denver, Colorado, the creator and host of The Confessional, and the author of three *New York Times* bestselling memoirs: *Pastrix: The Cranky, Beautiful Faith of a Sinner & Saint* (2013), *Accidental Saints: Finding God in All the Wrong People* (2015), and *Shameless: A Case for Not Feeling Bad about Feeling Good (about Sex)* (2019). She writes and speaks about personal failings, recovery, grace, faith, and really whatever the hell else she wants to. She always sits in the corner with the other weirdoes.

GREGORY BOYLE, SJ is a native Angeleno and Jesuit priest. From 1986 to 1992, Fr. Boyle served as pastor of Dolores Mission Church in Boyle Heights, then the poorest Catholic parish in Los Angeles. It also had the highest concentration of gang activity in the city. Fr. Boyle witnessed the devastating impact of gang violence on his community during the so-called "decade of death" that began in the late 1980s and peaked at 1,000 gang-related killings in 1992. In the face of law enforcement tactics and criminal justice policies of suppression and mass incarceration as the means to end gang violence, he and parish and community members adopted what was a radical approach at the time: treat gang members as human beings.

In 1988, they started what would eventually become Homeboy Industries, which employs and trains former gang members in a range of social enterprises, as well as providing critical services to thousands of men and women who walk through its doors every year seeking a better life. Fr. Boyle is the author of the 2010 *New York Times* bestseller *Tattoos on the Heart: The Power of Boundless Compassion.* His newest book, *Barking to the Choir: The Power of Radical Kinship*, was published in 2017.

He has received the California Peace Prize and been inducted into the California Hall of Fame. In 2014, President Obama named Fr. Boyle a *Champion of Change.* He received the University of Notre Dame's 2017 Laetare Medal, the oldest honor given to American Catholics. Currently, he serves as a committee member of California Governor Gavin Newsom's Economic and Job Recovery Task Force as a response to COVID-19.

REV. DR. MARK BOZZUTI-JONES, DMIN is an Episcopal Jamaican priest at Trinity Church Wall Street in New York City. A former Jesuit priest, Mark has missionary experience in Belize, Brazil, and Guyana. He is an avid reader and has taught at the elementary and university levels. He has a passion for the cultures in Latin America and the Caribbean.

Fr. Mark is an award-winning author whose recent books include *God Created, Jesus the Word, The Gospel of Barack Hussein Obama According to Mark* and *The Rastafari Book of Common Prayer.* Fr. Mark's intellectual interests include the impact of social issues on faith and spirituality, racism, and the plight of the poor. He is working on a book of poetry and loves flowers and Brazilian and Reggae music. He believes in the inculturation of religion. He is married to the Rev. Dr. Kathy Bozzuti-Jones and their son is Mark Anthony, the Negus.

REV. DR. MARGARET BULLITT-JONAS is an Episcopal priest, author, retreat leader, and climate activist. Her latest book, *Rooted and Rising: Voices of Courage in a Time of Climate Crisis,* is an anthology of essays co-edited with Leah Schade. She serves as Missioner for Creation Care in the Episcopal Diocese of Western Massachusetts and Southern New England Conference, United Church of Christ. She preaches and leads retreats in the USA and Canada on spiritual resilience and resistance in the midst of a climate emergency. She has been a lead organizer of many Christian and interfaith events about care for Earth, and has been arrested in Washington, DC and elsewhere to protest expanded use of fossil fuels. She is a graduate of Stanford (BA, Russian Literature), Harvard (PhD, Comparative Literature), and Episcopal Divinity School (MDiv). Her website, RevivingCreation.org, includes blog posts, sermons, multimedia, and articles.

DONNA L. CIANGIO, OP is a Dominican Sister of Caldwell, New Jersey, holds a doctorate with distinction from Drew University, and is the Chancellor of the Archdiocese of Newark. She has served as director of Church Leadership Consultation, working internationally and nationally in promoting parish vitality and pastoral direction, congregational and leadership development, faith formation, Small Christian Communities, planning with parishes and dioceses, and in many other areas. She also served as the International Coordinator for RENEW International, the Director of Pastoral Services of the National Pastoral Life Center, and as parish consultant for the Jesuit Conference USA.

In the parish setting, Sr. Donna has served as the Director of Adult Faith Formation, including RCIA and Baptism. She is an adjunct professor in Drew University's Doctor of Ministry program and a consultant for RCL Benziger Publishing Company. Sr. Donna also serves on the Board of Trustees of Caldwell University, the North American Forum for Small Christian Communities, and the Center for Ministry Development.

Her articles have appeared in *Today's Parish, Ligourian, CHURCH Magazine,* and in publications from Crossroad, Paulist Press, St. Anthony Messenger Press, and Catechetical Leader. Her most recent publication is *Waiting with Joy,* Advent reflection books for small group faith sharing from RENEW International.

RORY COONEY is in his twenty-sixth year as director of liturgy and music at St. Anne Catholic Community in Barrington, Illinois. Since 1984, he has composed or contributed to nearly twenty collections of music for worship with his wife, Theresa Donohoo, and friend Gary Daigle. Rory is a blogger and contributor to several periodicals including *Pastoral Music, Today's Parish,* and *GIA Quarterly,* and was the recipient of the 2014 Pastoral Musician of the Year award from the National Association of Pastoral Musicians. He is the author of *Change Our Hearts,* a book of Lenten reflections from Liguori Publications. Since 2015, he has served on the steering committee of the Liturgical Composers Forum, and currently acts as its chairperson. He is the father of six and grandfather of four. Rory lives in Lake Zurich, Illinois.

KATHERINE CORDOVA, SCHC is a special education teacher in Albuquerque, New Mexico, the caregiver of two amusing cats, and mother of two wonderful young people. She was born and raised in Albuquerque, a place that has been welcoming strangers for centuries and will for centuries more as an outpost on the Camino Real. Katherine has been a life-vowed member of the Society of the Companions of the Holy Cross since 1989. She is a believer in the power of love, committed community, and persistence.

REV. DR. DAVID DAVIS is currently the senior pastor of the Nassau Presbyterian Church in Princeton, New Jersey. He has served that congregation since 2000. David earned his PhD in Homiletics from Princeton Theological Seminary, where he continues to teach as a visiting lecturer. His academic work has focused on preaching as a corporate act and the active role of the listener in the preaching event. Before arriving in Princeton, he served for fourteen years as the pastor of the First Presbyterian Church, Blackwood, New Jersey. David grew up in Pittsburgh and did his undergraduate work at Harvard University, where he was a member of the University Choir, singing weekly in Memorial Church and listening to the preaching of Professor Peter Gomes. David is married to Cathy Cook, a Presbyterian Minister who is currently Associate Dean of Students and Director of Senior Placement at Princeton Seminary. They have two children: Hannah and Ben.

David has published two sermon collections: *A Kingdom You Can Taste* and *Lord, Teach Us to Pray*. He has served on the Board of Directors of the Presbyterian Foundation and the local Princeton YMCA. In addition to preaching in Presbyterian congregations around the country, David has preached to congregations in South Africa and Scotland and to the Samuel Proctor Child Advocacy Conference of the Children's Defense Fund, the Calvin Symposium for Worship, and on the campuses of Harvard and Duke Universities.

BECKY ELDREDGE is an Ignatian-trained spiritual director, retreat facilitator, and author who invites people deeper in their walk with Christ. Becky is the author of two books: *The Inner Chapel* (Loyola, 2020) and *Busy Lives & Restless Souls* (Loyola, 2017). She lives in Baton Rouge, Louisiana with her husband and three children.

Passionate about Ignatian spirituality and teaching people how to pray, Becky leans on her twenty years of ministry experience to help people make room for God in their daily lives and invite them into deeper relationship with God. Becky meets with men and women of all ages for monthly spiritual direction and guides people through the *Spiritual Exercises* of St. Ignatius. She directs both in-person and virtual retreats to make the Ignatian retreat experience accessible to all. Follow Becky and her blog, *Into the Deep: Exploring Ignatian Spirituality through the Voices of Women*, at www.beckyeldredge.com or on social media @beldredge98.

ROBERT ELLSBERG is the publisher of Orbis Books and the author and editor of many books, including *All Saints*, *A Living Gospel*, and editions of the writings of Dorothy Day, with whom he once served as managing editor of *The Catholic Worker*. For the past ten years he has written a daily column, "Blessed Among Us," for *Give Us This Day*.

MASSIMO FAGGIOLI, PhD is professor in the Department of Theology and Religious Studies at Villanova University (Philadelphia). His books and articles have been published in more than ten languages. He is columnist for the magazines *Commonweal* and *La Croix International*. His most recent publications include the books *A Council for the Global Church: Receiving Vatican II in History* (Fortress, 2015); *The Rising Laity: Ecclesial Movements since Vatican II* (Paulist, 2016); *Catholicism and Citizenship: Political Cultures of the Church in the Twenty-First Century* (Liturgical, 2017); and *The Liminal Papacy of Pope Francis: Moving toward Global Catholicity* (Orbis, 2020). He is co-editing with Catherine Clifford *The Oxford Handbook of Vatican II* (Oxford University Press, 2021), and is under contract with Oxford University Press for the book *God's Bureaucrats: A History of the Roman Curia*.

MICHELLE FRANCL-DONNAY is a professor of chemistry and an adjunct scholar at the Vatican Observatory. When not doing research in quantum mechanics she writes on the joys and struggles of attempting to live a contemplative life in the midst of the everyday chaos that being a wife, mother, and scientist brings. She is an occasional contributor to Give Us This Day and a regular columnist for the science journal Nature Chemistry. Her most recent book is Waiting in Joyful Hope, reflections on the readings of Advent. Michelle gives the occasional retreat and blogs about prayer, God, and laundry at Quantum Theology (quantumtheology.blogspot.com). More of her writing can be found at www.michellefrancldonnay.com.

RON HANSEN was ordained a deacon in the Catholic Church in 2007 and currently serves in the parish of Saint Joseph of Cupertino in northern California.

MARTY HAUGEN is a liturgical composer, workshop presenter, performing and recording artist, and author from Eagan, Minnesota. For the past thirty years, Marty has presented workshops and concerts across North and Central America, Europe, Asia, and the Pacific Rim. He has over forty recordings and more than 400 separate printed editions available through GIA Publications. A number of his published songs, including "Shepherd Me, O God," "Gather Us In" and "All Are Welcome" are well-known to many religious denominations. He has composed *Mass of Creation*, and several liturgical settings for Lutheran congregations, including *Holden Evening Prayer, Unfailing Light* (with Pastor Susan Briehl), and *Now the Feast and Celebration*, as well as a communion setting for the new *Evangelical Worship Book* (ELW-Augsburg Fortress).

Marty has served as an editor or consultant to a number of GIA hymnals and has been a contributor to hymnals or supplements for many denominational groups including the ELCA and ELCIC (Evangelical Lutheran Church of America and Canada), the United Methodist Church, the Presbyterian Church (USA), the Mennonite Brethren, the United Church of Christ, the United Church of Canada, the Anglican Church of Canada, the Church of England, the Church of Scotland, the Church of Jesus Christ of Latter Day Saints, and Roman Catholic groups in Great Britain, Canada, Ireland, and Australia.

FR. DANIEL P. HORAN, OFM, PhD is the Duns Scotus Chair of Spirituality at Catholic Theological Union in Chicago, where he teaches systematic theology and spirituality; serves as a columnist for the *National Catholic Reporter*; and is the author of more than twelve books, including *Catholicity and Emerging Personhood: A Contemporary Theological Anthropology* (Orbis), which received the 2020 First Place Award for Theology Book from the Association of Catholic Publishers. Fr. Daniel regularly lectures around the United States and abroad and serves on a number of university, academic, and publication editorial boards, including the St. Bonaventure University Board of Trustees, the Franciscan School of Theology Board of Regents, and the Board of Directors of the International Thomas Merton Society. He is co-host of *The Francis Effect* podcast.

FR. JAN MICHAEL JONCAS was ordained in 1980 as a priest of the Archdiocese of St. Paul-Minneapolis, Minnesota. Fr. Joncas holds degrees in English from the (then) College of St. Thomas in St. Paul, Minnesota, and in liturgical studies from the University of Notre Dame, and the Pontificio Istituto Liturgico of the Ateneo S. Anselmo in Rome. He has served as a parochial vicar, a campus minister, and a parochial administrator (pastor). He is the author of six books and more than two hundred fifty articles and reviews in journals such as *Worship, Ecclesia Orans,* and *Questions Liturgiques.* He has composed and arranged more than 300 pieces of liturgical music. He is currently Artist in Residence and Research Fellow in Catholic Studies at the University of St. Thomas, St. Paul, Minnesota.

GREG KANDRA is the creator of the popular blog "The Deacon's Bench." Additionally, he serves as the Senior Writer for Catholic Near East Welfare Association (CNEWA), a pontifical association founded by Pope Pius XI in 1926. Before joining CNEWA, Deacon Greg spent nearly three decades in broadcast journalism, most of that time at CBS News, where he was honored with every major award in broadcasting, including two Peabody Awards and two Emmy Awards. He's a regular contributor to *Give Us This Day,* the monthly prayer resource of Liturgical Press. In addition to contributing to the *Homilists for the Homeless* series, he's written several books, including *The Busy Person's Guide to Prayer* and *The Busy Person's Guide to an Extraordinary Life* (Word Among Us Press). Deacon Greg was ordained a deacon for the Diocese of Brooklyn in 2007. He and his wife, Siobhain, live in Forest Hills, New York.

JAMES J. KNIPPER is publisher of Clear Faith Publishing, which is focused on publishing books with a spiritual foundation. Their first three books, a series of homilies, have received several awards and raised over $100,000 for various charities.

Deacon Jim graduated from the University of Scranton with a degree in chemistry and received a Master's in Business in the Pharmaceutical Industry from Fairleigh Dickinson University in 1984. He received a Master's in Theology from Georgian Court University in May 2015 and an honorary degree from that institution in May 2017. He is currently a member of the Board of Trustees for the Basilica of the National Shrine of the Immaculate Conception in Washington, DC.

Today, he divides his time between Marco Island, Florida and Washington Crossing, Pennsylvania with his wife, Teresa. He is the proud father of four sons and four grandchildren. He was ordained a deacon in 2008 in the Diocese of Trenton and is a member of St. Paul's Catholic Church, Princeton, New Jersey, where he serves the parish. You can follow his preaching at http://teachbelief.blogspot.com/.

MICHAEL LEACH is publisher emeritus and editor-at-large of Orbis Books. A leader in religion book publishing for five decades, he has edited and published more than three thousand books. His authors include Nobel Prize winners, National Book Award winners, and hundreds of religion book award winners. He has served as president of the Catholic Book Publishers Association and the ecumenical Religion Publishers Group. Before joining Orbis as director and publisher in 1997, Mike was president of the Crossroad/Continuum Publishing Group in New York City, which he helped found in 1980. In 2007, the Catholic Book Publishers Association honored him with a Lifetime Achievement Award. Dubbed "the dean of Catholic book publishing" by *U.S. Catholic* magazine, Mike has authored or edited many books of his own, including *Why Stay Catholic?* which the Catholic Press Association voted "Best Popular Presentation of the Catholic Faith" in 2012, *The People's Catechism, I Like Being Married*, and *Soul Seeing*, a collection of his award-winning columns in the *National Catholic Reporter*. Mike lives in Connecticut with his wife of fifty-two years, Vickie.

RICHARD G. MALLOY, SJ, PHD, aka "Mugs," was born at Temple University hospital in Philadelphia, the friendly city of brotherly shove. He studied cultural anthropology at Temple, so he didn't go far in life. From 1988–2003, he lived and worked as a member of the Jesuit Urban Service team in Camden, New Jersey. During those years, he also taught at St. Joseph's University in Philadelphia, and from 2010–2019 at the University of Scranton, teaching anthropology, sociology, and theology. He lived for fifteen years in the first-year dorms (anthropological fieldwork!). In 2019, he began serving as director of Mission and Ministry at Cristo Rey Jesuit High School in Baltimore.

Fr. Malloy's books from Orbis, *A Faith that Frees: Catholic Matters for the 21st Century*; *Being on Fire: The Top Ten Essentials of Catholic Faith* and *Spiritual Direction: A Beginner's Guide*, were all recognized with awards by the Catholic Press Association. Fishing is his passion in life. He is convinced that catching a ten-pound trout, the Eagles winning (another!!!) Super Bowl, or the Phillies beating the Yankees in the World Series, are all sure signs that the second coming of Jesus is imminent. Follow him @FrMalloy.

REV. RICKY MANALO, CSP, PHD is a Paulist missionary priest, composer, theologian, and author. He is the recipient of the 2020 Distinguished Catholic Music Composer of the Year Award by the Association of Catholic Publishers, and the 2018 Pastoral Musician of the Year Award by the National Association of Pastoral Musicians. He studied composition and piano at the Manhattan School of Music, theology at the Washington Theological Union, and liturgy, culture, and sociology at the Graduate Theological Union (GTU), Berkeley, California. In addition to his books, *Chanting on Our Behalf* (revised edition, Pastoral Press, 2015) and *The Liturgy of Life* (Liturgical Press, 2014), he co-authored the entry "Contextual Preaching" with Stephen Bevans in *A Handbook for Catholic Preaching* (Liturgical Press, 2016). He is a theological consultor for the United States Conference of Catholic Bishops and the co-author of the official national pastoral plan for Asian Pacific Catholics, *Encountering Christ in Harmony* (2018). Fr. Manalo has been invited to six of the seven continents to do a variety of presentations, from academic lectures, keynotes, and pastoral workshops to preaching, presiding, and giving concerts. He resides at St. Paul the Apostle Church in New York City.

JAMES MARTIN, SJ is a Jesuit priest, editor at large of *America* magazine, consultor to the Vatican's Dicastery for Communication, and author of many books, including the *New York Times* bestsellers *Jesus: A Pilgrimage* and *The Jesuit Guide to (Almost) Everything*. His most recent book is *Learning to Pray: A Guide for Everyone.*

SHIRIN McARTHUR is an Episcopal laywoman, spiritual guide, retreat leader, writer, and editor who ponders the sacred through prayer, poetry, dance, photography, nature, and contemplation. She holds an MDiv from Boston University School of Theology and a Certificate in Spiritual Guidance from the Shalem Institute in Washington, DC. Shirin has been leading retreats since the early 1990s and offering spiritual guidance since 1995. Her award-winning Prayerful Pondering blog is part of the Christian Century network. Raised in New Mexico, she spent eighteen years in Massachusetts and now lives near Tucson, Arizona with her husband, the Rev. Henry Hoffman. Shirin copyedited this volume of *Homilists for the Homeless.* You can learn more about her atshirinmcarthur.comand see her photography at instagram.com/shirinmcarthur.

BROTHER MICKEY O'NEILL McGRATH, OSFS, an Oblate of St. Francis de Sales, is an award-winning artist, author, and storyteller. He is a popular presenter and frequent keynote speaker at conferences, parishes, and retreat centers throughout the United States and Canada. Using his own paintings and the stories which inspired them, Bro. Mickey makes deep and often humorous connections between art, social justice, and religious faith around a wide variety of themes and subjects.

Mickey's first and foremost love, however, is books, in all aspects: illustrating, writing, publishing, and promoting. His works have been honored over time by the Catholic Press Association and Association of Catholic Publishers. A copy of his first publication with Clear Faith Publishing, Good Pope John XXIII, was presented to Pope Francis soon after its launch. Bro. Mickey sees his work as being at the service of Catholic social teaching. To that end, he has created posters for the United States Conference of Catholic Bishops to promote immigration reform and home missions and has licensed his work to Catholic textbook publishers. He is a recipient of the Thea Bowman Black Catholic Education Award in recognition of his work on Sr. Thea Bowman, his great spiritual mentor and inspiration.

Bro. Mickey currently lives and works in Camden, NJ. You can visit his website at www.bromickeymcgrath.com.

MEGAN McKENNA is a native of New York City, but has lived in New Mexico for more than three decades. She is a theologian, storyteller, poet and scribe of the Scriptures, a teacher, preacher, and minor prophet. She has authored more than fifty books, drawn from her missionary work in Latin America, Southeast Asia, Africa. Her focus is on peace, reconciliation, and restorative justice among Indigenous peoples world-wide, with Native Americans and with Frist Nations of Canada.

Most groups she works with struggle with poverty, violence, forgiveness, peacemaking and community organizing in the face of change, trauma and shifting ways of life with multi-cultural and multi-religious groups. She seeks to pass on the wisdom of the universal Church and of human communities using the Word of God and stories from all people, through retreats, parish mission and transitional conferences for religious communities and groups that do justice in Europe and the US.

She has authored more than fifty books, including *And Morning Came: Scriptures of the Resurrection, Praying the Rosary, Send My Roots Rain, The New Stations of the Cross, On Your Mark: Reading Mark in the Shadow of the Cross,* and the recently released, *The Poor Will Save Us.*

BRIAN McLAREN is an author, speaker, activist, and public theologian. A former college English teacher and pastor, he is a passionate advocate for "a new kind of Christianity"—just, generous, and working with people of all faiths for the common good. He is a faculty member of the Living School for Action and Contemplation, which is part of the Center for Action and Contemplation, and co-hosts a podcast called *Learning How to See.* He works closely with Vote Common Good and with the Auburn Senior Fellows. His most recent projects include an illustrated children's book (for all ages) called *Cory and the Seventh Story,* and *The Galapagos Islands: A Spiritual Journey.* Two important new releases are in process: *Faith after Doubt* (January 2021) and *Do I Stay Christian?* (Spring 2022).

REV. PENNY A. NASH is a priest living in the Episcopal Diocese of Virginia. After twelve years of "regular" parish ministry in parishes in both Georgia (where she was ordained in 2007) and Virginia, Penny became certified as an intentional interim minister and now serves in the capacity of interim rector, guiding parishes through the time of wilderness between settled pastors as they rediscover who they are, who their neighbors are, and what God is calling them to next in their life as a beloved community.

Penny loves to travel and the beach (pretty much any beach) is her happy place. An avid photographer, she showcases her photography as sermon illustrations and occasional other posts on her blog: penelopepiscopal.blogspot.com. She also posts her sermons on her YouTube channel (https://www.youtube.com/channel/UCkTCjVSEyla89THIanCTpOg/) that isn't big enough to have its own custom URL yet. She and her husband, Tom Cox, are the parents of three wonderful adult children. They live in Richmond, Virginia with their two cats, Sally and Bella.

DENNIS PLUMMER has been involved with homelessness and housing issues since the late 1980s. His involvement has included undercover investigation of shelter conditions, working as emergency shelter staff, crafting public policy, leading program design, and teaching English as a second language. He now serves as CEO of Heading Home in Albuquerque, New Mexico, an agency focused on outreach, emergency shelter, and permanent housing. Prior to moving to Albuquerque, Mr. Plummer lived for three years as a monk in the Society of St. John the Evangelist and worked for seven years in the Office of the Canon to the Ordinary in the Episcopal Diocese of Massachusetts. He is a practiced hypnotherapist, enjoys extreme sports, and can really settle into reading a good book!

REV. JAN RICHARDSON is an artist, writer, and ordained minister in the United Methodist Church. She serves as director of The Wellspring Studio, LLC, and has traveled widely as a retreat leader and conference speaker. With her work described by the *Chicago Tribune* as "breathtaking," she has attracted an international audience that is drawn to the spaces of welcome, imagination, and solace that she creates in both word and image. Jan's books include *The Cure for Sorrow, Night Visions, In the Sanctuary of Women,* and the recently released *Sparrow: A Book of Life and Death and Life.* She is especially known as a crafter of blessings that enter deeply into our human experience.

A native Floridian several generations over, Jan grew up in Evinston, a small community near the university town of Gainesville. The rural landscape, community traditions, and lifelong relationships fostered a rich sense of place, imagination, and ritual that continue to shape Jan's life and infuse her work. Jan makes her home in Florida. She often collaborated with her husband, the singer/songwriter Garrison Doles, until his sudden death in December 2013. For more about her work, visit janrichardson.com.

RT. REV. V. GENE ROBINSON is Vice President of Religion and Senior Pastor at the Chautauqua Institution in western New York State, having served for nearly five years as a Senior Fellow at the Center for American Progress, Washington, DC. He was elected Bishop of the Episcopal Diocese of New Hampshire on June 7, 2003, becoming the first openly gay and partnered bishop in historic Christianity, and was consecrated a Bishop on All Saints Sunday, November 2, 2003.

Robinson graduated from the University of the South in 1969 with a BA in American Studies/History. In 1973, he completed the MDiv degree at the General Theological Seminary in New York and was ordained deacon and then priest in that same year. His book *In the Eye of the Storm: Swept to the Center by God* (Seabury) was published in 2008. In 2012, he authored *God Believes in Love: Straight Talk about Gay Marriage* (Knopf) contributing to the national debate about marriage equality. He has been the subject of two feature-length documentaries: *For the Bible Tells Me So,* premiering at the 2006 Sundance Film Festival, and *Love Free or Die,* also premiering at Sundance, in 2012, which won the Special Jury Prize. Bishop Robinson was invited by President-elect Barack Obama to give the invocation at the inaugural ceremonies at the Lincoln Memorial on January 18, 2009.

FR. RICHARD ROHR, OFM is a globally recognized ecumenical teacher bearing witness to the universal awakening within Christian mysticism and the Perennial Tradition. He is a Franciscan priest of the New Mexico Province and founder of the Center for Action and Contemplation (CAC) in Albuquerque, New Mexico. Fr. Richard's teaching is grounded in the Franciscan alternative orthodoxy—practices of contemplation and self-emptying, expressing itself in radical compassion, particularly for the socially marginalized.

Fr. Richard is the author of numerous books, including *Everything Belongs, Adam's Return, The Naked Now, Breathing Under Water, Falling Upward, Immortal Diamond, Eager to Love, The Wisdom Pattern,* and *The Universal Christ.* Find his audio conversation series *Another Name for Every Thing,* exploring themes from *The Universal Christ,* on most podcast platforms.

Fr. Richard is academic Dean of the Living School for Action and Contemplation. Drawing upon Christianity's place within the Perennial Tradition, the mission of the Living School is to produce compassionate and powerfully learned individuals who will work for positive change in the world based on awareness of our common union with God and all beings.

TIMOTHY SHRIVER is a lifelong educator, a founder of the movement of social and emotional learning, the leader of special Olympics for over two decades, and a seeker of mystics and the presence of God. Tim has produced movies, written books, and given far too many talks all centered on discovering the unimaginable beauty of everything. Most recently, he founded a new organization, Unite, dedicated to healing the painful divisions in our country through stories and solutions that unite.

MARY ELIZABETH SPERRY holds a master's degree in liturgical studies from the Catholic University of America and a master's degree in political science from the University of California, Los Angeles. She is the author of *Bible Top Tens* (Our Sunday Visitor), *Ten: How the Commandments Can Change Your Life* (Franciscan Media), *Scripture in the Parish: A Guide for Catholic Ministry* (Liturgical Press), *Real Life Faith: Bible Companions for Catholic Teens* (Liguori), and *Making Room for God: Decluttering and the Spiritual Life* (Ave Maria Press). Her articles have appeared in *The Liguorian, Emmanuel, Today's Parish Minister,* and other publications. She has spoken in the Arch/dioceses of Baltimore, Los Angeles, Dallas, Harrisburg, and Orange and has given talks and retreats in numerous parishes. She has been interviewed on National Public Radio, CBS Radio, NBC, EWTN, and other Catholic radio stations.

FRAN ROSSI SZPYLCZYN is a former corporate executive turned church worker. She graduated from St. Bernard's School of Theology and Ministry in May of 2013 with a Master of Arts in Pastoral Studies. By day she is the Pastoral Associate for Administration at the Church of the Immaculate Conception in Glenville, New York. Fran has extensive experience facilitating faith formation for both teenagers and adults, directing retreats, and public speaking.

A published writer, her work has appeared in numerous books, online forums, and publications. She was a charter contributor to the *Homilists for the Homeless* series. Fran has also been published in the *National Catholic Reporter, America* Media, *The Evangelist,* the *Albany Times Union,* and is a regular contributor to *Give Us This Day,* published by Liturgical Press. A longtime social media advocate, she has a blog called *There Will Be Bread.* Originally from the New York City area, Fran now lives in Clifton Park with her husband, Mark.

REV. PATRICK J. WENRICK graduated with an MDiv in Mission Specialization from Catholic Theological Union in 1982 and was ordained a priest in October of the same year. Since that time, he has been in various ministries within the Roman Catholic Tradition, including being Vocation Director and Assistant Pastor of two churches in New Jersey, as well as Assistant Rector of a Religious community. Graduating from LaSalle University in Philadelphia with a Master's Degree in Pastoral Counseling, Pat went to work first as a therapist and later as Program Director for a drug and alcohol outpatient facility in Bucks County, Pennsylvania. While Program Director, he also taught World Religions as an adjunct faculty member at Bucks County Community College. In 1998, he also established a clinical practice as a New Jersey licensed professional counselor.

In July 2003, Rev. Wenrick married his lovely wife, Susan, in Princeton, New Jersey and relocated to the Tampa area with their daughter, Allyson. He continues to witness marriages, perform baptisms, and to be available for visiting the sick and dying in hospitals and nursing homes as part of CITI Ministries. He has given numerous workshops and talks on lifespan development, spirituality, and bereavement issues, weaving a healthy spiritual-psychological approach to the problems that confront contemporary society.

PHYLLIS ZAGANO, PhD is an internationally acclaimed scholar and lecturer on contemporary spirituality and women's issues in the Roman Catholic Church. Her most recent book, *Women: Icons of Christ* (Paulist Press) traces the history of ministry by women, especially those ordained as deacons, and answers the question: Who can image Christ, the risen Lord? *Women: Icons of Christ* joins her award-winning books *Holy Saturday: An Argument for the Restoration of the Female Diaconate in the Catholic Church* (Crossroad), *Women & Catholicism: Gender, Communion, and Authority* (Palgrave-Macmillan), and *Women Deacons? Essays with Answers* (Liturgical). She is Senior Research Associate-in-Residence and Adjunct Professor of Religion at Hofstra University and was appointed by Pope Francis to the 2016–2018 Commission for the Study of the Diaconate of Women.

CHARITIES

WELCOMING THE STRANGER is an educational non-profit that offers free classes in English as a Second Language (ESL), computer skills, and United States citizenship exam preparation to adult immigrants and refugees in the Philadelphia metro region.

Founded in 1999, Welcoming the Stranger has taught over 4,000 students from 104 different countries. Welcoming the Stranger is a fully independent, IRS-approved, 501(c)(3) non-profit corporation. Financial support comes from individuals, places of worship, and local businesses, as well as grants from area foundations, which allows all programs to remain free of charge for students.

Using paid teachers and about 100 volunteers each term, they offer about fifteen to twenty classes each trimester. Classes are held both day and evening. Over the past several years, classes have been offered in Bensalem, Doylestown, Hatboro, Harleysville, Lambertville, Langhorne, Levittown, Morrisville, Newtown, Northeast Philadelphia, Southampton, and Warminster. Classes are often located in churches and community centers. Each year Welcoming the Stranger offers three 12-week terms of classes. Registrations for each term number approximately 300 students.

During the Coronavirus pandemic they are continuing their mission by holding classes via the Internet.

https://www.welcomingthestranger.org/

KINO BORDER INITIATIVE, located in Nogales, Sonora, and Nogales, Arizona promotes US-Mexico border and immigration policies that affirm the dignity of the human person and a spirit of bi-national solidarity. They carry out their mission through direct humanitarian assistance and accompaniment with migrants, social and pastoral education with communities on both sides of the border, as well as participation in collaborative networks that engage in research and advocacy to transform local, regional, and national immigration policies.

Since 2009, the Kino Border Initiative has been serving migrants arriving in Nogales, Sonora, regardless of the journey or circumstances that brought them there. Along the way and still today, KBI evaluates the shifting needs of migrants and responds by altering their humanitarian assistance and education and advocacy efforts.

kinoborderinitiative.org

FREEDOM UNIVERSITY is an award-winning human rights organization and modern-day freedom school for undocumented students banned from equal access to public universities in Georgia. In a hostile political environment, Freedom University provides a sanctuary of learning where undocumented students can study without fear. Through tuition-free college level classes, college application assistance, mental health and legal support, and social movement leadership training, Freedom University advances students' human right to education and empowers them to participate in the transformation of their world.

www.freedom-university.org

AL OTRO LADO is a bi-national, social justice legal services organization serving indigent deportees, migrants, and refugees in Tijuana, Mexico. Their mission is to provide legal services and to uplift our immigrant communities by defending the rights of migrants against systemic injustices in the legal system. Their comprehensive cross-border programming and litigation work integrate trauma-informed practices. They engage vital partnerships and thousands of volunteers to provide essential legal services to migrants at the Southern Border in Tijuana and throughout Southern California. Al Otro Lado's work is also centered in fighting for all families that have been torn apart by unjust immigration laws.

Al Otro Lado has assisted dozens of families with cross-border custody issues and helps connect family members residing in the United States to social, legal, medical, housing, and mental health services via a unique program in Los Angeles.

Al Otro Lado is a partner organization at the Wellness Center—Los Angeles, located in the historic LA County General Hospital building on the LAC+USC Hospital Campus. Housed where many of their clients and families are receiving care, they offer free immigration legal services to low-income individuals. This partnership allows clients to access a multitude of services (legal, medical, mental health, exercise, health, and others) in one place.

https://alotrolado.org/

ACKNOWLEDGMENTS

I am most grateful to all those in my life who said, "Yes!" to this project. With this being the fourth book of homilies that we have compiled, edited, and published, there is no doubt that it takes an expanded team of talented and supportive people in order to publish a volume of work that hopefully feeds the souls of our readers. So, I am most grateful to:

- **ALL OF OUR CONTRIBUTORS**, some who have been with us for all of our volumes and some who have joined us for the first time. Your talent for opening our eyes and hearts and souls to the Gospel is a true gift to all of us.
- **BROTHER MICKEY McGRATH**, whose inspiring art throughout the book visually brings life to the words on the page.
- **DOUG CORDES**, who continues to give beautiful style and design to the works we publish.
- **SHIRIN McARTHUR**, who has an incredible keen eye in technically editing the works of such a variety of authors, keeping to their individual styles, while enhancing the ability of the words to reach our readers.
- **MAUREEN EDORE**, who keeps me on track and helps bring order to my life and my ministry.
- **SERGIO HERNANDEZ** and **FRAN ROSSI SZPYLCZYN**, who support our social media presence each day.
- For my sons, **TIM**, **JON**, **PETER** and **JACOB**, and their wives, who are always there to support my work.
- For my beautiful grandchildren: **BODHI**, **BLOOM** and **OLIVER** who remind me how to see Christ through the eyes of a child.
- In memory of my beloved grandson, **JULIAN**, who will never be forgotten, and who, through every moment of his short life, reminded me how to love others.

- And for my wife, **TERESA**, who for over thirty years has endlessly provided me with love and support and spiritual wisdom.

And for you, **OUR READERS**, who support our work and thus support our charities. May you be blessed in all that you do as you remember to live with love for others so that, together, we can continue our call to welcome the stranger, to give nourishment to those who hunger, and to care for all those who live on the margins.

Made in the USA
Monee, IL
30 December 2020

55979983R00187